KT-197-931

THE COMPLETE ILLUSTRATED GUIDE TO

FENG SHUI

ELEMENT

Shaftesbury , Dorset . Rockport , Massachusetts
Brisbane . Queensland

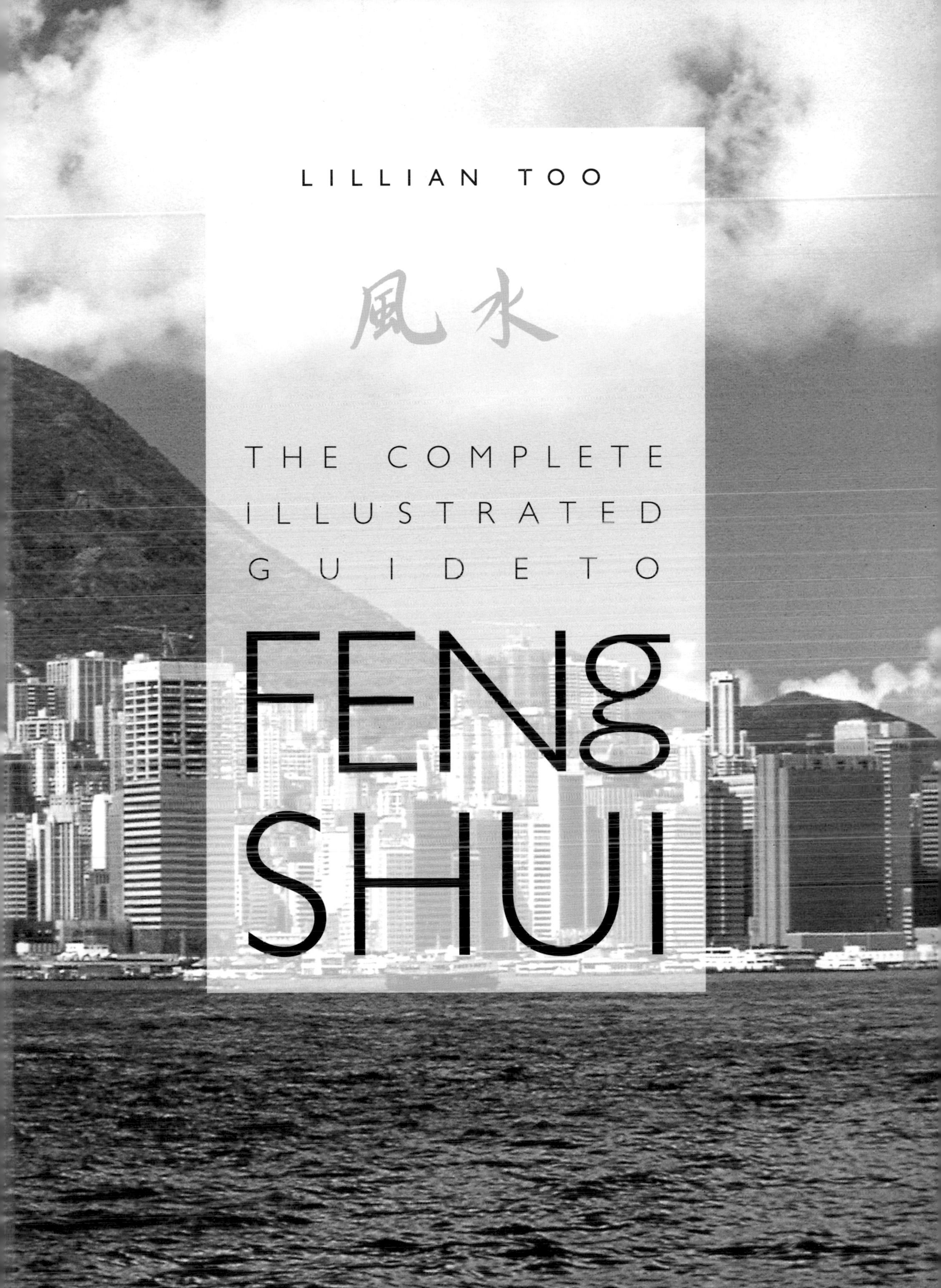
LILLIAN TOO
風水
THE COMPLETE
ILLUSTRATED
GUIDE TO
FENG
SHUI

I dedicate this beautiful book to my daughter Jennifer Too who, in essence, was the first brilliant blessing that Feng Shui brought to me and my husband; since her arrival into our lives, we have never looked back...

First published in Great Britain 1996 by
ELEMENT BOOKS LIMITED
Shaftesbury, Dorset, SP7 8BP

Published in the USA in 1996 by
ELEMENT BOOKS INC.
PO Box 830, Rockport, MA 01966

Published in Australia in 1996 by
ELEMENT BOOKS LIMITED
for JACARANDA WILEY LIMITED
33 Park Road, Milton, Brisbane 4064

First Published October 1996
Reprinted November and December 1996
February, April, June and November 1997

Designed and created with The Bridgewater Book Company

ELEMENT BOOKS LIMITED
Editorial Director: Julia McCutchen
Managing Editor: Caro Ness
Production Director: Roger Lane
Production: Sarah Golden

THE BRIDGEWATER BOOK COMPANY
Art Director: Terry Jeavons
Page layout/make-up: John Christopher
Managing Editor: Anne Townley
Picture Research: Bella Grazebrook
Three-dimensional models: Mark Jamieson
Studio photography: Guy Ryecart
Illustrators: Andrew Kulman, Lorraine Harrison and Alan Bridgewater

Printed by
Midas Printing Hong Kong Limited

British Library Cataloguing in Publication data available.

ISBN 1 85230 882 6

CONTENTS

ABOUT THIS BOOK

Feng Shui offers a method of living life in a harmonious relationship with the earth's environment and with its energy lines. Its practice can enhance your good fortune in many areas of your life, including your family relationships, your career and your business.

There are many different approaches to the practice of Feng Shui and the aim of this book is to provide the reader with an accessible guide to implementing its practices with advice that is based on sound experience.

The first part of the book describes the philosophy of Feng Shui and the second moves on to look at the principles of Feng Shui. The third part discusses the practical application of Feng Shui, looking at the location of your home and its interior design and decoration. The fourth part then describes how you can use Feng Shui to enhance your personal relationships.

The practice of Feng Shui is explored throughout the book in a clear, straightforward text with practical examples that are illustrated and explained with many unique images.

MODELS ILLUSTRATE THE PRACTICE OF FENG SHUI.

CLEAR EXPLANATIONS OF FENG SHUI FORMULAS AND PRACTICAL ADVICE ON HOW TO APPLY THEM.

The Complete Illustrated Guide to Feng Shui

EAST-HOUSE/WEST-HOUSE THEORY

This Feng Shui theory suggests that the eight directions of the eight-sided Pa Kua symbol represent eight types of houses. These are divided into two categories of four houses each, known as the east houses and the west houses. The names of the houses, their front and back door directions, and the elements associated with them are summarized on page 89.

To identify the kind of house you have, first check the direction of your front and back doors. Take these directions from the inside looking out. When in doubt, use the back door as the determining factor to identify what type of house it is. For example, if your back door faces northwest while your front door faces southeast, yours is a Chien house. It belongs to the west group and its element is metal. If your back door faces south and your front door faces north, yours is a Li house. It belongs to the east group of houses and its element is fire. If the front door faces north and the back door faces southwest, the back door takes precedence, so it is a Kun house (and not a Li house), belonging to the west group.

East-group houses are associated with the elements water, wood, and fire. The houses are thus in a harmonious relationship with each other, since water produces wood, which produces fire. East-group houses clash with west-group houses because the elements form a destructive relationship (the metal of a west house destroys the wood of an east house, for example).

The Feng Shui of east-group houses can be enhanced with plants, flowers, bright lights, and water structures. Place these enhancers near the front door, or in the corresponding element sectors identified on the Pa Kua *(see pages 80–81)*.

West-group houses are associated with the elements metal and earth. To enhance the Feng Shui of west-group houses, use wind chimes and crystals.

WEST GROUP: TUI HOUSE

WEST GROUP: KEN HOUSE

WEST GROUP: KUN HOUSE

88

RECOGNIZABLE BUILDINGS ARE ANALYZED.

CONCEPTS EXPLAINED THROUGH UNIQUE PLASTER MODELS.

FENG SHUI DEMONSTRATED THROUGH A RANGE OF EXAMPLES SHOWING HOW DIFFERENT STYLES OF ARCHITECTURE CAN BE AUSPICIOUS OR INAUSPICIOUS.

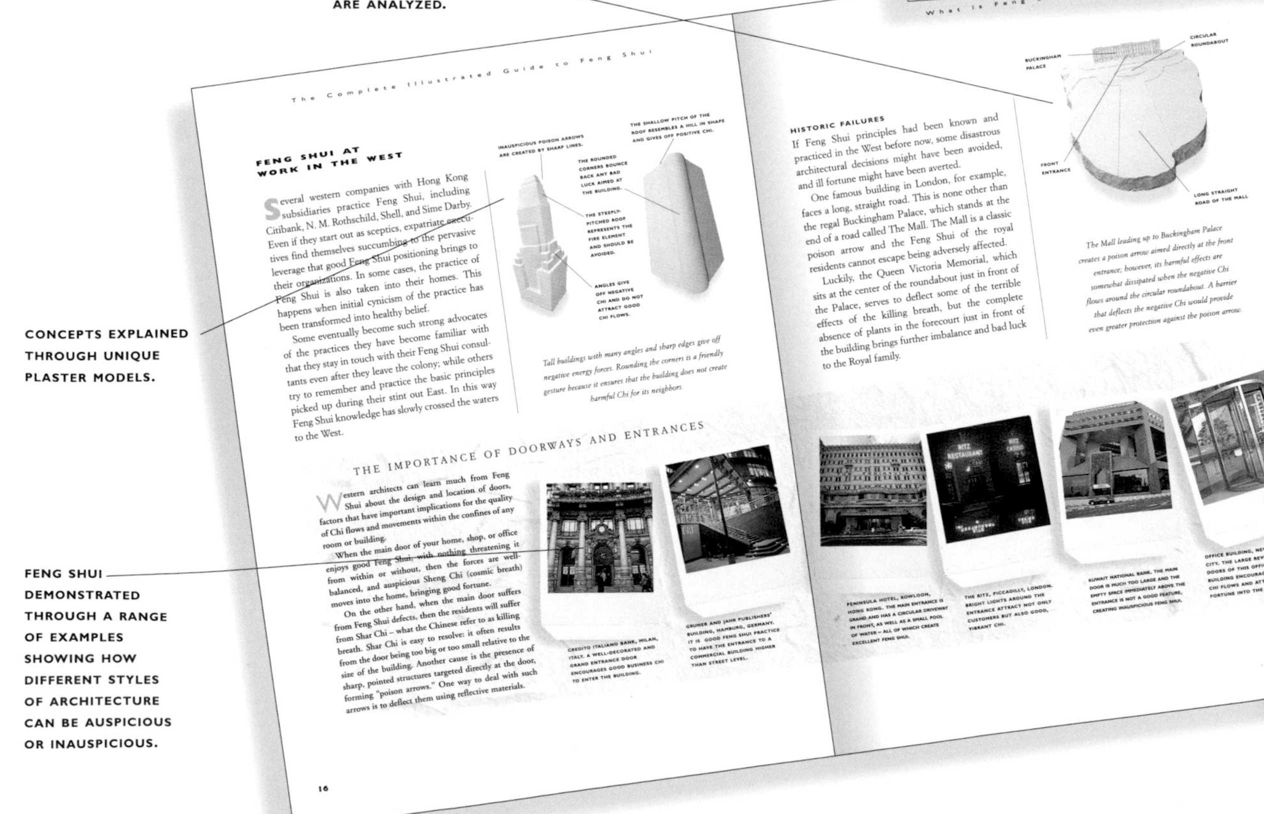

The Complete Illustrated Guide to Feng Shui

FENG SHUI AT WORK IN THE WEST

Several western companies with Hong Kong subsidiaries practice Feng Shui, including Citibank, N. M. Rothschild, Shell, and Sime Darby. Even if they start out as sceptics, expatriate executives find themselves succumbing to the pervasive leverage that good Feng Shui positioning brings to their organizations. In some cases, the practice of Feng Shui is also taken into their homes. This happens when initial cynicism of the practice has been transformed into healthy belief.

Some eventually become such strong advocates of the practices they have become familiar with that they stay in touch with their Feng Shui consultants even after they leave the colony; while others try to remember and practice the basic principles picked up during their stint out East. In this way Feng Shui knowledge has slowly crossed the waters to the West.

Tall buildings with many angles and sharp edges give off negative energy forces. Rounding the corners is a friendly gesture because it ensures that the building does not create harmful Chi for its neighbors.

THE IMPORTANCE OF DOORWAYS AND ENTRANCES

Western architects can learn much from Feng Shui about the design and location of doors, factors that have important implications for the quality of Chi flows and movements within the confines of any room or building.

When the main door of your home, shop, or office enjoys good Feng Shui, with nothing threatening it from within or without, then the forces are well-balanced, and auspicious Sheng Chi (cosmic breath) moves into the home, bringing good fortune.

On the other hand, when the main door suffers from Feng Shui defects, then the residents will suffer from Shar Chi – what the Chinese refer to as killing breath. Shar Chi is easy to resolve: it often results from the door being too big or too small relative to the size of the building. Another cause is the presence of sharp, pointed structures targeted directly at the door, forming "poison arrows." One way to deal with such arrows is to deflect them using reflective materials.

CREDITO ITALIANO BANK, MILAN, ITALY. A WELL-DECORATED AND GRAND ENTRANCE DOOR ENCOURAGES GOOD BUSINESS CHI TO ENTER THE BUILDING.

GRUNER AND JAHR PUBLISHERS' BUILDING, HAMBURG, GERMANY. IT IS GOOD FENG SHUI PRACTICE TO HAVE THE ENTRANCE TO A COMMERCIAL BUILDING HIGHER THAN STREET LEVEL.

16

What is Feng Shui?

HISTORIC FAILURES

If Feng Shui principles had been known and practiced in the West before now, some disastrous architectural decisions might have been avoided, and ill fortune might have been averted.

One famous building in London, for example, faces a long, straight road. This is none other than the regal Buckingham Palace, which stands at the end of a road called The Mall. The Mall is a classic poison arrow and the Feng Shui of the royal residents cannot escape being adversely affected.

Luckily, the Queen Victoria Memorial, which sits at the center of the roundabout just in front of the Palace, serves to deflect some of the terrible effects of the killing breath, but the complete absence of plants in the forecourt just in front of the building brings further imbalance and bad luck to the Royal family.

The Mall leading up to Buckingham Palace creates a poison arrow aimed directly at the front entrance; however, its harmful effects are somewhat dissipated when the negative Chi flows around the circular roundabout. A barrier that deflects the negative Chi would provide even greater protection against the poison arrow.

PENINSULA HOTEL, KOWLOON, HONG KONG. THE MAIN ENTRANCE IS GRAND AND HAS A CIRCULAR DRIVEWAY IN FRONT, AS WELL AS A SMALL POOL OF WATER – ALL OF WHICH CREATE EXCELLENT FENG SHUI.

THE RITZ, PICCADILLY, LONDON. BRIGHT LIGHTS AROUND THE ENTRANCE ATTRACT NOT ONLY CUSTOMERS BUT ALSO GOOD, VIBRANT CHI.

KUWAIT NATIONAL BANK. THE MAIN DOOR IS MUCH TOO LARGE AND THE EMPTY SPACE IMMEDIATELY ABOVE THE ENTRANCE IS NOT A GOOD FEATURE, CREATING INAUSPICIOUS FENG SHUI.

OFFICE BUILDING, NEW YO[RK] CITY. THE LARGE REVOLVIN[G] DOORS OF THIS OFFICE BUILDING ENCOURAGE PO[SITIVE] CHI FLOWS AND ATTRACT FORTUNE INTO THE BUIL[DING].

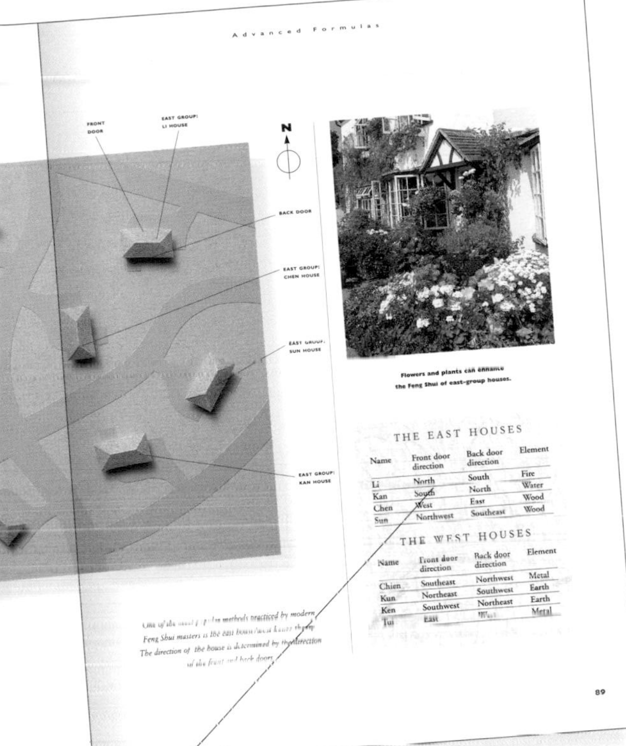

THE EAST HOUSES

Name	Front door direction	Back door direction	Element
Li	North	South	Fire
Kan	South	North	Water
Chen	West	East	Wood
Sun	Northwest	Southeast	Wood

THE WEST HOUSES

Name	Front door direction	Back door direction	Element
Chien	Southeast	Northwest	Metal
Kun	Northeast	Southwest	Earth
Ken	Southwest	Northeast	Earth
Tui	East	West	Metal

LILLIAN TOO

Lillian Too began her preoccupation with Feng Shui in the early 1970s when she began to learn *kung fu* with Master Yap Cheng Hai. He told her many fascinating stories about Feng Shui and its potent effect on families and households. Her research into the subject then began and led her through a fascinating study of the whole spectrum of Chinese cultural practice, which was intensified in the 1980s.

She has actively used Feng Shui to enhance her own career and family life, preferring to test out alternative methods if something she has tried does not work, and always basing her practice on the fundamentals of the science.

TABLES SUMMARIZE AUSPICIOUS DIRECTIONS AND LOCATIONS.

BOXED FEATURES INTRODUCE DETAILED ADVICE.

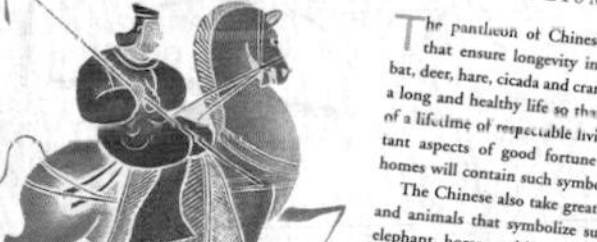

PRACTICAL EXAMPLES ARE ALL BASED ON EXPERIENCE.

SPECIALLY COMMISSIONED PHOTOGRAPHY SHOWS HOW TO IMPLEMENT FENG SHUI.

PART ONE

INTRODUCING FENG SHUI

Chapter One

WHAT IS FENG SHUI?

The study of Feng Shui takes us on a fascinating journey of discovery that blends several aspects of Chinese cultural practice. Feng Shui is an enticing composite of mystical beliefs, astrology, folklore, and common sense. As we look in more detail at this ancient practice, our investigation will reveal Feng Shui to be a very complex wisdom, based on the Chinese understanding of the dynamic flow of energy throughout the universe, and described through colorful symbolism.

We will enter into the intangible world of dragons and tigers, wind and water, positive and negative forces, Yin and Yang, energy flows, cosmic breaths, and the interactions of nature's elements, constantly changing, constantly in a state of flux.

FENG SHUI means "wind and water." In its literal sense this refers to the topography of the earth, its mountains, valleys, and waterways whose shape and size, direction and levels are created by the continuous interaction of these two powerful forces of nature. To people of Chinese origin all over the world, Feng Shui is a mystical practice that blends ancient wisdom with cultural tradition, a body of knowledge that lays down guidelines for life's different situations.

The laws of Feng Shui are, for example, used to differentiate between auspicious and inauspicious land sites, and they provide instructions for positioning homes and designing room layouts in ways that promise to enhance the quality of their owners' lives in surprising and dramatic ways.

In the family home, good Feng Shui positioning creates harmonious relationships between husband and wife, fosters good health, attracts abundance and prosperity, and helps to build good reputations. In Chinese cultures, where family life and honor are very strong, good Feng Shui is seen as helping husbands and wives beget many good and loving children who will bring honor to the family name.

In business, observing Feng Shui rules in the selection and design of your premises is a sound way of creating opportunities for growth, raising your business profile and your standing in the community, of attracting customers, raising profits, and expanding turnover. Employees will stay loyal and a pervasive aura of goodwill will create smooth working relationships.

Bad Feng Shui, by contrast, brings illness and disaster, accidents and financial loss. Bad Feng Shui causes opportunities to slip away, careers to fade, wealth to be squandered, and reputations to collapse. Above all, bad Feng Shui causes grave unhappiness, and sometimes even results in tragic consequences for the family and its well being.

FENG SHUI REVIVAL

Feng Shui practice is enjoying a spectacular revival in the country of its origin. Plans for new buildings and huge property developments around southern China and in many of its coastal cities now bear testimony to the Feng Shui practitioner's input. Like their fellow Chinese in Hong Kong, Taiwan, Singapore, and elsewhere, increasing numbers of Chinese in present-day China now actively look to Feng Shui to give them an additional edge in business.

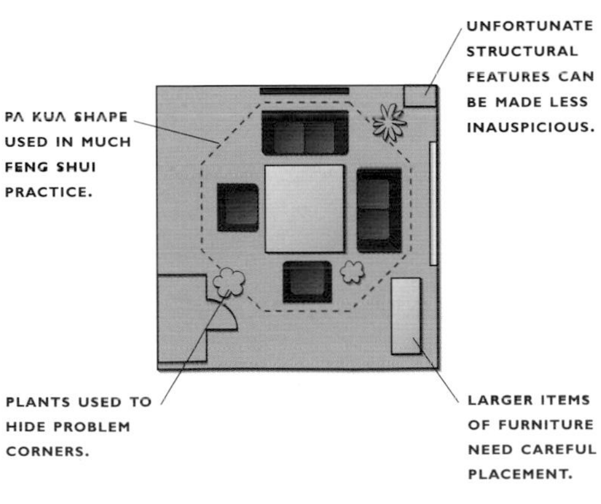

FAR LEFT **Making small adjustments to your room layouts following Feng Shui guidelines can improve your family relationships.**

LEFT **The ancient science of Feng Shui can create advantageous results when applied to modern interiors.**

ENERGY LINES

Feng Shui advocates living in harmony with the earth's environment and its energy lines, so that there is a proper balance between the forces of nature. Feng Shui contends that the environment is crowded with invisible but powerful energy lines – some auspicious and some pernicious – and that these energy lines carry with them either harmony or discord, health or sickness, prosperity or poverty.

The practice of Feng Shui is concerned with harnessing the energy lines that are auspicious – what the Chinese refer to as "the Dragon's cosmic breath" (or Sheng Chi). Auspicious energy lines travel in a meandering fashion. Feng Shui is also about avoiding inauspicious energy lines that represent "killing breath" (or Shar Chi). Feng Shui experts strenuously warn against sleeping, sitting, working, eating, and living in places that are hit or attacked by this pernicious and invisible killing breath, which is usually described as "poison arrows."

The eight roads radiating from the Arc de Triomphe in Paris create excellent Feng Shui for the city, with energy able to flow along the broad avenue of the Champs Elysée to the open spaces of the Place de la Concorde.

The energy flowing along the two arms of the Y-shaped road in front of the Flatiron building in New York City could be overwhelming. The triangular shape of the building itself suggests inauspicious Feng Shui, although this is somewhat mitigated by the rounded corners.

Killing breath is caused by the presence of sharp, pointed objects or structures that channel bad Feng Shui. Individuals are inadvertently harmed if these poison arrows happen to be aimed directly at front doors, or at rooms, chairs, desks, or beds where they sit or sleep.

POISON ARROWS

The offending arrow structures can be straight roads, the sharply pointed angles of roof lines, a single tree, electricity pylons or towers, the edges of a tall building, a cross, a protruding corner, an overhead beam, or any object that has a threatening appearance. The foul energy that emanates from poison arrows travels in straight lines, carrying with it ill fortune and other odious effects.

If the front door or sitting and sleeping position of an individual lies in the direct path of such energy forces, the consequences are believed to be extremely negative, and sometimes can even be disastrous, causing grave misfortune to the resident or individual concerned.

DIRE CONSEQUENCES

The sharper and more threatening the poison arrow, the more dire the consequences of being hit. Misfortune caused by such arrows takes the form of illness, missed opportunities, legal disputes, quarrels, financial loss, and many other types of bad luck. Feng Shui offers a variety of solutions for combating or avoiding poison arrows, and knowledge of Feng Shui enables practitioners both to diagnose bad Feng Shui situations and then to find ways of taking proper precautions against their malevolent effects.

The consequences of poison arrows can be quite clearly demonstrated. Many highly visible and important public buildings are, for example, exposed to poison arrows, simply because, in western architecture and town planning, it is thought desirable to have a straight avenue leading directly to the grand ceremonial entrance. Such is true in the case of the White House in Washington, where negative energy is channeled down 16th Avenue straight to the door of the President's home. It is also true of Buckingham Palace in London, the home of the British royal family, and numerous stately homes in Great Britain.

Is it any wonder, then, that American influence in the world is in decline (compared with the Pacific Rim and Orient, which is on the ascendancy), and that people in Great Britain are talking about the end of the monarchy and the reform of the House of Lords?

GOOD FORTUNE SYMBOLS

Good Feng Shui is associated with certain objects because of their colors or the material from which they are made, or because their name in Chinese is similar to desirable conditions, such as tranquility or longevity. Having these objects in your home, or hanging a painting on the wall depicting these objects, will help to bring good fortune. Some of the most important objects and their symbolism include:

- Wealth, which is symbolized by gold, antique coins, and the presence of clean, clear, rippling water.

The crane denotes longevity.

The elephant symbolizes wisdom.

- Wisdom is represented by the elephant, which is regarded with great respect in many Asian countries.
- Longevity and good health, which is represented by bamboo, pine trees, and cranes, which are often depicted in Chinese art. Peaches also symbolize longevity.

FENG SHUI AT WORK IN THE ORIENT

Feng Shui is a vital and exciting component of a wisdom from ancient China – a science that goes back at least four thousand years – to the days of emperors and mythical legends.

That it has survived the centuries, and is today widely practiced by Chinese businessmen in Hong Kong, Taiwan, Singapore, and Malaysia, is a powerful testament to its efficacy and potency. In many parts of Asia, Feng Shui is regarded as a vital part of everyday life. Top executives and humble stall-keepers, tycoons and taxi drivers alike believe in and practice Feng Shui.

Very few Hong Kong residents would run the risk of having bad Feng Shui. Consulting a Feng Shui expert before buying a new home, relocating an office, or rearranging floor layouts is very much taken for granted. Skilled Feng Shui masters do a brisk business, providing consultations to rich and poor alike, basing the fees they charge on the square footage of the space they survey. Needless to say, fees usually escalate in proportion to the wealth and status of the client.

HONG KONG'S PROSPERITY

The residents of Hong Kong believe that the former colony will continue to prosper, despite the handover from British to Chinese rule that will take place in June, 1997. They believe that Hong Kong

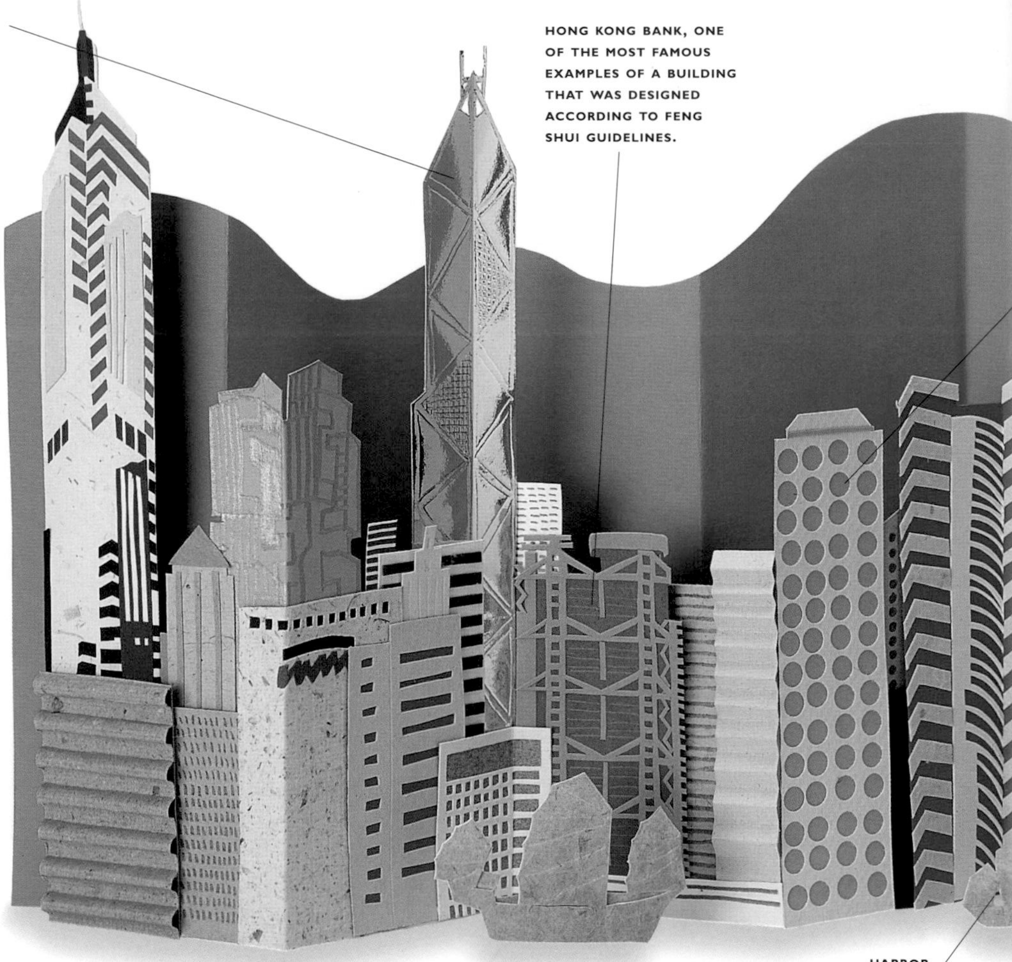

Almost every high-rise building in Hong Kong has design features that were determined by good Feng Shui practices. Often a Feng Shui master works alongside the architect and engineer in the initial phases of a building's design. If an established business is failing, a Feng Shui expert may be called in to assess the building and suggest alterations to improve the flow of prosperous energy.

will always enjoy good Feng Shui because, they say, the shape of its harbor resembles a money bag. The "mouth" of this money bag is so small that whatever prosperity has been achieved, whatever riches and wealth have been accumulated, will stay safe forever within the bag. Residents also point to the safeguard provided by the presence of the nine dragons that give their name to Kowloon island. The same auspicious nine dragons are also represented in a wall on the seafront of the island, a replica of the Nine Dragon Wall found in the Forbidden City in Beijing.

In recent years, as China has opened its doors to the outside world, businessmen from Hong Kong have moved their operations into southern China and they have reawakened the practice of Feng Shui in that country. Feng Shui, along with so much else from China's past, had taken a back seat to the politics of Communism and was considered outdated and inappropriate to latter day aspirations. It is thus ironic that Chinese emigrants, who have kept alive their cultural and traditional beliefs, such as Feng Shui, are now reminding China of its old wisdoms and cultural practices.

THE CONNAUGHT BUILDING, WITH ITS ROUND WINDOWS, WAS ORIGINALLY THOUGHT TO HAVE BAD FENG SHUI, BUT IT COULD BE SAID THAT THE WINDOWS SYMBOLIZE COINS, AND INDEED COMPANIES HAVING OFFICES IN THE BUILDING HAVE FLOURISHED AND ENJOYED GOOD FENG SHUI.

VICTORIA PEAK LIES BEHIND HONG KONG, SYMBOLIZING SUPPORT AND REPRESENTING GOOD FENG SHUI.

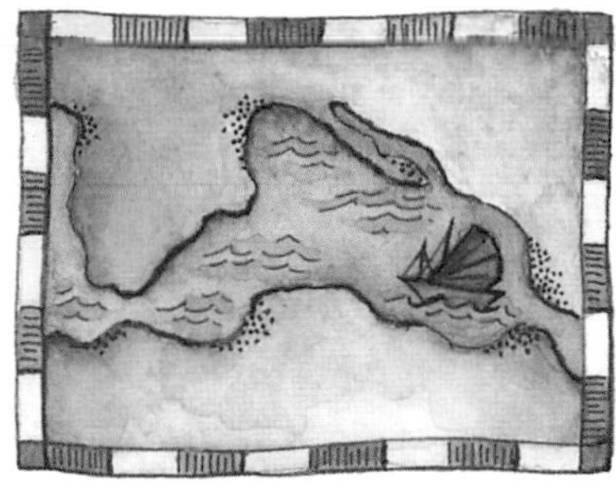

Hong Kong's prosperity is believed to be safeguarded for the future because the shape of the harbor resembles a money bag.

Meanwhile, across the South China Sea, experts point to an abundance of auspicious Feng Shui for the Malaysian capital, Kuala Lumpur, and for Singapore. In both cases, they say, excellent balance has been achieved in the interaction of Feng Shui's five elements. The earth and metal elements, represented by roads and high-rise buildings, are perfectly balanced by healthy vibrant trees lining the major thoroughfares. Efforts to clean up the rivers flowing across the cities have brought additional good luck, while the essential water element – symbolizing the flow of money – is present in the numerous artificial waterfalls and fountains in the public parks and in front of buildings. At night, the thoroughfares are brightly lit, creating beautiful "fire," thus attracting plenty of intangible business luck to the two cities.

FENG SHUI AT WORK IN THE WEST

Several western companies with Hong Kong subsidiaries practice Feng Shui, including Citibank, N. M. Rothschild, Shell, and Sime Darby. Even if they start out as sceptics, expatriate executives find themselves succumbing to the pervasive leverage that good Feng Shui positioning brings to their organizations. In some cases, the practice of Feng Shui is also taken into their homes. This happens when initial cynicism of the practice has been transformed into healthy belief.

Some eventually become such strong advocates of the practices they have become familiar with that they stay in touch with their Feng Shui consultants even after they leave the colony; while others try to remember and practice the basic principles picked up during their stint out East. In this way Feng Shui knowledge has slowly crossed the waters to the West.

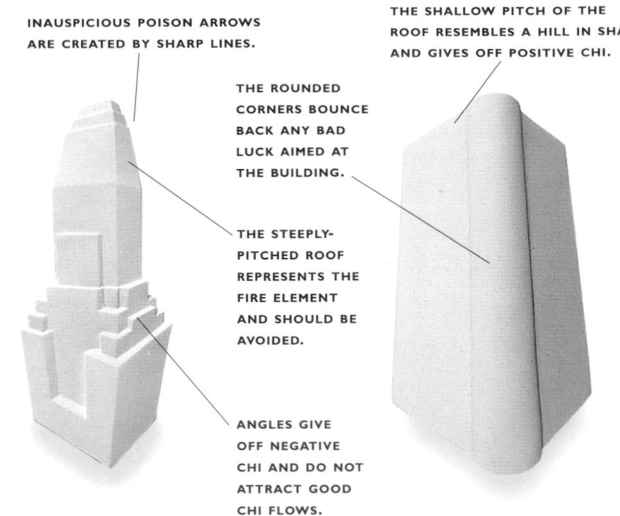

Tall buildings with many angles and sharp edges give off negative energy forces. Rounding the corners is a friendly gesture because it ensures that the building does not create harmful Chi for its neighbors.

THE IMPORTANCE OF DOORWAYS AND ENTRANCES

Western architects can learn much from Feng Shui about the design and location of doors, factors that have important implications for the quality of Chi flows and movements within the confines of any room or building.

When the main door of your home, shop, or office enjoys good Feng Shui, with nothing threatening it from within or without, then the forces are well-balanced, and auspicious Sheng Chi (cosmic breath) moves into the home, bringing good fortune.

On the other hand, when the main door suffers from Feng Shui defects, then the residents will suffer from Shar Chi – what the Chinese refer to as killing breath. Shar Chi is easy to resolve: it often results from the door being too big or too small relative to the size of the building. Another cause is the presence of sharp, pointed structures targeted directly at the door, forming "poison arrows." One way to deal with such arrows is to deflect them using reflective materials.

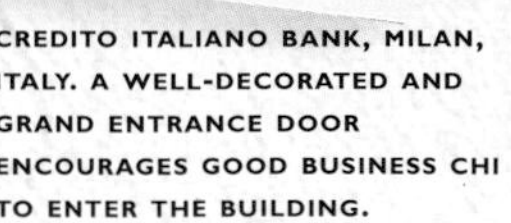

CREDITO ITALIANO BANK, MILAN, ITALY. A WELL-DECORATED AND GRAND ENTRANCE DOOR ENCOURAGES GOOD BUSINESS CHI TO ENTER THE BUILDING.

GRUNER AND JAHR PUBLISHERS' BUILDING, HAMBURG, GERMANY. IT IS GOOD FENG SHUI PRACTICE TO HAVE THE ENTRANCE TO A COMMERCIAL BUILDING HIGHER THAN STREET LEVEL.

HISTORIC FAILURES

If Feng Shui principles had been known and practiced in the West before now, some disastrous architectural decisions might have been avoided, and ill fortune might have been averted.

One famous building in London, for example, faces a long, straight road. This is none other than the regal Buckingham Palace, which stands at the end of a road called The Mall. The Mall is a classic poison arrow and the Feng Shui of the royal residents cannot escape being adversely affected.

Luckily, the Queen Victoria Memorial, which sits at the center of the roundabout just in front of the Palace, serves to deflect some of the terrible effects of the killing breath, but the complete absence of plants in the forecourt just in front of the building brings further imbalance and bad luck to the Royal family.

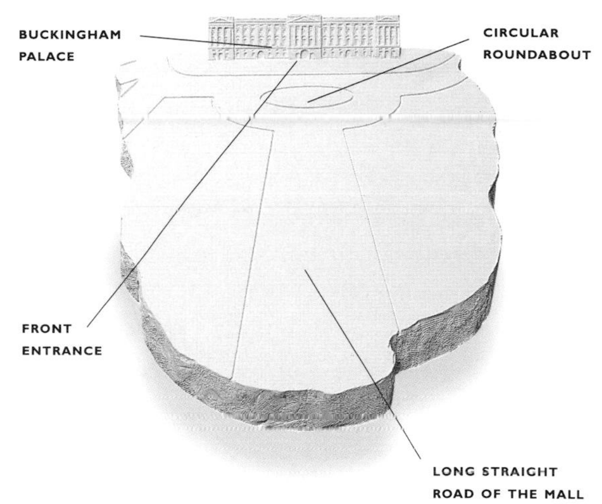

The Mall leading up to Buckingham Palace creates a poison arrow aimed directly at the front entrance; however, its harmful effects are somewhat dissipated when the negative Chi flows around the circular roundabout. A barrier that deflects the negative Chi would provide even greater protection against the poison arrow.

PENINSULA HOTEL, KOWLOON, HONG KONG. THE MAIN ENTRANCE IS GRAND AND HAS A CIRCULAR DRIVEWAY IN FRONT, AS WELL AS A SMALL POOL OF WATER – ALL OF WHICH CREATE EXCELLENT FENG SHUI.

THE RITZ, PICCADILLY, LONDON. BRIGHT LIGHTS AROUND THE ENTRANCE ATTRACT NOT ONLY CUSTOMERS BUT ALSO GOOD, VIBRANT CHI.

KUWAIT NATIONAL BANK. THE MAIN DOOR IS MUCH TOO LARGE AND THE EMPTY SPACE IMMEDIATELY ABOVE THE ENTRANCE IS NOT A GOOD FEATURE, CREATING INAUSPICIOUS FENG SHUI.

OFFICE BUILDING, NEW YORK CITY. THE LARGE REVOLVING DOORS OF THIS OFFICE BUILDING ENCOURAGE POSITIVE CHI FLOWS AND ATTRACT GOOD FORTUNE INTO THE BUILDING.

ANCIENT SOURCES: THE CLASSIC FENG SHUI TEXTS

Until recently, much of the extensive literature written on Feng Shui has only been available in Chinese and the principles are not well known in the West, even though much of this literature is freely available in Taiwan and Hong Kong. The origin of these texts goes back thousands of years, at least to the fourth century B.C.

In the past, Feng Shui practice was confined to the ruling classes – to the emperor and his ministers. Many of the early records and ancient texts were (and remain) obscure. Their definitions were hidden in archaic language, their meanings locked in symbolic explanations that sometimes give rise to multiple interpretations. Court advisors had to pass imperial examinations that involved acquiring a profound knowledge of the classical Chinese texts. One of these was the *I Ching* – known in the West as the *Book of Changes* – and those who sought to attain high positions had to be able to interpret the divinations and predictions revealed in the *I Ching*, an important component of which entailed knowledge of Feng Shui.

LEARNED MANDARINS

Those who acquired this knowledge enjoyed privileged positions at court, and were revered as learned mandarins. These were the men who were consulted when palaces and tombs were built and when new cities and capitals were planned. They conscientiously studied landscapes, carefully calculated compass directions, and diagnosed the positioning of buildings within land sites. They also worked out appropriate dimensions for new buildings, a science that also involved investigating individual birthdates, to ensure that human energy flows could be harmoniously aligned to that of the home, its residents, and the environment.

MASTER YANG

In China, Feng Shui has been practiced since at least the Tang Dynasty (A.D. 618–907). The most ancient practitioner of Feng Shui was Master Yang Yun-Sang, who is universally acknowledged as its founder. Master Yang was the principal advisor to the court of the Tang emperor, Hi Tsang (A.D. 888). Master Yang left a legacy of classical texts that have

Learned mandarins were the Feng Shui practitioners of the imperial Chinese court. Much revered, they advised on all building projects.

Feng Shui symbolism has a long history, dating back thousands of years. Here a golden lion guards the entrance to the former Imperial Palace in Beijing.

been preserved and which continue to be studied to this day. His books on Feng Shui make up the major texts on which generations of practitioners have based their knowledge and practices.

CROSSING THE WATERS

Much of the rich heritage of the Feng Shui textbooks (and there are presently about two to three thousand of these texts) has made its way to Taiwan. It is believed that when General Chiang Kai-shek fled to the island from the Communists in China in 1949, he not only took with him thousands of tons' worth of Chinese treasures, paintings, art objects, and imperial treasures from the Forbidden City, but that his entourage also brought with them valuable old texts pertaining to Chinese scholarship and ancient wisdoms. Thus books on Feng Shui crossed the waters and made their way to the tiny island.

In Taiwan, Feng Shui is taken very much for granted and here the science is so advanced that many of the detailed and very potent advanced formulas of Feng Shui are practiced. It is no coincidence that Taiwan today stands among the richest and wealthiest nations of the world, with foreign reserves larger than the whole of mainland China and a per capita income that easily matches that of the developed world.

SCIENCE AND CIVILIZATION

Feng Shui is often described in the classical texts using a simple six-character phrase – "tian ling di li ren he" – which is full of resonance and meaning. Literally translated it means: "auspicious heavenly influence, beneficial topography, harmonious human actions."

These are the three factors that contribute to auspicious Feng Shui, but, as with so much in Chinese thought and science, far more lies behind this simple phrase than appears on the surface.

To understand heavenly influence it is necessary to learn astronomy and astrology and to study the *I Ching*. To become an expert on topography means studying various topographical features, such as hills, valleys, and watercourses, and understanding their influence on rain, floods, and tides. Knowledge of human actions requires an understanding of social, cultural, political, and religious forces, the hierarchical structure of society, the place of religion, and the moral obligations on both society and the individual.

Mastering Feng Shui involves careful study of topography.

ANIMAL SYMBOLISM AND THE FORM SCHOOL

In the works of Master Yang, the founder of Feng Shui practice, great emphasis is placed on the shape of hills and mountains, on the direction of watercourses and, above all, on the careful location and understanding of the lair of the dragon, China's most revered celestial creature.

Indeed, to the Chinese, the almighty dragon symbolized great power, and many natural phenomena were explained in the old days as manifestations of the dragon's moods. Thus, droughts were caused by thirsty dragons, typhoons and floods that brought chaos and death indicated the dragon's wrath, and life-giving rain was brought by happy, satisfied dragons.

Master Yang's doctrines were detailed in three classical Feng Shui texts, and each of these describes the practice of Feng Shui in terms of colorful dragon metaphors. The first of these, *Han Lung Ching,* describes the "Art of Rousing the Dragon." The second, *Ching Nang Ao Chih*, offers guidelines and methods for locating the dragon's lair, while the third book, *I Lung Ching,* explains the techniques for finding the dragon in areas where "they do not prominently stand forth."

The white tiger hills on the right, or the west, merge with the green dragon to create auspicious Chi.

The black turtle hills should lie behind to act as back support and protection.

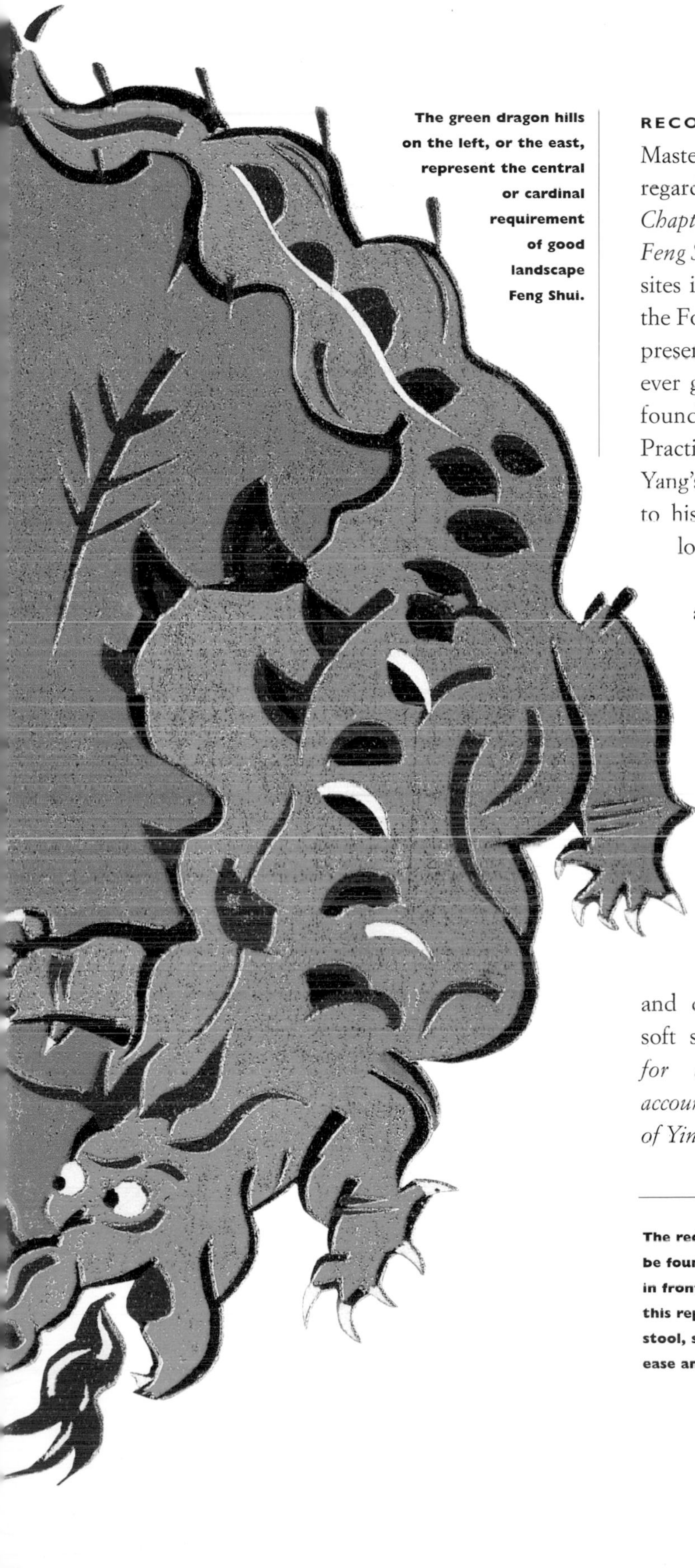

The green dragon hills on the left, or the east, represent the central or cardinal requirement of good landscape Feng Shui.

RECOGNIZING LANDSCAPES

Master Yang's principles eventually came to be regarded as the Form School of Feng Shui *(see Chapter Four for a fuller discussion of the different Feng Shui schools)*, rationalizing good and bad land sites in terms of dragon symbolism. According to the Form School, auspicious locations required the presence of the green dragon. Furthermore, wherever genuine dragons lived, there, too, would be found the important white tiger companion. Practitioners of Feng Shui who followed Master Yang's descriptions of a landscape and subscribed to his theories thus began their investigation of locations by searching for the dragon.

Dragons, tigers, and all other celestial animals that feature in the language of Feng Shui are to be construed in a symbolic sense. These animals refer to hills and landforms. Whether dragons and tigers are actually considered to be present depends, among other things, on the shape of hills and mountains, on the presence and directions of waterways – such as lakes and rivers – on the type of soil in the terrain, on how lush the vegetation is and, finally, on the perceived balance of Yin and Yang – expressed in terms of light and dark, sunlight and shade, hard rock and soft soil *(see Chapter Three for a more detailed account of the concept of Yin and Yang).*

The red phoenix hill should be found in low-lying land in front of the site and this represents the footstool, signifying a life of ease and luxury.

THE PA KUA AND THE COMPASS SCHOOL

While dragon symbolism was the principle mainstay of the Form School, eventually there emerged a second major system that approached the practice of Feng Shui from a quite different perspective. This second system laid stress on certain calculations, using the symbols of the *I Ching* or *Book of Changes* and the directions of the compass, and was based on door directions and individual dates of birth. Good or bad Feng Shui was then interpreted according to the placement of the symbolic hexagrams and trigrams of the *I Ching* around an eight-sided symbol called the "Pa Kua."

One trigram was placed on each side of the Pa Kua, and, according to where each of the eight trigrams were placed, corresponding attributes and symbols were further identified, referring to colors, to different members of the family, to specific compass directions, to one of the five elements, and to other attributes.

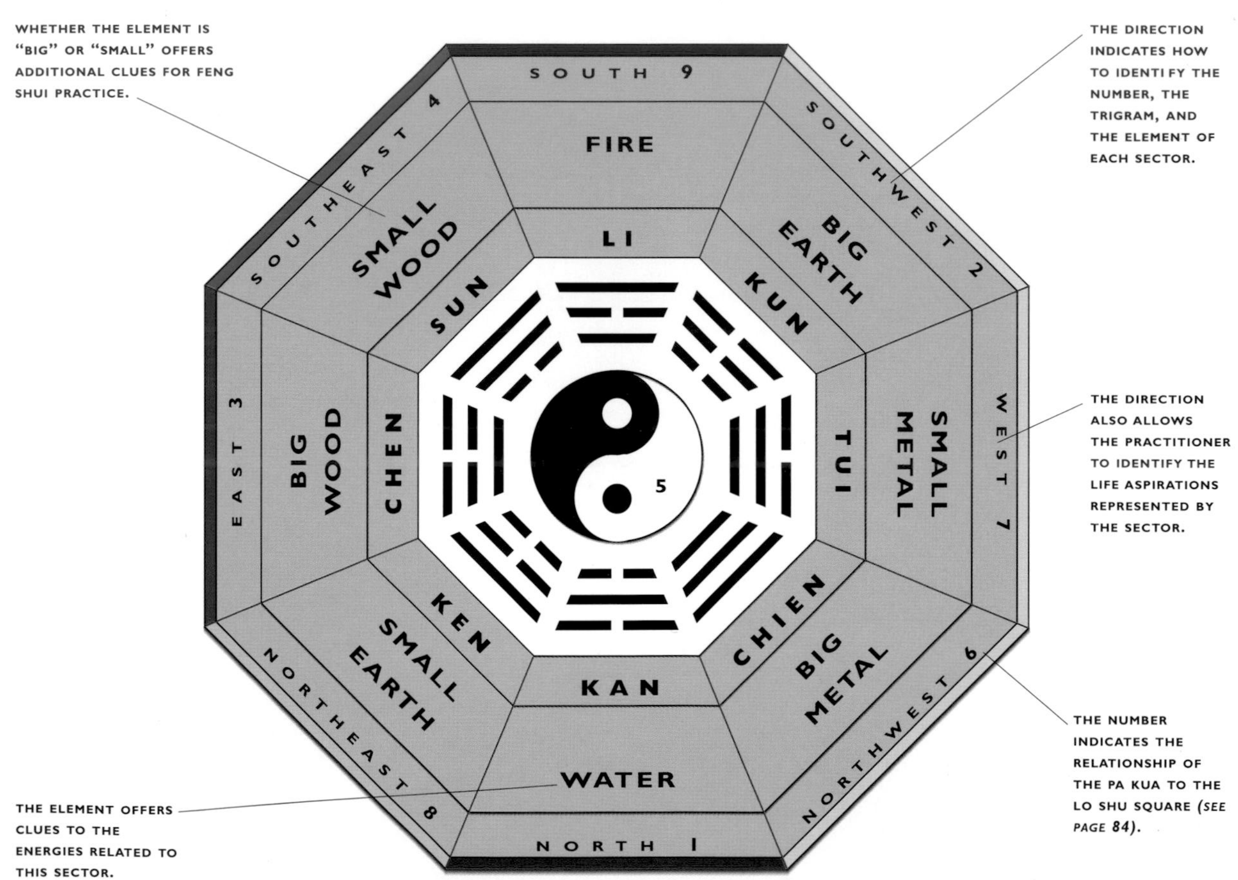

The eight-sided Pa Kua is used by the Compass School of Feng Shui. Symbols and meanings attributed to each sector offer clues for the practice of Feng Shui.

THE LUO PAN

The Luo Pan, or Chinese Feng Shui compass, is an elaborate reference compass which contains all the clues and symbols that indicate good and bad Feng Shui. Each of the symbols will have different meanings for different masters, and, once a master has gained great expertise, he or she will usually have their own Luo Pan designed containing all their own trade secrets. Furthermore, the Chinese always place south at the top of the compass but north is still magnetic north. For the layman practitioner, however, any Western compass will suffice.

DESIGNING THE HOME

Each of these symbols and attributes are supposed to offer clues for designing the interiors and exteriors of houses or palaces, for allocating different rooms to different purposes and for assigning different corners of the home to different individuals in order to maximize auspicious Feng Shui for every member of the family.

This second major system came to be known as the Compass School of Feng Shui, although this school now has many different branches. Each branch has a different method, and uses different equations for its Feng Shui calculations; some concentrate on numerology, while others concentrate on a time dimension. Certain branches of the Compass School also emphasize the influence of the planets on the quality of good landscape locations.

A traditional Luo Pan compass used in the Compass School of Feng Shui. The signs and symbols on each ring represent reference words that could have different meanings for different masters.

MODERN FENG SHUI

By the late nineteenth and early twentieth centuries, the two major schools of Feng Shui had begun to merge completely. Theories of the Form School – including beliefs in the use of dragon symbolism – gained wider acceptability and began to be practiced by followers of the Compass School. Modern Feng Shui practitioners today practice a hazy combination of the two.

FORM OR COMPASS?

In Taiwan, where Feng Shui practice is very advanced, the predominantly Hokkien dialect group of Chinese practitioners use potent Compass School formulas, but they also take landscape considerations into account.

Indeed, the Taiwanese believe that despite what the compass formulas may be indicating, landscape considerations override Compass School indications. Thus, for instance, if according to certain formulas your main door would bring you auspicious luck if it faced south, but by doing so you would be facing a small hill or, worse still, a mountain, then despite what the formula says, you will suffer ill fortune. This is because the effect of the hill or mountain would be too awesome, and would completely override Compass School indications. Facing a hill directly is always bad Feng Shui. If you live in the vicinity of a hill, always place your home in such a way that the hill lies behind you. This allows you to tap the hill for support, and not

Feng Shui considerations can be applied to any home. If you live in the country, you will be more likely to take landscape considerations into account and concentrate on exterior Feng Shui. In Taiwan, the effect of the terrain is deemed to be more powerful than Compass School calculations.

If you live in an apartment, you will look to Feng Shui interpretations that are closely connected to the interior of your home. Here the room is flooded with light and has abundant greenery, but the poison arrows created by the edge of the bookcase as well as the exposed bookshelves will create Shar Chi.

to have to confront it. This tenet is based on the belief that humankind is not strong enough to take on the power of a hill or mountain.

NEW DEVELOPMENTS

There are now many different Compass School formulas and the methods favored in Hong Kong and Taiwan differ. These differences can be interpreted in the light of the predominant type of living conditions of the population in each country. In Hong Kong, the method used for calculating individual auspicious and inauspicious directions is generally based on the Four Pillars method, which is linked to Chinese astrology. In Taiwan they use the Pa-Kua Lo-Shu formula. Furthermore, in Hong Kong more emphasis is placed on the interiors of houses in the practice of Feng Shui, especially for creating wealth. In contrast, the Taiwanese use the Water Dragon formula for outdoor Feng Shui to attract prosperity. This is probably due to the fact that in Hong Kong, 90 percent of the population now live in high-rise apartments and few have the necessary gardens in which to build a water dragon. This has encouraged Feng Shui masters to develop new interpretations more applicable to the needs of the population living in apartments.

INTERPRETATION

Irrespective of the method or formula used, however, all the symbols and tools of Feng Shui are the same. It is only in the interpretation of the symbols that they differ. Thus, how good the professional Feng Shui practitioner is depends almost entirely on the superiority of his or her interpretations of the symbols, and on how creative and clever he or she is in finding solutions to Feng Shui problems. The best masters are those who interpret the formulas correctly and then make suggestions that do not require too much redesign of one's home.

FENG SHUI EFFICACY

On December 24, 1992, the *Asian Wall Street Journal* carried an interesting story on its front page. "A kind of crystal ball" is how it labeled the "Feng Shui Index" devised by staff at the Credit Lyonnais bank. This was an index that had accurately forecast the major turning points of the Hang Seng index (the Hong Kong stock market's index of share price performance) 12 months in advance of the events.

The newspaper reported that stock analysts working at the Hong Kong arm of Credit Lyonnais Securities had consulted a trio of Feng Shui experts on how they thought the Hong Kong stock market would perform in the year of the Monkey (1992).

In Hong Kong, the securities arm of Credit Lyonnais has, since 1992, commissioned a Feng Shui forecast on the Hong Kong stock market's performance over the coming year. Termed the "Feng Shui Index," this report has proved to be remarkably accurate.

These experts used a combination of astrological and geographical calculations to measure and redress the imbalances of Hong Kong's natural and man-made environments, and they had used this to create their "Feng Shui Index." By December, it had become clear to the analysts that this same Feng Shui Index was an "almost perfect map of the market's turning points."

Spurred on by this incredible performance, Credit Lyonnais has commissioned similar indexes every year since. To practitioners familiar with the Feng Shui's potency, the accuracy of these predictions comes as no surprise. To the Westerner, ignorant of the practice, much of the Feng Shui analysis must have sounded like "bulletins from a psychedelic zoo," since much of the index described the interactions between the twelve animals of the Chinese zodiac and the five elements of fire, water, metal, wood, and earth.

According to the project's head at the securities firm, however, the Feng Shui analysis can very easily be compared to the mathematical market forecasting methods widely used on Wall Street.

ADVICE TO THE PRESIDENT

For an even more dramatic tale of Feng Shui, we move over to the Philippines. On January 4, 1993, the Reuters press agency flashed the headline: "Ramos to heed Geomancy advice." It proceeded to report the fact that President Fidel Ramos had said he would look into reports that three misplaced trees were to blame for the continuing misfortunes and natural calamities afflicting the Philippines. According to Feng Shui analysis, the report stated, three huge trees standing in front of Malacanang, the presidential palace, were blocking the flow of cosmic energy, thereby keeping good fortune from the president and the country. Experts suggested that these trees should be felled.

Philippine President Fidel Ramos took seriously the warnings from Feng Shui experts that three huge trees in front of the presidential palace were preventing positive Chi flows and good fortune from reaching the President and the country.

They also pointed to the presence of unlucky symbols on the presidential seal and on the country's bank notes. The sea lion in the presidential seal had an inauspiciously crooked tail, while the stars surrounding it suggested darkness, signifying disaster. The 500 peso bill was considered unlucky because it contained 13 stars, showed 13 people, and the number 500 appeared 13 times.

CARRIAN CAN OF WORMS

These and other stories are the stuff of folk tales in the cities of Asia. Feng Shui stories that relate to the rise and fall of powerful politicians, billion-dollar corporations, and wealthy business leaders are almost always taken seriously. When the infamous Carrian Group of Hong Kong collapsed in the early 1980s, revealing a complex web of intrigue, murder, corruption and scandal, many attributed its demise to a newly built road flyover whose shape resembled that of two crab claws tightly crushing the Carrian headquarters building in its grip. With such Feng Shui, it was just a matter of time before the Carrian can of worms was exposed and its key executives placed under arrest.

The Philippine 500 peso bill and its association with the number 13 is considered very unlucky for the Philippines.

FORTUNE'S RISE AND FALL

In the late 1980s, a highly popular Malaysian Chinese politician was placed under arrest and imprisoned by the Singapore authorities. Many attributed his downfall to the bad Feng Shui of his palatial mansion, that had been newly built in one of the more fashionable suburbs of Kuala Lumpur. Gossip had it that he was arrested shortly after moving into the new house, which had a winding staircase in its center, carpeted in red. The staircase, it was speculated, resembled a corkscrew boring into his heart, while the red carpet was said to symbolize blood flowing from the wound.

Bruce Lee, the well known Kung Fu movie star, was at the height of his career when he died suddenly in Hong Kong. Popular gossip attributes his death to Feng Shui, blaming his Chinese name, "siau loong," which means "little dragon," for his demise. In making his home in Kowloon, the place of the nine dragons, Bruce Lee is said to have shown disrespect for his elders. Warned of this, he installed a protective Pa Kua symbol above his main door to ward off inauspicious forces, but during a particularly fierce typhoon, the Pa Kua fell, leaving him at the mercy of the fierce wind dragons. When the Pa Kua collapsed, Bruce Lee lost his protection and his life.

Hong Kong at night. Good Feng Shui practices have helped to make this city one of the most prosperous business centers in the world.

FENG SHUI SUCCESSES

Not all Feng Shui stories, however, are tales of misfortune. There are also stories that relate how Feng Shui has brought great abundance to cities and great leaders. Sun Yat Sen, the leader of the October 10th revolution that overthrew the Qing dynasty in China in 1911, is believed to have enjoyed tremendous good luck because of the excellent position of his mother's grave.

One of Malaysia's richest men, Lim Goh Tong, is an ardent believer in Feng Shui. He made his fortune after successfully building the Genting Highlands Casino, Hotel and Resort in the mountains located on the outskirts of Kuala Lumpur. Many speculated that he positioned the Genting Hotel so perfectly according to the principles of Feng Shui that it was profitable from the start. Today, almost 30 years later, the Genting Group is a household name in Malaysia and has assets all over the world.

So, too, with the fast-growing Hong Leong Group, which has assets in Hong Kong, London, the United States, and Australia. In the early 1980s, when the company was not yet very large, I was Group Managing Director, and one of my main concerns was to have the company logo of a dragon

The Genting Highlands Resort, Kuala Lumpur, Malaysia. Good Feng Shui design ensured success from the start.

redrawn. The dragon is a very popular and powerful symbol, and many Chinese use it as a corporate logo, but the Hong Leong dragon looked thin and hungry and, worse, it was enclosed in a circle. I was told by a Feng Shui master in Hong Kong that the circle would make it difficult for the dragon to fly and hence for the group to grow and expand. He recommended that I draw a fat, pregnant-looking dragon and advised that I remove the circle... which I did. The group has never looked back, successfully growing by acquisition (signifying lots of offspring), and today it is one of the most profitable and successful conglomerates found in the region.

Good Feng Shui has also helped many of Hong Kong's Chinese business leaders, including the legendary Li Ka Shing, owner of Hong Kong Electric, the Hutchison group, and many other billion-dollar businesses around the world; the charitable Y K Pao (deceased); Run Run Shaw, the Chinese cinema tycoon, and even the British-controlled Swire and Jardine groups. All have respect for the practice of Feng Shui – as can be easily discerned from the favorable positioning of their business premises and buildings.

A CITY'S FENG SHUI AWARENESS

Feng Shui is becoming increasingly popular all over Asia, especially in countries where Chinese people have settled. In Taipei – the capital of Taiwan and one of Asia's most vibrantly successful and wealthy cities – most of the high-rise buildings have been conscientiously designed with the corners smoothed round or cut off so that neighboring buildings do not have their Feng Shui hurt by the intangible forces of killing breath caused by "poison arrows."

The new Hong Leong corporate logo of the smiling, pregnant dragon that brought great success to the company.

MODERN SCIENCE VERSUS ANCIENT LORE

There are those who say that the subjective elements of Feng Shui analysis suggest that it is best regarded as an art – one requiring an understanding of mysticism and even having spiritual connotations. But the practice of Feng Shui does not require faith or fervent belief, nor does it require the compromise of any religious convictions or personal values. It is suggested here that Feng Shui should be regarded as a science – one that is based on the ancient Chinese view of the universe with its own novel explanations of the forces that shape it – and that its practices have many parallels with Western science, so that it requires far less of a leap of faith to justify many of its more obscure customs to the Western mind.

CULTURAL CONSIDERATIONS

Feng Shui is an oriental science insofar as it is a model of the world that allows those who use it to make certain predictions and achieve certain goals. It is based on practice, rather than the principles of theory upon which much of Western science is founded.

Feng Shui is not a complete science, just as chemistry describes only the chemical aspects of Western science. Since it is only part of a complete system, the practitioner can only understand it fully by also studying the other sciences, such as the *I Ching* or *Book of Changes* which is at the root of almost all traditional Chinese philosophy.

Feng Shui seeks to explain the behavior of the world in relation to the lives of individuals. Thus, it is a social science, but since it appears to deal with the behavior of external forces, it is also a physical science. It is a study of how the environment in which people live may affect their lives. But, beyond this, it is a study of how to use the environment to influence the quality of a person's life. This combination of sciences merely illustrates the huge difference between Western and oriental sciences, and explains why many Western scientists consider that there is no such thing as oriental science – the frame of reference is simply too difficult.

FENG SHUI THEORY

Feng Shui is described in a completely allegorical manner. The use of symbolism is rich: dragons, tigers, tortoises, compasses, and the five elements. These allegories serve to allow the practitioner easier access to, and learning of, the methods. It is, after all, a practical skill, and has been used by every member ot society in the orient. These allegories and symbolic mechanisms are rather like mnemonics to aid learning. Such symbolism, however, has the effect of hiding its relationship with Western thought because there is a cultural barrier to understanding the meaning of such symbolism.

Western science may have discovered how to split the atom, but there are still many pervasive sources of energy in the environment that it has yet to comprehend and learn how to harness.

The earth's atmosphere reverberates with unseen energy forces such as radio waves, which modern science has only recently begun to recognize and utilize. The ancient Chinese understood these forces and were able to harness their influences through the practice of Feng Shui.

INVISIBLE ENERGIES

Feng Shui seeks to harness Chi, or "dragon's cosmic breath." Chi is invisible, and so it should be, coming as it does from a mythical creature. It is also, apparently, all around us.

Parallels can be drawn between Chi and various forms of energy described in Western science where energy fields are investigated using various instruments. Compasses, for instance, are sensitive to magnetic fields. Feng Shui masters also use compasses. Electrical fields can be felt as static. Feng Shui also takes notice of these fields. Gravitational fields can be seen in the passing of the tides. Feng Shui takes an individual's year of birth into consideration, and predicts cyclical influences that change with the years and months, which may indicate particular concerns with the gravitational configuration of the solar system.

The fact of the matter is that the documentation upon which Feng Shui methods are based has been lost – only the methods remain. But this does not stop them from being effective. It only prevents a more profound understanding until the origins can be rediscovered. In order to do that, it is necessary to find hypotheses and sensible speculations about its mechanisms.

Much of Feng Shui practice is based on symbolism. This often involves descriptions of mythical beasts peculiar to that culture. This creates a cultural barrier between Eastern and Western scientific understanding.

PARALLELS WITH WESTERN SCIENCE

Feng Shui is concerned with very subtle effects – translated as luck. Western scientists might consider these as subtle levels of probability. Probability effects are not precise predictions – they indicate that certain things are more likely to happen if certain Feng Shui methods are used. Feng Shui describes several classes of events, some of which are deemed desirable and are thus labeled auspicious, while others are labeled inauspicious. The classes of events are roughly summarized as:

- production of wealth
- enhancement of health
- improvement of relationships
- protection from misfortune or harm
- mild misfortune
- serious loss
- serious injury
- death.

These classes describe the kind of Chi that certain environments and Feng Shui methods generate. It is, therefore, necessary to link the energy of Chi with human conditions.

THE HUMAN COMPONENT

As the biological systems of people and most animals are mainly reliant upon electrical energies, it is not difficult to see why we may well react in subtle ways to minute changes in our electrical environment. Many such correlations are being investigated by Western science: for instance, the much publicized connection between high electromagnetic fields under electrical pylons and the incidence of cancer. If we look at Feng Shui practice, we find that Feng Shui masters advise against living too near to transmission lines and towers, but explain the reason as being the likelihood of being hit by Shar Chi or "killing breath."

Thus it may be argued that Western science is well acquainted with invisible energies, some or all of which may be a component of the Chi said to affect individuals in Chinese terms.

MAGNETIC FIELDS

Feng Shui investigates living and working spaces with respect to their orientation in the magnetic field of the earth. Feng Shui masters will use compasses to determine the orientation of such spaces and the location, in particular, of the main door used for entry and exit. This initial information allows them to locate where particular elemental influences exist. This implies that Feng

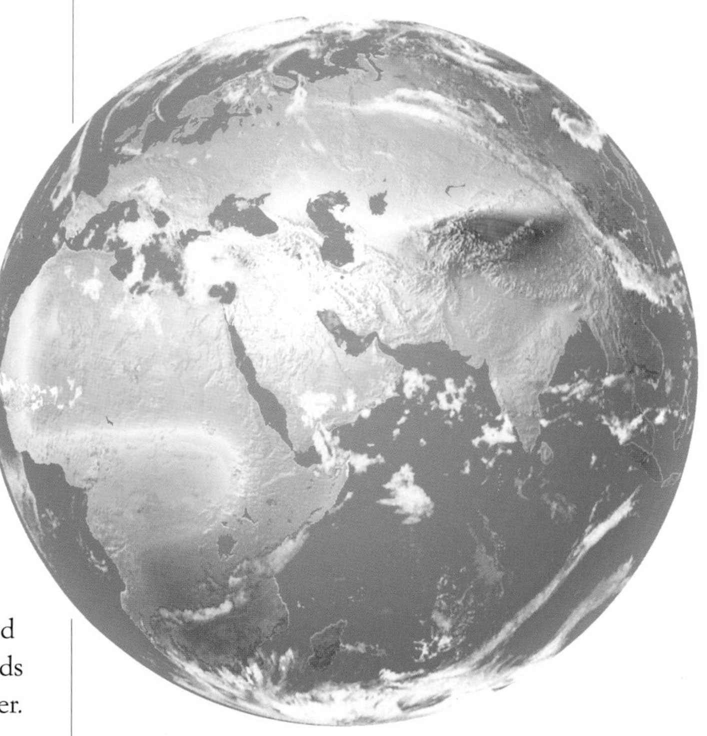

Much of Feng Shui practice is based around the earth's gravitational and magnetic fields.

Hills and valleys can affect climatic conditions – the symbolism of dragon shaped hills is, therefore, based on sound common sense.

Shui masters are concerned with the relationship between the magnetic fields and electrical or generally energetic materials.

Western science documents the interaction between magnetic fields and moving electrical charges. This is exactly the situation when an individual walks around in the earth's magnetic field. The effect is very weak; nevertheless, it exists. It is, therefore, not surprising that Feng Shui masters are interested in the magnetic field where an individual spends most of his or her time, whether at home or at work.

TIEN TI REN – HEAVEN, EARTH, AND MAN LUCK

According to Chinese tradition, humankind has three types of luck: these are known as Tien Ti Ren, or heaven luck, earth luck, and man luck. Balance these three types of luck harmoniously, so the ancient sages tell us, and we can enjoy enormous good fortune. Heaven luck is beyond our control. It determines whether we are born rich or poor, destined for greatness or success, or fated to suffer tragedies and misfortunes.

Feng Shui can be used to influence earth luck, which is within our means of control, so long as we try to live in balance with the natural forces of the environment. Good Feng Shui helps to overcome difficulties experienced during times of inauspicious heaven luck and softens predicaments caused by unfavorable man luck, bringing abundance and prosperity, good health, and an abundance of personal happiness.

GEOGRAPHICAL CONSIDERATIONS

The basic practice of Feng Shui sometimes ignores biology and the use of compasses, and concentrates on the symbolism of terrain. Good terrain on which to site one's home should exhibit the symbolic existence of the dragon, the white tiger, the black tortoise, and the red phoenix. These might be indicated by buildings, mountains, hills, lakes, and rivers. This symbolism may simply be common sense that indicates that certain locations are instinctively unhealthy while others are particularly pleasing. This is seen in the search for a better home location, which is known to enhance the quality of life.

However, there are probably deeper implications existing in the ancient practices of Feng Shui because the symbolic coupling of the dragon and tiger, which creates Chi, is said to be the mechanism of enhancing luck. This is perhaps an indication of one source of Chi that is somehow related to the lie of the land.

The parallel may be drawn with Western science in which the existence of charged particles and particles of water vapor in the atmosphere is well documented, and so are the effects of such particles upon people. The study of weather effects shows that mountains, valleys, and other geographic factors do give rise to various climatic conditions, including winds and eddies, temperature gradients, and humidity conditions. The lie of the land will, therefore, affect the prevailing weather conditions around the home. Parallels may, therefore, be drawn between Western science and Feng Shui practice.

Chapter Two

WHAT CAN FENG SHUI DO FOR YOU?

The promise of Feng Shui is exciting and mysterious, yet the fundamental philosophy underlying its practice is simple: "live in harmony with the elements of nature," it gently advises. Reside in surroundings that properly balance these elements and tap into the auspicious energy lines of the earth. By so doing, you will activate the invisible but powerful energies of the natural environment to work strongly in your favor, bringing you tremendous good fortune and protecting you against ill luck, bad health, and lost opportunities.

FENG SHUI is neither difficult to understand nor hard to practice. Once you appreciate its underlying and basic tenets, you will begin to see that Feng Shui adopts a sensible approach toward your relationship with the environment and your personal living space.

The most important of Feng Shui doctrines spring from its core philosophy – that humankind must live in harmony with the environment. This is an age old wisdom that advocates living in equilibrium and symmetry with the earth and its mountains and rivers, its winds and its waters. Feng Shui encapsulates this in a broadly based body of principles that promise prosperity and abundance, peace and serenity, and health and longevity to those who build their homes according to its guidelines, which advocate harmony and balance.

In places where the population is predominantly Chinese – such as Hong Kong, Taiwan, and Singapore – businessmen who want that extra edge unfailingly consult the Feng Shui master before building their business and residential premises. The results – in terms of good or bad fortune – have convinced them that Feng Shui can do a great deal to help them – as it can also do for you.

When Feng Shui guidelines are successfully applied to your home, the harmony and balance of your surroundings will ensure a happy and fulfilling family life.

MIGRATIONS AND THE CHINESE WORLD

Throughout the long history of the Chinese people, migration has been a constant theme. Chinese people have moved away from their homeland to carve out new lives for themselves and their families. Wherever they have settled, they have continued to arrange the direction of their homes, and the rooms within them, according to Feng Shui guidelines. Thus, Chinese people living in Hong Kong, Taiwan, and Singapore, and even those who have migrated to America, Canada, and Australia, nearly all practice some form of Feng Shui. Most do so unknowingly, for much Feng Shui practice was passed on from generation to generation by word of mouth from father to son.

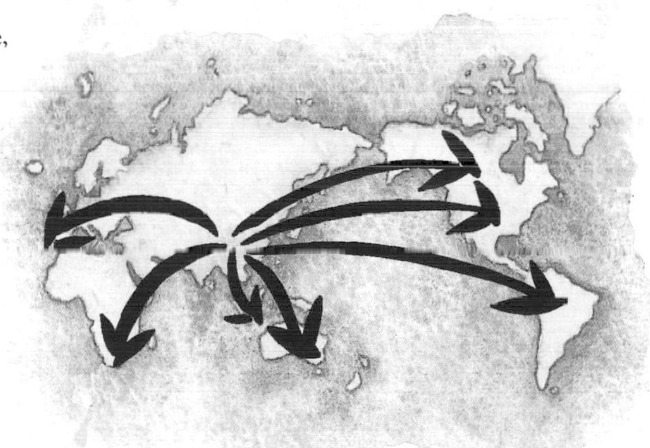

Chinese migration has introduced Feng Shui to various parts of the world.

WORKING FOR SUCCESS

You do not need to believe in Feng Shui for it to work. Many of its guidelines are pragmatic and make sound common sense. Implement the Feng Shui changes to your life that you feel are necessary, based on the guidelines of this book, and then observe whether it works.

Once you start to practice Feng Shui principles, however, you have to allow time for the results to manifest themselves. It is also necessary to remember that Feng Shui is an aspect of earth luck and, as such, is only one of three types of luck to have an influence over our lives.

Feng Shui is especially potent in attracting auspicious luck for your career or business, and there are several ways of activating this type of good luck.

The singer and actress Madonna. For those professions that require fame and popularity, the correct use of Feng Shui tools can be used to attract fame and recognition luck. One way of doing this it to keep the south corner of your home brightly lit at all times.

Good Feng Shui helps to alleviate suffering and misfortune during periods of bad luck caused either by our own actions (man luck) or by fate (heaven luck). Feng Shui mitigates problems and minimizes difficulties, often by creating circumstances that give you a way out of your problems. When your reputation, your health, or even your livelihood is threatened, having good Feng Shui will afford you some protection; it can even open new doors for you, thereby creating fresh opportunities that will eventually help you out of unwelcome situations.

During times of neutral or good man luck and heaven luck, however, good Feng Shui brings abundant good fortune. When the other aspects of your birth chart are favorable, good Feng Shui brings wealth, success, prosperity, and happiness. It creates vibrant good health, promotes a happy and harmonious family life and, in addition, ensures that your children enjoy success and academic honors.

Feng Shui enhances the chances of success in whatever you do – at work, in college, and even in competitive sports.

In business, good Feng Shui enhances turnover, attracts good business, and swells profits. Opportunities for growth and expansion are also enhanced, and employees will all work together harmoniously.

Good Feng Shui expands your career, presents opportunities for promotion, and helps to attract mentors and other patrons who can improve your prospects. It also opens up opportunities for you to improve yourself: travel, the acquisition of knowledge, responsibility, and authority are all enhanced. Good Feng Shui also brings fame and power if all other aspects of your birth chart allow this kind of success into your life.

GOOD RELATIONSHIPS

Feng Shui can bring good vibrations to romance and marriage, smoothing over and enhancing relationships and thereby bringing happiness to your personal life. Bad Feng Shui, however, causes severe problems and missed opportunities. Sometimes bad Feng Shui can even cause death through accidents and chronic disease. Bad Feng Shui also causes reputations to fall, businesses to collapse, and just about everything that can go wrong in your life to go wrong.

The study of Feng Shui, therefore, involves recognizing when you are suffering from disagreeable positioning or some other unbalancing defects. Often, for instance, when a marriage suddenly goes sour, the cause can usually be traced to bad Feng Shui emanating from a new house or apartment into which the couple has recently moved.

IMPROVING THE MARRIAGE

One very difficult problem that afflicts modern families is the appearance of a third party from outside who threatens to break up the family. This can be the case if a husband or wife becomes the target of an aggressive female or male and is encouraged to "stray." Usually a situation like this would never arise if the Feng Shui of the house had been positioned correctly in the first place, particularly the location of the bedroom and/or the sleeping direction of the husband and wife. In such cases, suitable Feng Shui changes should be made to address the specific problem.

SOLVING CHILDREN'S PROBLEMS

Another common problem facing families pertains to wayward or disobedient children. Such children often

A happy, healthy family life is often the result of good Feng Shui that reverberates throughout the home.

Good Feng Shui practice, along with personal effort, can bring academic achievement and honors into your life, if that is your heart's desire.

mix with unsuitable peer groups or indulge in other anti-social behavior. Provided that the problem is genuine, once again Feng Shui can be instrumental in resolving the situation. Often, after changing sleeping or sitting directions, a change can be seen and felt quite speedily.

Academic success has long been a part of Chinese culture. In the old days, passing the imperial examinations was one of the surest ways of making a quantum leap upwards in terms of social status and career advancement. Often, merely having a single brilliant son was sufficient to "pull" an entire family from a lower social strata to a higher one. Thus, many of the Chinese cultural definitions of happiness or success always included "scholastic success" for the sons of the family.

Feng Shui texts, therefore, proclaim that good Feng Shui can often improve the scholastic performance of the children of the household, by aligning their rooms and sleeping positions according to their birth charts.

JAMES AND MARYANNE

Take, for example, the case of James and Maryanne, who had been married for six years when James got promoted. Up to then they had been extremely happy living with Maryanne's parents, and their two children, Todd (aged two) and Eva (five), were growing up well. Shortly after James's promotion, they found a three-bedroom apartment in London. Thrilled with the prospect of at last having their own place, Maryanne worked hard with the interior decorators, and they moved into their new home just before Christmas.

In the summer of the following year, when I came to visit, I was appalled to learn from Maryanne that James was having an affair with someone at the office and had considered moving out! He worked late most nights and had stopped taking her out. Maryanne was very near to having a breakdown.

The story has a happy ending. Fortunately, the cause of their marital problems was immediately obvious and easy to resolve. First of all, in her zeal for their home to look modern, Maryanne had installed a huge mirror in the bedroom, which had created the Shar Chi (killing breath), which was affecting the marriage. In addition, one of the toilets was located in the southwestern corner of their apartment – a part of the building that, in Feng Shui terms, can symbolize marriage. The siting of the toilet was literally flushing away all their happiness.

I advised them to remove the mirror and to stop using the toilet altogether. Today, nearly a decade later, James and Maryanne are still together, happier than ever.

THE HEAD OF TREASURY

Mr Gordon, the Head of Treasury at a Hong Kong investment bank, was appalled at the spate of resignations he was experiencing. There was an air of constant tension in the office. Employees seemed reluctant to cooperate with each other. There was unabashed politicking going on and careless mistakes seemed to have become a common occurrence. Dealing profits suffered greatly as a result.

Mr Gordon's assistant, a bright young MBA graduate, suggested that they consult a Feng Shui expert to improve the layout of the dealing room. The Feng Shui master who was brought in strenuously objected to the seating arrangements of the dealing staff, and suggested changes, which were implemented at once.

To Mr Gordon's surprise, things improved almost immediately, and, within three months, all the previous losses had been recovered. More important was the air of friendly cooperation that now seemed to prevail in the office. Two troublemakers had resigned of their own accord, but those who stayed – as well as three new employees – settled happily into the newly designed office. Peace prevailed and Mr Gordon has become a fervent supporter of Feng Shui!

BUSINESS AND PROSPERITY

Just as bad Feng Shui can emanate from the home, so the Feng Shui of a new office can be the cause of problems at work, either in a career or in a business context. Usually the problem can be corrected, so it is advisable to check various aspects of your workplace from a Feng Shui perspective. In the same way, if you have just invested funds to start up a new business, it makes sense also to make the effort to "tap into the Chi flows of the earth," if that is what it takes to harness a little bit of luck as well.

Stock Exchange in Madrid, Spain. Feng Shui experts have been able to predict with great accuracy the major fluctuations in the stock market based on calculations that measure the physical environment of stock exchange buildings.

THE RESTAURANT

A friend of mine once started an Italian restaurant in Kuala Lumpur. She had been lucky in finding the perfect location in a very busy part of a wealthy suburb, and the grand opening was a great success. She received favorable publicity, and, in the days immediately following the opening, she was kept busy with plenty of customers. Business soon died down, however, so that, after the first month, she could barely break even. By the sixth month she was desperate. Night after night, the restaurant stayed empty, and staff morale collapsed.

On the night I visited her restaurant, the food was delicious, but Stella herself looked worn out. I remarked casually that the entrance to her restaurant was most inauspicious. I had noticed that it was being hit by a large poison arrow caused by the sharp edge of the roof across the road. With such Shar Chi (killing breath) directed at her restaurant, it would be difficult for her to attract any customers.

Stella confided that she was so discouraged that she was on the verge of closing the business down. No need, I said. Instead, reorientate your door and hang up a Pa Kua mirror to deflect the poison arrow. Stella implemented both changes immediately. I also offered a few more tips to activate her business luck. Today I get the best table and a complimentary meal each time I visit, even though the restaurant is almost always full!

Delicious food and a welcoming atmosphere could not compensate for the misfortune caused by a restaurant's inauspicious main entrance.

COUNTERING BAD FENG SHUI

Sometimes events in your life warn you that something is going badly wrong, especially when members of your family start getting sick, one after the other, for no apparent reason, or you find yourself becoming depressed and feeling uneasy, or when things at the office suddenly become extremely difficult.

Bad Feng Shui is generally caused by the bad positioning of doors and by the inauspicious location of rooms and doors. Often this results in poison arrows creating Shar Chi (killing breath). Sharp pointed objects and threatening structures pointing at your place of work, especially at its main entrance or front door, can cause all kinds of difficulties and misfortunes. Feng Shui offers solutions for counteracting poison arrows; indeed, much of Feng Shui practice has to do with countering or diffusing the pernicious effects of poison arrows.

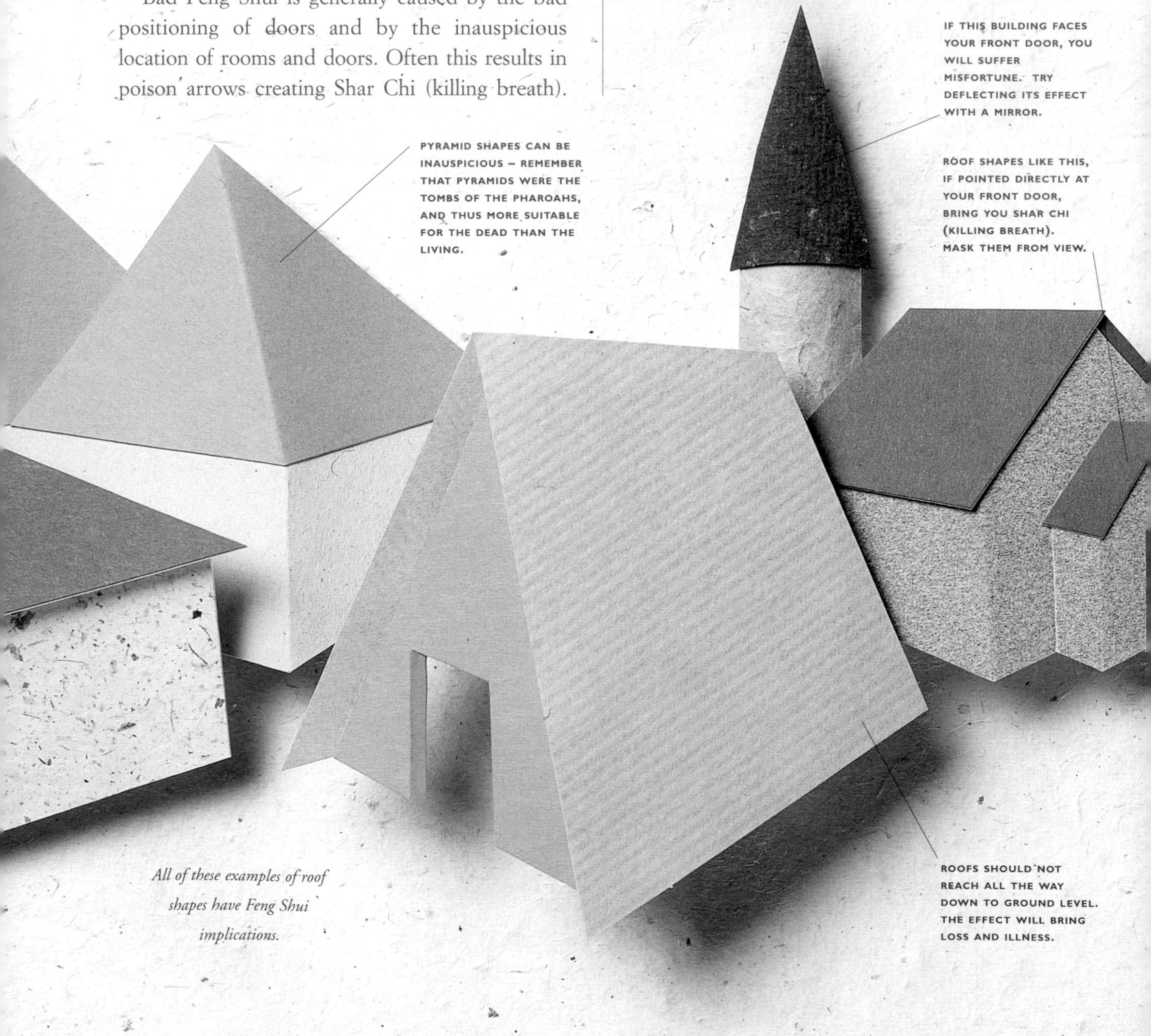

IF THIS BUILDING FACES YOUR FRONT DOOR, YOU WILL SUFFER MISFORTUNE. TRY DEFLECTING ITS EFFECT WITH A MIRROR.

PYRAMID SHAPES CAN BE INAUSPICIOUS – REMEMBER THAT PYRAMIDS WERE THE TOMBS OF THE PHAROAHS, AND THUS MORE SUITABLE FOR THE DEAD THAN THE LIVING.

ROOF SHAPES LIKE THIS, IF POINTED DIRECTLY AT YOUR FRONT DOOR, BRING YOU SHAR CHI (KILLING BREATH). MASK THEM FROM VIEW.

All of these examples of roof shapes have Feng Shui implications.

ROOFS SHOULD NOT REACH ALL THE WAY DOWN TO GROUND LEVEL. THE EFFECT WILL BRING LOSS AND ILLNESS.

EIFFEL TOWER

The Eiffel Tower in the center of Paris is a beautiful and imposing structure, but if your house faces such a building, or if you have a large picture window directly facing one, the Chi created will be too strong and the Feng Shui will not be auspicious. If you cannot move away, the best solution to countering such a poison arrow is to try to block it off visually. If yours is an apartment facing it, try to keep the windows closed, or use heavy curtains. If your house is facing it, try changing the direction of your front door, or, if this is not possible, try growing some leafy trees to hide it from view. The first method deflects the arrow's killing breath before it reaches your house and the second dissolves it. Remember, the killing breath of poison arrows always travels in a straight line, so that it is not difficult to take measures to avoid its effects.

The Eiffel Tower is striking and beautiful to look at, but if it directly faces your front door it transforms into a poison arrow.

There are several different methods used by various schools of Feng Shui to counteract poison arrows. Naturally, it is vital to be alert to their presence so that they may be avoided altogether. If this is not possible, then other ways must be found to neutralize them. This is what Feng Shui is about: first the diagnosis of the problem and then the attempt to improve matters by trying one or more of the suggestions that you will find explained in greater detail in later chapters.

RIGHT **Land situated below or close to tall structures, such as transmission towers, could suffer from the effects of negative, unbalanced Chi. Trees could disperse Shar Chi.**

ACTIVATING GOOD FENG SHUI

In addition to taking a defensive approach to the practice of Feng Shui, it is also possible to work actively towards enhancing your good luck using Feng Shui principles. It is possible, for instance, to energize different aspects of your life, thereby improving the parts of your life that represent happiness to you.

For example, if money is what you want, there are specific corners of your home that you can activate by using Feng Shui enhancers. These can range from good lighting effects to healthy green plants and decorative objects. By energizing the parts of your home that represent wealth, the likelihood of increasing your income will be considerably improved. Likewise, it is also possible to enhance your career opportunities, attract mentors or helpful people into your life, assist your children in their studies, improve your love life, enhance your marriage possibilities, or attract romance into your life.

The different formulas used by Feng Shui masters for activating good Feng Shui according to compass directions have long been regarded as trade secrets, and some of the most potent of these formulas are discussed in more detail in Chapter Five. In addition, Feng Shui also offers guidance on auspicious and inauspicious dimensions.

There are many specific dimensions that attract good Feng Shui as well as dimensions that bring misfortune. There are also Feng Shui formulas that offer auspicious and inauspicious directions and positions that are based on ancient texts. These use your birth dates to decipher personalized directions that work by aligning the Chi flows within the human body with the Chi flows of the environment, thereby enhancing harmony and good fortune.

Thus Feng Shui also offers specific measures for improving your own health, or that of a family member, even if they are suffering from chronic illness.

WHERE THERE IS BRIGHT LIGHT IN THE SOUTHERN AREA OF YOUR HOUSE, YOU WILL ENJOY EXCELLENT FENG SHUI LUCK, ESPECIALLY IF YOU ARE IN POLITICS OR SHOW BUSINESS.

SILK FLOWERS ARE EXCELLENT FENG SHUI ANYWHERE IN THE HOME. THEY ARE COLORFUL AND HAPPY, AND THEY NEVER DIE. BUT DO KEEP THEM CLEAN AND FREE FROM DUST.

THE FISH IS AN EXCELLENT SYMBOL OF SUCCESS. PLACE IT NEAR THE ENTRANCE OF YOUR HOME TO SIGNIFY ATTAINMENT.

CRYSTALS ARE ENERGIZERS AND AND SHOULD BE DISPLAYED IN THE SOUTHWEST, NORTHEAST, OR CENTER OF THE HOME OR ROOM.

WIND CHIMES ARE EXCELLENT FOR COUNTERING OVERHEAD BEAMS AND PROTRUDING CORNERS.

MIRRORS ARE EXCELLENT WHEN PLACED IN THE DINING ROOM, BUT QUITE BAD WHEN PLACED IN THE BEDROOM.

ROUND TABLES ARE EXCELLENT, BECAUSE THEY DO NOT GIVE OFF BAD SHAR CHI. ROUND SHAPES ALSO REPRESENT THE LUCK FROM HEAVEN.

THE SIZE OF YOUR DESK

Even altering the size and proportion of desks, tables, windows, and doors can contribute to good Feng Shui. I can testify from personal experience to the power of such formulas. In the year in which I changed the size of my desk at the office, I was promoted three times. That was also the year I was appointed to the position of Chief Executive Officer of a bank in Hong Kong, making me the first woman to hold such a position in Asia.

MAKE YOUR DESK **60** TO **61** INCHES IN LENGTH TO ENJOY CAREER AND POWER LUCK.

60 – 61"

40 – 42"

MAKE YOUR DESK **40** TO **42** INCHES WIDE TO ENJOY MENTOR LUCK.

33"

MAKE YOUR DESK **33** INCHES HIGH TO ENJOY MONEY LUCK.

The dimensions of your desk can be very influential in bringing you career, power, mentor, and money luck.

LEFT *This corner has been activated by a Feng Shui expert using modern Western products that are associated with good luck, success, and affluence.*

THE VALUE OF EXPERIMENTATION

The practice of Feng Shui does not require the drastic reconstruction of rooms or houses. It would be a mistake to equate the potency of the practice with the scale or subtlety of the changes made. Often, all that is required is a shift of a few degrees in the placement of a door, a tiny difference in the dimensions of tables, a tree here, a plant there, a small pool or water fountain nearby, or some light in a corner. The objective is to create and attract good Chi and to ensure that it settles.

If you are a beginner in the science of Feng Shui, experiment and monitor the results of any changes that you make in the layout or decoration of your house. Be alert to the possibility of quite delicate transformations in your fortunes and in your own behavior.

Be honest with yourself. Guard against either imagined improvements or a presumed worsening of your circumstances. Remember that the effects of Feng Shui are not instantaneous. The appearance of good fortune is often subtle and takes place over time. It is necessary to be patient, and to be wary of becoming too obsessed with results. Allow time for the benign Chi currents to enter your home or office, and slowly attract harmony and balance into your life.

Sometimes when the Feng Shui "enhancer" used is too strong, you may feel yourself becoming more aggressive than usual – this is because the vibrations, or Chi, created are too powerful. If this is the case, make some changes and experiment further. Perhaps your mirror is too large, your silk flowers too tall, your wind chimes too big in relation to your room. Balance is essential.

CONSULTING A MASTER

Much of Feng Shui, be it Form or Compass Feng Shui, can be learned without too much difficulty. Like any other discipline or profession, practical experience does improve performance. Viewed from this perspective, Feng Shui masters and consultants offer an important service. In recent years, however, as Feng Shui enjoys such a spectacular revival of interest, so many consultants have set up shop that it has become difficult for the amateur practitioner to judge who is and who is not sufficiently experienced.

I have known and consulted many Feng Shui masters in my own personal study of the subject. I seldom accept everything they recommend, preferring instead to put my own interpretation into practice. In other words, I do my own Feng Shui,

A simple remedy to counterbalance the effects of negative Chi could be to install a small fountain. Clean, flowing water brings good fortune.

A WORD OF WARNING

Finally, a word of warning. It is a very ambitious person indeed who would offer to check out the Feng Shui of someone else's home or office. Studying the subject for personal use is one thing. It is useful and effective and also very interesting. Practicing it for others is something else.

Lillian Too with her Si Fu, Master Yap Cheng Hai. Those masters who are genuinely knowledgeable and experienced are worth their weight in gold.

often with quite spectacular results. Thus I am convinced Feng Shui is something that can be learned if one has access to good books or good teachers on the subject.

Almost all the Feng Shui masters I have been privileged to meet have themselves studied from old masters (Si Fus), who not only apprenticed them in the practice, but also provided old texts for them to study and discuss. They are all strongly grounded in the basic fundamentals, and their interpretations of the ancient texts are often based on years of practical experience. One of my Feng Shui Si Fu is Master Yap Cheng Hai, a very knowledgeable and experienced master who is also brilliantly articulate and generous in providing explanations for any recommendations that he gives. Master Yap studied Feng Shui with revered masters from Taiwan, Hong Kong, and Singapore, and he has made countless trips to China, exchanging notes with other practitioners. Someone like him is worth consulting. But, of course, he is expensive and not easily available, as are others like him.

My advice, therefore, is that if you cannot afford a genuine and experienced master, it is far better to invest some time and effort to study the basic fundamentals of Feng Shui yourself. The science is not difficult, and you will be amazed at how easy and effective Feng Shui can be.

CHECKLIST

As you embark on changes inspired by Feng Shui teaching, ask yourself the following questions at regular intervals as a way of monitoring progress.

- Is your family quarreling less?
- Are you achieving better communication with other members of your family, or with your colleagues at work?
- Has your luck improved?
- Do you see fresh opportunities opening up for you?
- Has your income increased?
- Is your business improving?
- Are your children performing well at school?
- Are you feeling healthier and more energetic?

PART TWO

THE PRINCIPLES OF FENG SHUI

Chapter Three

YIN AND YANG

Feng Shui is an ancient Chinese science, more easily understood when seen from the perspective of the Chinese view of the universe and of heaven and earth. The Chinese believe there are two cosmic forces, two opposing yet complementary energies that shape the universe and everything in it. They refer to these two energies as "Yin" and "Yang." Together Yin and Yang constitute a balanced whole known as Tao – or "the Way" – the eternal principle of heaven and earth in harmony. Good, auspicious Feng Shui can only be created when there is balance and harmony between Yin and Yang.

ALL CHINESE beliefs, traditions, cultural practices, and superstitions are based on the principle of dualism, or opposites. Yin and Yang are, respectively, the negative and positive principles that govern all human existence. These primordial forces are in opposition, and yet, when combined, they symbolize perfect harmony. Yin and Yang are represented pictorially by the universally known symbol of an egg with the yolk and the white strongly differentiated, the black and white colors distinguishing between the two forces.

Everything in the universe contains varying degrees of Yin and Yang. Observe how, in the Yin/Yang symbol there is a tiny bit of Yang in the Yin and a tiny bit of Yin in the Yang. This symbolizes the transient nature of Yin and Yang and emphasizes that these two forces are always in a state of flux, thereby creating change, even as they interact.

The Chinese characters for Yin and Yang.

Yin and Yang together constitute the Tao – "the Way" – the eternal principle of heavenly and earthly harmony, the universe whose life and breath is called Chi. Yin and Yang depend on each other and give meaning to the existence of man. Thus, without dark, there can be no light. Without hot, there is no cold. Without death, there is no life. Without stillness, there can be no movement.

The Yin and Yang exist in a state of ever-changing interplay of opposites. Without Yin, there can be no Yang; without Yang, there can be no Yin.

THE CHARACTERISTICS OF YIN AND YANG

In Feng Shui, applying the Yin and Yang concept brings about balance and harmony, which in turn brings good fortune. When either too much Yin energy or too much Yang energy prevails, imbalance is created, thereby bringing abundant misfortune.

Yin and Yang symbolize many different aspects of our universe, and have been used by Chinese philosophers in order to account for human emotions, character, and behavior. Yin represents the moon and the more despondent side of human nature; Yang is the sun and the bright, solid, energetic side of humankind.

Yang also symbolizes heaven, vigor, and positive energy. It is hard, fiery, and hot. Even numbers, movement, and life itself is Yang. Yang is the dragon in Feng Shui, representing mountains and raised landforms. Tall buildings, large structures, and noise create Yang energy.

Yin symbolizes the earth, the moon, darkness, and negative energy. It governs the cold, the soft, the dead, and odd numbers. Yin is the tiger in Feng Shui. Valleys, streams, and water possess Yin qualities. Burial grounds, places of worship, and flat, contourless land emanate Yin energy.

Yin and Yang continually interact, creating change. Thus, summer gives way to winter, which in turn gives way to summer once again. Night follows day. The moon gives way to the sun. Darkness becomes light.

The forces of Yin are powerful during the cold winter months when darkness prevails, but they weaken when the Yang of the summer sun asserts its influence. Likewise, Yang prevails in the summer months, when the warmth of the weather brings life, sunshine, and good harvests.

Situations with too much Yin are too quiet and lifeless, and, hence, are to be avoided, just as a place with too much Yang energy spells misfortune and imbalance, because it is too strong.

The Yin/Yang symbol shows that the two complementary components of life intertwine to make up the whole. There is a bit of Yin in the Yang area and a bit of Yang in the Yin area to symbolize the fact that neither component stands completely on its own.

YIN/YANG ATTRIBUTES

YIN IS DARK	YANG IS LIGHT
YIN IS FEMALE	YANG IS MALE
YIN IS PASSIVE	YANG IS ACTIVE
YIN IS THE MOON	YANG IS THE SUN
YIN IS THE RAIN	YANG IS THE SUNSHINE
YIN IS THE ODD NUMBERS	YANG IS THE EVEN
YIN IS THE EARTH	YANG IS THE HEAVEN
YIN IS THE WATER	YANG IS THE MOUNTAINS
YIN IS THE WINTER	YANG IS THE SUMMER
YIN IS THE COLD	YANG IS THE HEAT
YIN IS THE TIGER	YANG IS THE DRAGON

ACHIEVING BALANCE AND HARMONY

The beauty of nature is a reflection of the harmonious and balanced interplay that is the essence of natural forces – the Yang of the sun (left) follows the Yin of the moon (right) in a never ending cycle.

The Yin and Yang of Feng Shui is reflected in our surroundings – where we eat, where we sleep, and where we work. Where our environment demonstrates a good balance between the symbols of Yin and Yang, the forces are in harmony, bringing good fortune. Where they are imbalanced, ill fortune follows.

Achieving good Feng Shui, therefore, has much to do with balancing the Yin and Yang elements. Applying the Yin/Yang principle, bad luck can improve, giving way to good fortune, just as good fortune can also turn sour. Man's fortunes fluctuate: sometimes they are good, and sometimes they are bad. This is referred to as the Tao of mankind. Thus, man's luck is affected by the cycles of nature's forces.

The practice of Feng Shui thus has two important dimensions – a space dimension, which concerns the physical environment, and a time dimension, which concerns changing forces in the atmosphere caused by nothing other than the passage of time.

Because the intangible forces that determine environmental balance are continually changing, practitioners of Feng Shui must constantly be alert to these alterations – whether they are man-made or caused by natural phenomena. Feng Shui is thus not a static science. It requires constant adaptation, and a true Feng Shui practitioner will be constantly alert to the need for change. When a little tree grows into a big tree, for example, the effect it has on one's fortunes also changes. Similarly, the presence of boulders whose colors alter as a result of the rain and sun can affect the balance of Yin and Yang, as can the shifts in the sun's rays as the seasons change or, more to the point, when progress and development create massive reconstructions to one's suburbs and surrounding landscapes.

It is this aspect of Feng Shui practice that provides the rationale for all those who would like to tap into the earth's luck to make a general study of Feng Shui, and in the process become more aware and more attuned to the changes that take place in their physical environment. Instead of relying on Feng Shui consultants, the serious student should have no difficulty in understanding the Feng Shui dos and don'ts. Such awareness of your environment will definitely make your life more pleasant and your efforts more rewarding.

YIN AND YANG IN THE LANDSCAPE

It must be clear by now that Feng Shui is the science of divining Yin and Yang in one's immediate environment – the landforms and landscapes around one's home, such as rivers, roads, mountains, hills, surrounding buildings, and every kind of man-made structure.

All these physical structures create varying amounts of Yin or Yang energy that affect one's Feng Shui. When the Yin symbols and the Yang symbols are in balance, the Chi created is auspicious, bringing prosperity and abundance. When they are unbalanced, they can become fierce and threatening, and the Chi created is obnoxious and poisonous, bringing misfortune and ill luck to the residents.

For example, a completely flat landscape is said to be too Yin. Raised landforms should be introduced onto such a landscape, which can represent Yang. Likewise, a completely hilly landscape with no rivers or plants cannot be balanced because it is too Yang. There must be valleys and waterways to bring balance to the environment. In any landscape there should also be shady sides and sunny sides. Think of the desert, which is too Yin – how can it be balanced? How can a harmony of nature's forces be created? Think of the craggy peaks of high mountain ranges. How also can these be balanced? By extension, how can such environments contain the promise of wealth and happiness? How can they be regarded as having good Feng Shui?

A varied, balanced landscape is the most favorable Feng Shui environment. On the left-hand side of this diagram, the Yang mountains are balanced by the Yin meandering river. On the right, the flat barren plains create an excess of Yin and, therefore, do not suggest auspicious Feng Shui.

Hills that follow the outline of the dragon's back are said to be Yang, and should appear on the left-hand side of the house.

Gently undulating landscapes are the type of terrain that best represent a good Yin/Yang balance, which is so crucial for harmony. This principle of balance is a central rule of Feng Shui. In practical terms, a completely flat yard can be balanced with shrubs, plants, ponds, boulders, and trees. But if any of these structures is too large, thereby overwhelming the yard or the house, then disharmony is once again created, leading to bad Feng Shui.

Residents then suffer from the consequences of imbalance, which are manifested in the form of illness and other kinds of bad luck.

Feng Shui offers a set of guidelines that enable the practitioner to read a landscape in such a way that homes and work places, and even gravesites and burial grounds of one's departed ancestors, are positioned in a way that facilitates the creation and trapping of auspicious Chi that bring benefits to residents or descendants. It goes further. Feng Shui also offers suggestions for ensuring that this vital and precious Chi circulates and settles, thereby bringing even more good luck to residents.

FLAT, ARID LANDSCAPE IS TOO YIN.

THE FOUR CELESTIAL ANIMALS

Yin/Yang balance should always be maintained inside and outside the home or workplace. There are many old Feng Shui texts (most of which are written in old Chinese) that offer colorful descriptions of perfect sites or locations. These descriptions often use symbolic representations that were, perhaps, more easily understood in ancient times. Thus, rather than describing locations in Yin/Yang terms, the shape of the landscape was compared to the appearance of both real and mythical creatures, including dragons and tigers, turtles and phoenixes.

The dragon, one of the celestial animals. Sites imbued with the dragon's cosmic breath are areas of abundance and prosperity.

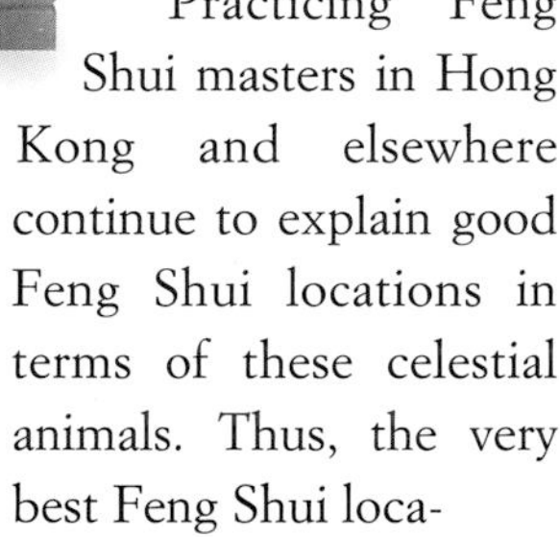

Practicing Feng Shui masters in Hong Kong and elsewhere continue to explain good Feng Shui locations in terms of these celestial animals. Thus, the very best Feng Shui locations are described as green dragon/white tiger formations ("Cheng Lung Pak Fu" in Chinese), where the dragon is Yang and the tiger is Yin, and this phrase is used so often that it has become a synonym for the practice of Feng Shui.

Along with the tiger and the dragon, the black turtle of the north and the crimson phoenix of the south make up the four celestial animals of Chinese mythology. Dragons are particularly important as symbols of great good fortune. In landscape Feng Shui, the green dragon is ideally placed on the east, or on the left side of the house looking out from the front door. This is not, however, as vital a requirement as its overall relationship with the other symbolic animals. Dragon hills are usually higher than tiger hills, and as long as they are on the left-hand side of the house, the symbolism is complete and auspicious.

Chinese-style porcelain often features the dragon symbol as decoration.

In Feng Shui the black turtle is symbolized by a range of hills that should ideally be placed behind an abode or dwelling place. They serve to provide protection against the harsh north winds, and represent good Feng Shui by providing the vital ingredient of solid support.

Auspicious Feng Shui is also enhanced by a small hillock in front of the home, which symbolizes the crimson phoenix. This also represents the fire energy of the south and symbolizes a footstool

The turtle, another of the celestial animals, is symbolized in landscape, by protective hills behind a house.

supporting the feet, signifying a life of leisured ease and happiness.

The ancient texts also contain descriptions of good locations based on the notion that certain shapes relate to one of the five main elements of fire, earth, wood, water, and metal. Thus the shapes of mountains, river flows, and contours are expressed in elemental terms and Feng Shui analysis is used to assess how they interact with each other to generate good or bad Feng Shui.

By going back to the source books of Chinese thought, especially the *I Ching* and the commentaries of Confucius, modern Feng Shui masters have penetrated the veil of the language of the ancient texts, thereby successfully unlocking the meaning of their symbolic language.

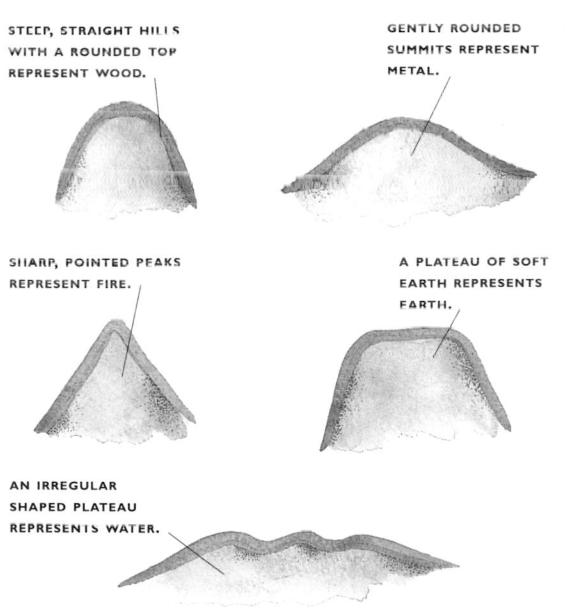

The five elements can be found represented in the landscape. Practitioners may not always agree on their interpretation, and, therefore, experience is required.

THE WHITE TIGER

In Landscape Feng Shui the white tiger is usually placed on the west, or on the right-hand side of the house. Tiger hills are always lower than dragon hills. One important guideline of Feng Shui is that the tiger must not be disturbed or activated, since this would transform it into a malevolent creature. It is, therefore, important to identify the tiger hills and, having done so, to make sure that no major structure or activity is placed there. The right-hand side of the building should also ideally be peaceful and quiet. Roads on the tiger side of the house, for example, should not be too busy. It is considered foolish to activate the tiger as you could direct its ferocity at the residents of your home.

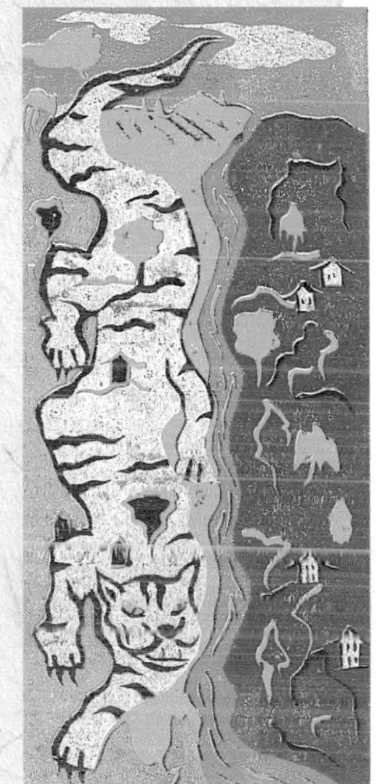

The tiger is represented by lower hills on the right.

They have also been able to translate ancient Feng Shui analysis and practice into terms more relevant to today's needs. Thus, buildings have been substituted for mountains, roads for rivers, and many of the structures of the modern world – such as power station towers, transmission lines, and the sharp corners of massive high-rise buildings – have been incorporated into the way the landscape is now analyzed.

HARMONY AND BALANCE IN TOWNS AND CITIES

Feng Shui operates on the principle that the landscape is alive with hidden forces and energy lines that are caused by the shape, size, and color of physical structures that make up the landscape, as well as the directions of main doors and entrances. The study of Feng Shui enables the amateur practitioner to recognize auspicious and inauspicious shapes, features, and directions, thereby incorporating only good luck arrangements, forms, and patterns into their building plans.

In towns and cities, the natural landscape – hills, mountains, vegetation, and water – have been affected or replaced with roads, high-rise edifices, and all kinds of man-made structures. The shapes and dimensions of buildings, drains, flyovers, sewerage pipes, and other constructions often mean that the practice of Feng Shui must confront a totally new kind of environment that differs sharply from that which had been in existence when the practice was first formulated thousands of years ago.

All manner of structures can affect Feng Shui in the city. In Stockholm, Sweden, residents need to beware of tall towers and flyovers.

Modern practitioners need to adapt traditional principles in an intelligent, logical, and sensitive manner to present-day circumstances. Because of the subjectivity involved in the practice of modern, city-type Feng Shui, there are variations in the way Feng Shui rules are explained and interpreted. Viewed from this perspective, one can understand the sometimes apparently conflicting opinions and judgements of Feng Shui experts. In spite of this, if one applies a sensitive appreciation of underlying Feng Shui concepts when assessing potential locations for one's home in the city, one will not go far wrong.

IDENTIFYING YIN AND YANG IN THE CITYSCAPE

For city dwellers who live in houses and apartments, Feng Shui rules, principles, and influences must be considered – including the search for places with good Chi for the balancing of Yin and Yang and for a natural, harmonious relationship with nature. In looking for a good Feng Shui location the qualities of the general surroundings need to be considered. If it is in the suburbs, near hilly or undulating land, are there possible green dragon and white tiger formations? Study the shapes and dimensions of elevated landforms. Also look for waterways, rivers, mining pools, and other natural bodies of water. In doing this, take account of man-made constructions and include these in an overall assessment of locations. If the land being appraised is in the city center, use creative imagery and develop an awareness for details. Neighboring buildings – their shapes, sizes, color, and other characteristics – can represent dragons, tigers, turtles, and phoenixes.

At the same time one must also be aware of poison arrows and Shar Chi caused by both natural and man-made objects, which can precipitate inauspicious consequences. Where it is not possible to avoid the offending structures, they must be neutralized at all costs by using Feng Shui cures or antidotes, such as a line of trees to hide a conical tower exhibiting too much Yang.

In New York, the Olympic Tower dwarfs this church, whose twin steeples could emanate Shar Chi for its neighbors.

INVASIVE CONSTRUCTION

Special care needs to be taken by those living in towns and cities as, inevitably, constant building work can drastically alter the environment and disturb one's carefully constructed Feng Shui. Highways and flyovers, giant steel structures, big buildings, transmission lines, and massive cutting of hillsides all affect the balance of the surrounding environment (for good and bad), and therefore the Feng Shui of those who live nearby. One day the view may be clear and uncluttered, the next it may be marred by a telegraph pole or street light sending inauspicious Shar Chi directly into your home through the front door.

Even those living in villages in the middle of the country should beware. Stories abound in China of whole villages having been adversely affected when rivers changed course or when vast tracts of land were flattened as part of land reclamation schemes. In Hong Kong, a Feng Shui expert is almost always consulted when the authorities are planning new road schemes, to ensure that the landscape is not adversely affected.

Hong Kong is fortunate in its natural surroundings. The hills behind the city serve as protection and are very auspicious.

BALANCING YIN AND YANG IN THE HOME

Ensuring balance and harmony within the home is just as important as assessing the external landscape. Those living in apartments should be alive to the balance of Yin and of Yang in their interiors when arranging furniture and deciding on color schemes.

SHADE OR SUNLIGHT

Always ensure that some part of the interior gets some sunlight, preferably the living area. However, Chi can become unbalanced if this is too strong,

The lobby of a house should be spacious and welcoming. Here, the figurines of Chinese gods provide symbols of health, wealth and prosperity.

YIN AND YANG IN THE GARDEN

It is probably in the garden that Yin/Yang balance can best be manipulated to create good Feng Shui. Remember that anything that seems to suggest activity and brightness is symbolic of Yang, while anything dark and quiet suggests Yin energy. Thus a well-balanced garden will always have stones or boulders placed in between plants. The presence of water provides balance to the boulders, while the simultaneous presence of lights makes the environment even more harmonious. An undulating garden, perhaps with different levels, is always preferable to one that is completely flat and seemingly lifeless. One should always remember to throw away rotting and dead plants, as these give off a tremendous amount of Yin energy. Indeed, one way of gaging quality of the Feng Shui in any home is to see how well the garden, the grass, and plants grow. Flourishing plants are one of the best indicators of good Feng Shui.

The Feng Shui of these gardens perfectly balances Yin and Yang, greenery and stone, shade and sunlight.

and the glare of direct afternoon sun should therefore be avoided. A balance needs to be made between completely shading the home from the sun and allowing too much sunlight in during the day. In the former case, the atmosphere will become damp, contributing to the creation of stagnant, tired Chi, which will bring bad luck. It is best at all times to achieve a good balance of Yin and Yang where sunlight is Yin and dampness is Yang.

If there is too much sunlight, residents will suffer from too much Yang, causing oppressive headaches, bad tempers, and other problems. Chi can also become tired and faded in the same way that furniture and furnishings can be affected by strong sunlight. To counteract these problems, hang a well-cut lead crystal ball from a window. This has the effect of transforming the oppressive sunlight into a rainbow of colors, immediately enhancing the room with Chi that is revitalized and healthy.

WALLS AND FLOORS

Colors also work wonders for Yin/Yang balance. Thus, a red sofa would generate Yang energy, while a blue, gray, or black sofa would generate Yin energy. Colors of walls and ceilings should be balanced in order to create healthy amounts of Yin and Yang, with the use of dark and light colors. Having a preponderance of a single color overwhelms the home with too much Yin or too much Yang, and, while this may sometimes look good and conform to some interior design dictates, it can be harmful from a Feng Shui point of view. If an entire apartment is painted a light color, such as white, for example, then this can be balanced by using darker shades in the furniture, carpets, and other floorings, such as wood.

Offices can often display an excessive amount of Yang energy if they are furnished with a preponderance of dark furniture and bright flourescent lights. Where problems of excessive disharmony occur, Feng Shui solutions include the addition of flowers, plants, and even crystals – in the form of paperweights, for instance – to soften the atmosphere with Yin influence.

This room demonstrates a healthy balance of Yin and Yang with dark furniture complemented by light-colored walls.

The cardinal rule to remember is that there must be balance, and that this balance can be created in a number of ways so that visually the end result is pleasing. For instance, horse sculptures could be displayed in a corner of a home that is too dark and therefore too Yin, as the horse is deemed to be a Yang animal and has fire as its natural element.

Chapter Four

FUNDAMENTAL CONCEPTS OF FENG SHUI

Over many centuries of Feng Shui practice, numerous different schools have arisen. Each school differs from the others in the interpretation of the symbols contained in classical texts and in the emphasis they place on these various symbols. The differences are also colored by dialect and other regional influences. Despite this, the differences are generally superficial. When analyzed in depth, almost all practitioners subscribe to the same fundamental principles. The only real divergence in approach and method that is of any significance to modern practitioners is between the Form School and the Compass School of Feng Shui.

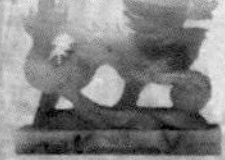

FORM COMPASS

THE FORM SCHOOL concentrates its focus on dragon symbolism. According to this school, good Feng Shui locations require the presence of the dragon, and where the true green dragon is found, there too will be the presence of the white tiger. Feng Shui masters who subscribe to this school begin their search for favorable locations by first looking for the dragon. Great emphasis is thus placed on land formations – such as the contours and shapes of hills and mountains – and the position, shape, and direction of waterways.

The Compass School, on the other hand, lays far greater stress on metaphysical speculation and uses the eight trigrams of the *I Ching*, the eight-sided Pa Kua symbol, and the Lo Shu magic square to diagnose the quality of Feng Shui positions.

The Compass School also emphasizes the influence of the planets on the quality of locations. Based on perceptions of these influences, a number of quantitative specifications have been formulated for use by practitioners of the Compass School. In contrast to the Form School, Compass School formulas assign only minor importance to landscape configurations, relying instead on complex calculations and symbolic associations.

It is important to note, however, that no matter how good the compass indications are, good Feng Shui cannot be achieved if the overall landscape represents truly harmful configurations. If door directions, for instance, adhere to sophisticated compass formulations, but the door opens so that the occupant faces the side of a hill, then the Feng Shui will be inauspicious. Form School Feng Shui should never be totally ignored.

The dragon is the principal symbol of Feng Shui. The spirit, or cosmic breath, of the dragon is believed to influence natural forces intangible in the environment, which translate into auspicious and inauspicious luck.

KEY CONCEPTS

Initially, the doctrines associated with the Form School and the Compass School developed independently. Today, however, the difference between the two schools is no longer so marked. Form School theories, including dragon symbolism, have gained wide acceptance amongst followers of the Compass School, and modern practitioners customarily use a combination of practices drawn from both schools.

Generally, the Form School, with its heavy emphasis on the natural landscape, requires a greater amount of intuitive insight, and is considered harder to practice, even though the green dragon/white tiger hill formations are relatively easy concepts to comprehend.

Compass School methods are much harder to learn, and the formulas of this school are more difficult to grasp and apply. Once mastered, however, Compass School Feng Shui is easier to practice because of its more precise formulaic methodologies. This book reproduces the principles fundamental to both schools, reflecting the more significant aspects of each school as practiced by today's masters.

In addition to the two different Feng Shui schools, there are also space and time dimensions to Feng Shui. The spatial element is concerned with the direction and dimensions of physical structures. It is rooted in a form of Chinese numerology that identifies lucky and unlucky corners of a building according to specific numerical calculations.

The time dimension to Feng Shui is considered a very advanced form of the practice and is not covered in great depth in this book. This is because, despite the important influence that time has on everybody's fortune, the physical characteristics of structures are generally held to be far more important in the long term.

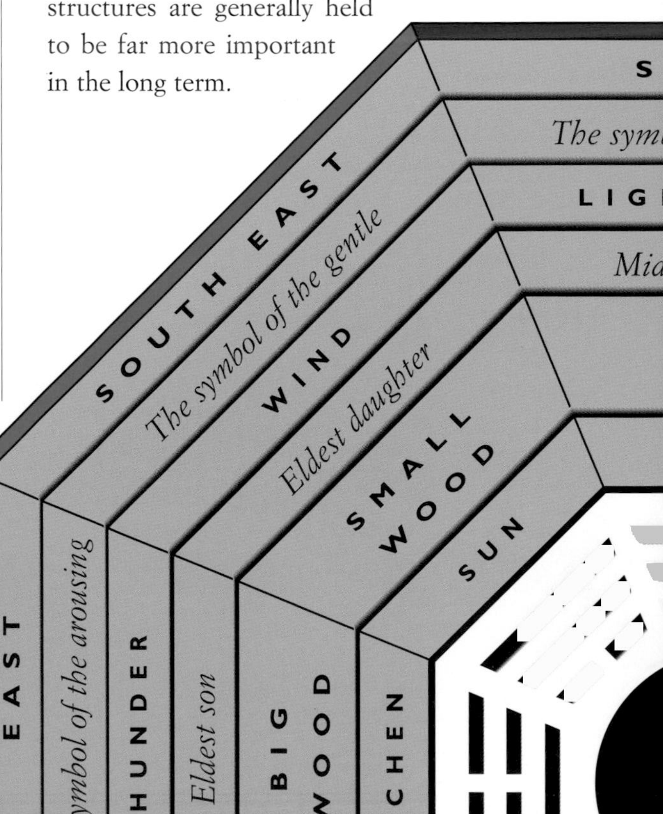

ABOVE **Enamelled tiled dragon motif from the Imperial Palace, Beijing. The symbol of the dragon is associated with the emperors of China and is a sign of strength, goodness, and male fertility. Imperial dragons have five claws.**

The Forbidden City in Beijing, China, displays much of the symbolism of Feng Shui practice.

BASIC PRINCIPLES AND SYMBOLS

As amateur practitioners, it is essential to understand the basic principles of spatial Feng Shui concepts first, before moving on to time concepts. The best way to start is to develop an understanding of the significant principles and symbols that govern the practice. In particular, there are two principles central to Feng Shui. These are:

- the concept of the cosmic breath or Chi
- the five elements and their relationships.

Feng Shui is also about symbols, of which the most important are:

- the Pa Kua
- the eight trigrams of the *I Ching*
- the Lo Shu magic square.

These principles and symbols permeate all Feng Shui practice, irrespective of which school is being followed. They are fundamental to understanding the Chinese view of the universe and the forces that affect human destiny.

SOUTH WEST
The symbol of the receptive
YIELDING
Mother
BIG EARTH
KUN

WEST
The symbol of the joyous
THE LAKE
Younger daughter
SMALL METAL
TUI

LEFT **The Pa Kua, probably the most important reference tool in Feng Shui practice.**

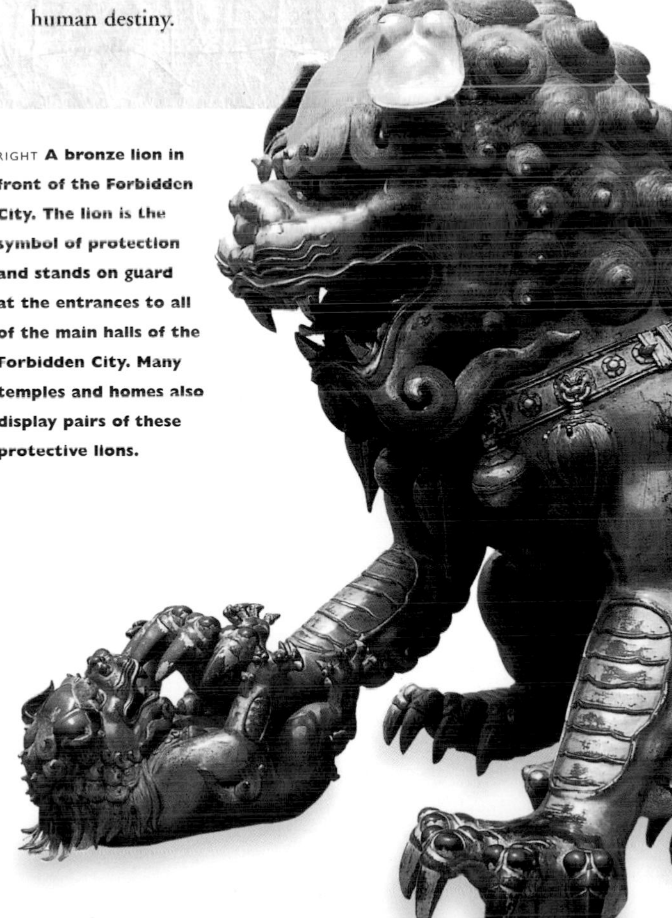

RIGHT **A bronze lion in front of the Forbidden City. The lion is the symbol of protection and stands on guard at the entrances to all of the main halls of the Forbidden City. Many temples and homes also display pairs of these protective lions.**

DEFENSIVE AND ACTIVATING FENG SHUI

The amateur practitioner needs to understand that there are essentially two different ways to practice Feng Shui: you can either be defensive or aggressive. Being defensive means taking steps to protect the home and workplace against bad Feng Shui, whilst being aggressive means taking active steps to encourage good Feng Shui. It is possible, however, to be both defensive and active at one and the same time.

Defensive measures ensure that manifestations of ill fortune – in the form of lost opportunities, illness, accidents, burglaries, loss of money, and so forth – do not befall you. Following this course also means that, even if ill fortune does befall you, the effects are mitigated and you are protected against the most serious consequences that could have occured. In short, the aim is to insulate you and your family against severe misfortune.

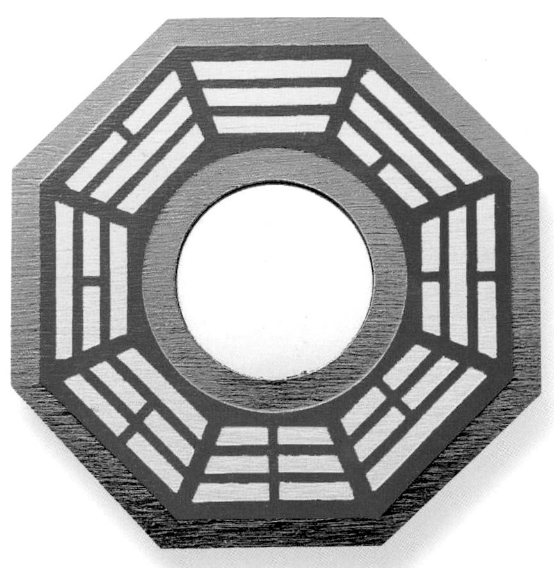

The Pa Kua mirror should always be placed outside buildings to deflect harmful Chi. It should never be placed inside a dwelling and should always be used with great care as it is a very powerful symbol.

ACTIVATING GOOD LUCK

Activating good Feng Shui involves energizing the excellent Chi flows that create and generate good luck. According to Feng Shui, good luck comes in many different guises. There is good luck in the form of wealth accumulation, in the form of recognition and fame, or in promotion to positions of power, status, and authority.

Good fortune can also mean enjoying marital bliss, being blessed with a wonderful family, having loving and respectful children, and generally being able to enjoy easy, happy relationships with the people around you.

Good luck can also mean having vibrant good health, living to a ripe old age, or having the ability to concentrate effectively and thus acquiring useful skills or knowledge.

Feng Shui offers guidelines and, in some instances, specific measures that you can adopt for activating any or all of these different types of good luck in your life.

Being both defensive and aggressive in your approach are simply two sides of the same coin, and, theoretically, there is nothing to prevent you from pursuing both kinds of Feng Shui at the same time. For beginners, it is advisable to start by being defensive, thereby guarding yourself against bad Feng Shui, before thinking about moving on to activate good luck.

COMBATING BAD LUCK

The cures that are used to combat bad Feng Shui require accurate diagnosis of the problem to begin with. Feng Shui cures need not entail elaborate changes. Often, the solution is simple, and merely involves using certain symbols, or changing the position or layout of important rooms and doors.

Once your Feng Shui is properly insulated against bad luck or bad intangible forces, you can

Carefully chosen and arranged decorative objects can be used to enhance a room. Here, a pair of vases which are rounded in shape, encourage Chi to meander.

In this bright, welcoming hallway, a fish pond has been placed to the left of the front door (as you look out) creating excellent Feng Shui and attracting wealth into the house. Problem columns, creating potentially harmful poisonous arrows, have been covered with healthy green plants, effectively minimizing harmful Chi flows.

then begin to think seriously about deliberately activating the Chi in different parts or corners of your house or workplace. At its most basic, this is again easily managed with the help of symbolic representations of the elements or can be achieved by rearranging rooms and doorways to tap into auspicious directions and locations, which are defined in such Feng Shui formulas as the Eight Locations theory and the Pa-Kua Lo-Shu theory *(see pages 78–81 and 98–103)*.

FENG SHUI CURES

Throughout this book you will find mentioned various Feng Shui cures that can be used in a number of different contexts: in the home, in the office, for attracting good fortune, jazzing up your social life, or guarding against ill health.

Paying attention to the direction in which you sleep, for example, can affect both your career and your marriage prospects. Guarding against the effects of poison arrows from sharp, angled corners or beams can improve your overall welfare, as well as play a pivotal role in your family relationships and business success. Choosing colors carefully can have dramatic effects upon your wealth, success, and personal happiness.

THE CONCEPT OF THE COSMIC BREATH, OR CHI

Central to the practice of Feng Shui is the concept of the dragon's cosmic breath – the flow of Sheng Chi. Feng Shui is all about capturing this vital Chi so that its magical qualities can be fully tapped to your advantage. Chi is the energy and the life force that pervades human existence. Chi is created when a monk sits in meditation and breathes correctly, when a Kung Fu expert gives a well-aimed blow and when a master artist or calligrapher makes a brushstroke. Chi is created in nature by the gentle, meandering flow of water, by the shape of a mountain, or by the symmetry and cosmic balance of the elements in the environment.

In symbolic terms, Chi is described as the cosmic breath of the dragon. This is simply a way of saying that certain landscape formations thought to resemble the dragon in appearance act as a source or fount of Chi, a place where this valuable breath can be created and accumulated, and where good fortune can be tapped. The Chi accumulation is strongest near the dragon's genitals, the organs of generation, while the Chi is likely to be most feeble and ineffective near its extremities.

Cosmic Chi is the source of prosperity, peace and abundant wealth, honor and good health. Homes built in areas where Chi exists and accumulates can be relied upon to benefit the people who live in them for several generations. Businesses with abundant Chi expand, prosper, and grow.

Chi must not be scattered or blown away. If this happens, there can be no good luck. In places where fast and strong winds blow, Chi is scattered and dispersed, hence the Chinese saying that "Chi rides the winds and disperses." Windy, unprotected sites exposed to the elements, are generally considered unfavorable.

When bounded by water, Chi usually halts and accumulates. Thus, watery places are generally regarded as auspicious locations. The water must be conducive to the accumulation of Chi, however. Straight or fast-flowing rivers carry Chi away almost as soon as it is created. Good luck thus evaporates into the atmosphere.

But it is not sensible to allow Chi to stagnate. If Chi grows stale or tired, all of the good luck will dissipate. In fact, analyzing the effect that the landscape has on the quantity and flow of Chi and whether it accumulates, stagnates, or is rapidly dispersed at any particular location, is the crux of landscape Feng Shui.

Yoga practice places great emphasis on the correct use of the breath (Chi) to benefit the body and produce a sense of well-being. This body Chi is similar to environmental Chi.

Practitioners of the Chinese martial arts such as Chi Kung or T'ai Chi tap into the flow of Chi within their bodies, rather than using aggressive force to overpower their opponents.

AUSPICIOUS SITES

For a site to be auspicious, it must have access to, or be near, a good, strong supply and flow of Chi. This need not necessarily be on the main vein or artery of the "dragon." The essence of Feng Shui investigation is to find a location where it is possible to trap the Chi energy flowing through and to accumulate it, without allowing it to go stagnant. Where the dragon's breath can be contained or where a permanent supply can be built up, will be the energy lines that bring wealth and prosperity.

Feng Shui guidelines thus focus on the methods that can be employed to harness the dragon's breath. The accepted theory is that this cannot happen where there are straight, vertical ridges or hills. Waterways and rivers should be slow and meandering, and the site must be protected from the effects of harsh winds.

CREATING AND DESTROYING CHI

Where environmental Chi is completely absent, it is possible to create elevations and structures that simulate the dragon, the tiger, and the turtle, and, in the process, actually cause Chi to be created or attracted to the site. This is because Chi is regarded as intangible energy and can be man-made. By the same token, through ill-informed ravaging of the landscape, Chi can also be destroyed. Creating a straight road would bring Shar Chi to the landscape, whereas a winding road would encourage meandering, auspicious Sheng Chi. Hence, the terrain and landscape must always be respected and care taken not to "injure the dragon."

A small cottage nestling in a valley is surrounded by dragon-shaped hills – the most auspicious of landscape configurations.

THE FIVE ELEMENTS

Both Form and Compass School Feng Shui are greatly influenced by the theory of the five elements. The Chinese believe the interactions of these five elements – earth, wood, fire, metal, and water – can be combined in different quantities to create all the permutations that are found in the forces of nature.

The element of fire is associated with the color red.

A significant portion of Feng Shui practice is based on interpreting how these elements interact in the physical environment to create good or bad luck. The elements are, in fact, involved in two kinds of cyclical relationship: the productive and the destructive cycles. In the productive cycle, fire produces earth, which produces metal, which produces water, which produces wood, which in turn produces fire. In the destructive cycle, wood destroys earth, earth destroys water, water douses fire, fire melts metal, which in turn will chop down wood.

Understanding these two cyclical relationships enables Feng Shui practitioners to incorporate individual symbolic elements into the positioning of homes and workplaces using the Chinese system of categorizing everybody's date and hour of birth according to the elements.

For instance, it would not be beneficial for someone born in a fire year to have too much water in the home, so ponds, fountains, aquariums, and objects colored black or dark blue (the water colors) should be avoided, because water destroys fire. On the other hand, plants and green objects (representing wood) would be considered auspicious, since wood produces fire. Additionally, it would be beneficial if one slept in the room located on the south side of the house or apartment.

Having too many plants in the home would not be very auspicious if you were born in an earth year, because wood destroys earth. Instead, decorating with red objects and bright lights would be conducive, since fire produces earth. Since earth is the central element of the five, earth people should sleep at or near the center of the house.

These examples demonstrate the various combinations that would or would not work from a Feng Shui point of view. In the case of a family, where each member is born under a different element, it is the element of the breadwinner or the head of the household that is

Earth, wood, metal, water – four of the five natural elements.

THE FIVE ELEMENTS AND THEIR PROPERTIES

Fire is red, an auspicious color. Fire is also summer and represents the south.

Water is black or dark blue. It represents winter and is placed north.

Wood is the east and is represented by the color green. Its season is spring.

Metal is white, and sometimes gold. Metal symbolizes the west. It represents fall.

Earth is yellow or brown. It represents the center.

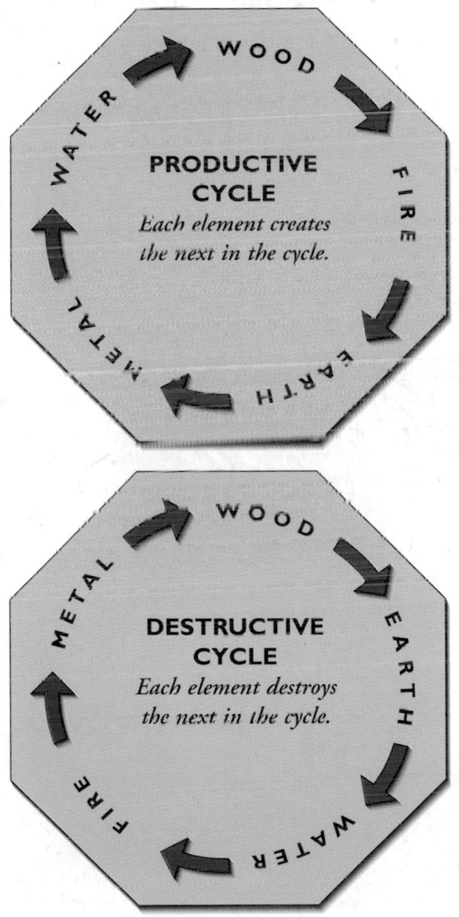

deemed the most significant. It is his or her element that should thus be considered when diagnosing for appropriate positions and furnishings. Other rooms in the house can be designed to benefit their principal occupant.

Each of the main compass directions is also identified with one of the elements. Knowledge of the interactions of the five elements is, therefore, also invaluable for creating a harmony of energies within a home, since decorative items symbolizing the different elements can be placed in corners of the home that correspond to that element to create auspicious Feng Shui *(see page 81 for the elements associated with each corner of the home)*. A metal wind chime in the west or northwest is auspicious.

Decorative items symbolizing water should be placed in the north, east and southeast corners of the home.

Decorating with red objects is very auspicious for people born in an earth year, because fire, associated with red, produces earth.

THE PA KUA

The Pa Kua is the principal reference symbol in the practice of Feng Shui. It is an octagonal-shaped symbol that corresponds to the four cardinal points of the compass, and the four sub-directions. In accordance with the conventions of the Chinese compass, south is placed at the top and north is at the bottom. However, as south is still south and north is magnetic north, it is not necessary to "flip" the directions around. The Pa Kua symbol derives its significance from the eight trigrams of the *I Ching*. These trigrams are placed around the edges of the symbol, thereby imparting symbolic meanings to each of the eight compass directions. The knowledgeable practitioner is able to use these symbols and directions to enhance the Feng Shui of specific corners and sectors of the home, encouraging good luck.

The Pa Kua shape itself plays a powerful and central role in the practice of Feng Shui, since it is regarded as one of the most important symbols of protection against poison arrows or other harmful structures. The Pa Kua symbol of the Early Heaven arrangement is also credited with having the power to ward off malevolent spirits.

YIN AND YANG DWELLINGS

According to modern interpretations, the Early Heaven arrangement represents the ideal universe, while the Later Heaven arrangement represents the practical applications of the trigrams to the earth,

The Feng Shui of Yin dwellings to house our ancestors should be designed using the Pa Kua Early Heaven arrangement.

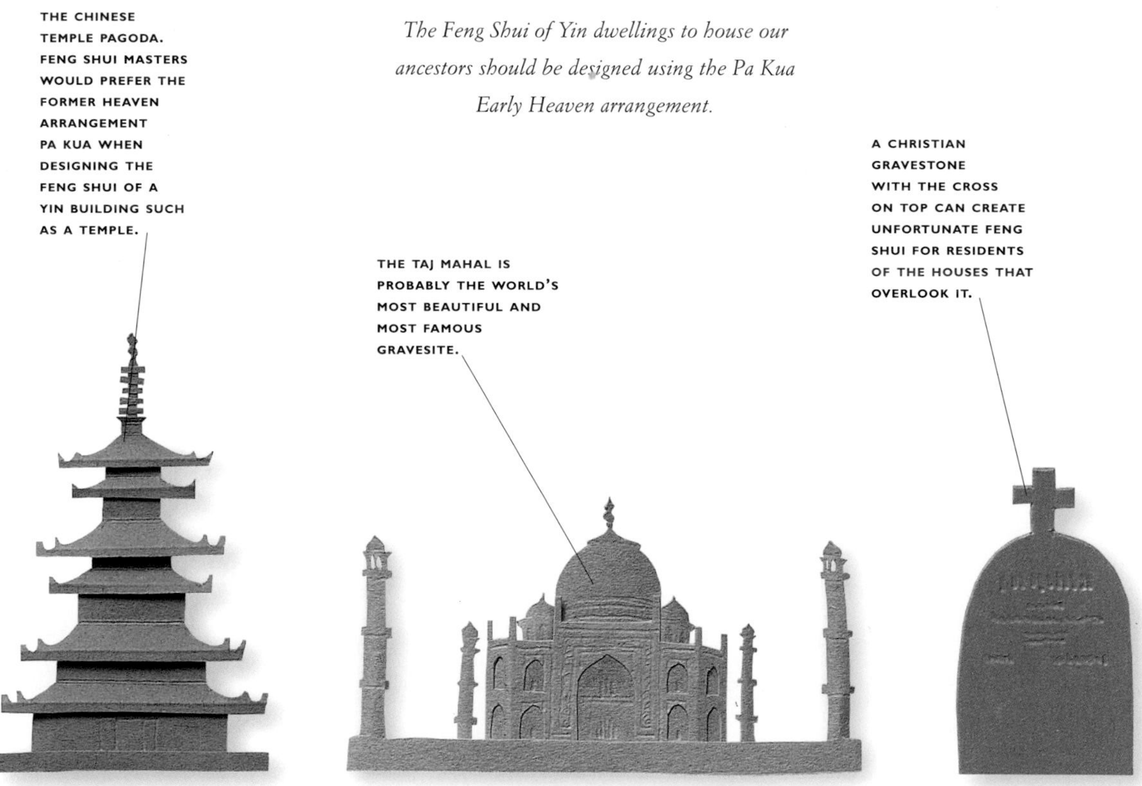

THE CHINESE TEMPLE PAGODA. FENG SHUI MASTERS WOULD PREFER THE FORMER HEAVEN ARRANGEMENT PA KUA WHEN DESIGNING THE FENG SHUI OF A YIN BUILDING SUCH AS A TEMPLE.

THE TAJ MAHAL IS PROBABLY THE WORLD'S MOST BEAUTIFUL AND MOST FAMOUS GRAVESITE.

A CHRISTIAN GRAVESTONE WITH THE CROSS ON TOP CAN CREATE UNFORTUNATE FENG SHUI FOR RESIDENTS OF THE HOUSES THAT OVERLOOK IT.

EARLY AND LATER HEAVEN ARRANGEMENTS

The Chinese believe that it is the special arrangement of the eight trigrams that gives the Pa Kua its potency and power. These trigrams are three-tiered combinations of broken and unbroken lines. Each of the trigrams is symbolic of several things, and they are arranged around the Pa Kua in either the "Early Heaven arrangement" or the "Later Heaven arrangement." The difference in the sequences lies in the placement of the trigrams. This changes the meaning of each of the compass directions, thereby affecting the Feng Shui solutions indicated.

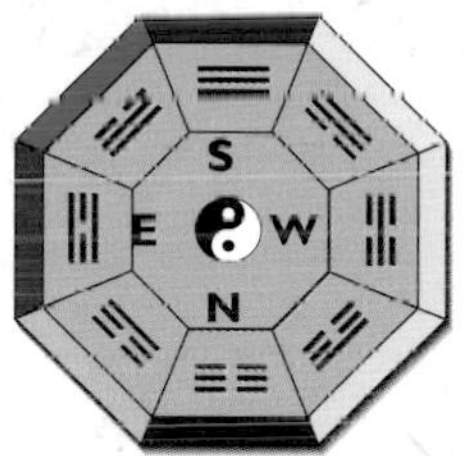

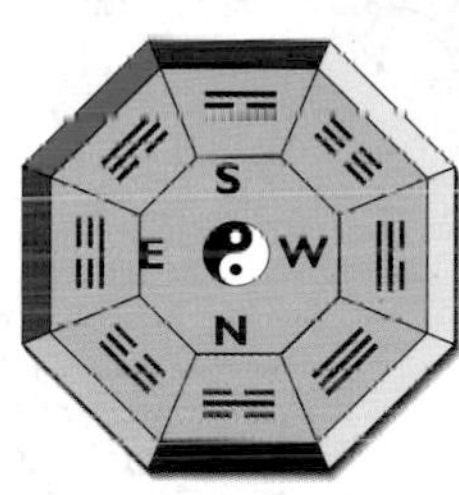

The positioning of the eight trigrams of the I Ching *in the Early (left) and the Later (right) Heaven arrangements of the Pa Kua*

and thus, by extension, it is strategically more important for the earth's Chi. As a result of this widely held view, Feng Shui masters generally prefer the Early Heaven arrangement of the Pa Kua to use as a protective symbol and hang it on doorways to ward off the killing breath of poison arrows. It is also preferred for designing the Feng Shui of Yin dwellings, such as gravesite positions for one's ancestors. The Chinese place special significance upon gravesites, as they believe that the quality of the Feng Shui of their ancestors' graves determines the destiny luck of descendants. It is for this reason that wealthy Chinese families in Taiwan guard their ancestral graves with care, since they do not want their Feng Shui to be adversely disturbed by jealous competitors.

The Later Heaven arrangement is used for Yang dwellings, or the abodes of the living. It is the arrangement referred to when using advanced Compass School formulas, or when making correlations between the five elements and directions for homes and offices. It is, therefore, this arrangement that will be referred to throughout the course of the rest of this book.

There are many variations of Yang dwellings – or abodes of the living – around the world

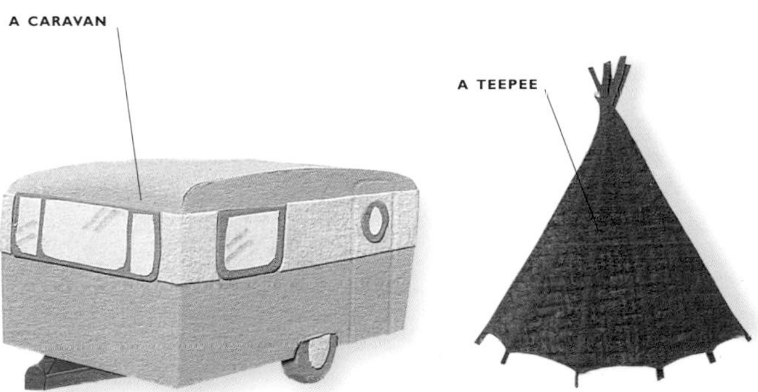

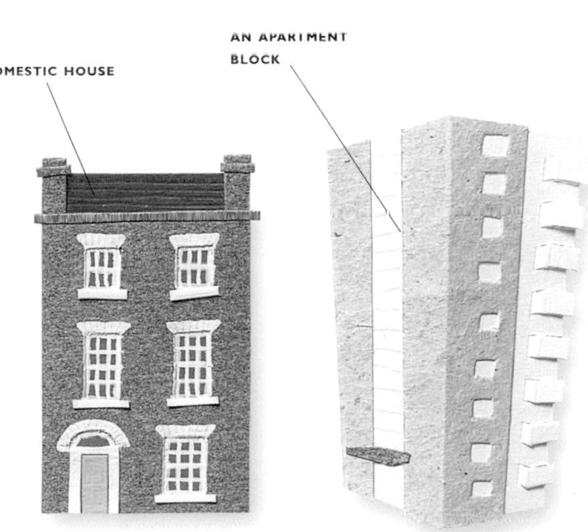

THE EIGHT TRIGRAMS OF THE I CHING

The eight primary trigrams are the roots of the *I Ching's* 64 hexagrams. Each trigram is made up of three straight lines which are either broken (– –) or complete (—). These trigrams collectively symbolize the trinity of heaven, earth, and man. The lowest place in the trigram is that of earth; the middle place belongs to man, while the upper place is the domain of heaven.

Each of the eight trigrams has its own multiple sets of meanings, as well as supplementary symbols and connotations. Each trigram has a corresponding cardinal point and compass direction. They each also represent one of the elements and at the same time epitomize a specific member of the family. As we have already observed, the meanings also change according to whether they are arranged around the Pa Kua in the Early Heaven or the Later Heaven arrangement.

IMPROVING FENG SHUI

The meanings of the trigrams can give valuable clues for improving and enhancing the Feng Shui of your dwelling or workplace. When examining the Feng Shui of these Yang dwellings, you should always interpret the Pa Kua directions according to the trigrams as they are arranged in the Later Heaven arrangement. This enables you to study the attributes and characteristics of any direction and therefore any corner of your house, merely by interpreting the trigram of that direction, its compass direction, element, symbolic color, and Yin or Yang characteristics. The meaning and implications of the trigrams are not immediately obvious, because they often suggest multiple definitions. With practice, however, they offer valuable clues, which can be implemented to create balance and attract auspicious Feng Shui.

Heaven, earth, and humanity are all represented in the trigrams of the I Ching. Earth inhabits the lowest place, the middle belongs to humanity, and the highest place belongs to heaven.

Ancient Chinese coins represent the metal element and symbolize wealth.

I CHING AS ORACLE

Confucius, one of the many hands involved in evolving the philosophy of the I Ching.

The *I Ching*, or *Book of Changes*, is one of the most important books in the world's literature. Its origins go back to mythical antiquity and nearly all that is greatest and most significant in the 5,000 years of Chinese cultural history and practice has either taken its inspiration from the *I Ching* or has exerted an influence on the interpretation of its texts and meanings.

The *I Ching* was originally formulated over 4,500 years ago by Fu Hsi, the legendary Chinese ruler who is said to have invented the linear signs manifested as the eight three-lined trigrams. King Wen, the progenitor of the Chou Dynasty (1150–249 B.C.), took the trigrams further and formulated 64 hexagrams. King Wen was also said to have appended brief judgments to each of the hexagrams, thereby laying the groundwork for much of the acknowledged wisdom of *I Ching* philosophy.

King Wen's son, the Duke of Chou, wrote the texts pertaining to each of the individual lines of the hexagrams, assigning meanings to them. His contributions were entitled the Changes of Chou, and these subsequently came to be used as oracles. These Changes, which are contained in a number of ancient historical records, drastically altered the

I Ching, expanding its philosophy to take on the colorings of divination. This was the status of the book when Confucius began his lifetime study of its texts, judgments, and images. He too expanded the book's scope with a series of commentaries that are generally referred to by the term "Wings."

The *Book of Changes* escaped the fate of other classics at the time of the famous burning of books under the tyrant emperor Chin Shih Huang Ti. By that time it had become firmly established as a book of divination and magic. It was not until around A.D. 226 that the *Book of Changes* came to be regarded as a book of wisdom, and by the time of the Sung period (A.D. 960–1279), the book had evolved further, this time as a textbook relating to statecraft and the philosophy of life.

During the time of the last Chinese dynasty, interpretations and commentaries of the book were once again influenced by theories of magic, and today it is regarded as one of the exalted divination texts of China.

Finally, during the K'ang Hsi period, a comprehensive version of the book finally took shape.

Each of the trigrams of the I Ching *is composed of three complete or broken straight lines.*

TRIGRAMS AND THEIR PROPERTIES

The eight primary trigrams are so important to Feng Shui practice that each has been given a name and each has been assigned a direction according to either the Early or Later Heaven arrangement of the Pa Kua. Special tables exist for you to check whether you and your house are in balance *(see Chapter Five)*.

In the *I Ching*, or *Book of Changes*, there are additional symbols associated with these trigrams. For the purposes of Feng Shui, however, the significant aspects of the trigrams relate mainly to their compass directions, and their corresponding numbers based on the pattern of the Lo Shu square *(see pages 84–85)*.

CHIEN: THE CREATIVE

This trigram comprises three unbroken Yang lines. It is often associated with the father, the head of the household, a leader, the male, or the patriarch. Chien symbolizes heaven, the sky, energy, and perseverance. Chien's element is big metal and its direction, under the Later Heaven arrangement, is northwest. Its number is 6.

Chien represents heaven.

KUN: THE RECEPTIVE

Kun comprises three broken Yin lines. It is associated with the mother, the matriarch, and the maternal female. Kun's element is the earth and its direction is southwest. Kun symbolises the perfect complement for Chien and, according to the *I Ching*, Kun must be led and activated by Chien if it is to maximize its potential. Its number is 2.

Kun represents the earth.

CHEN: THE AROUSING

This trigram is made up of two broken Yin lines above an unbroken Yang line. It represents the eldest son. Its image is thunder. It is also symbolic of the dragon, which, rising out of the depths, soars magnificently up to the stormy skies. Thus, the strong Yang line pushes upward below the two broken lines, which give way. Its element is wood and its direction is east. Its number is 3.

Chen is symbolic of the dragon.

SUN: THE GENTLE

This trigram is formed by two unbroken Yang lines above a single broken Yin line. It represents the eldest daughter, and its attribute is summed up in the word "penetrating." Sun's colors are brown or green and its element is wood. Its direction is southeast and its number is 4.

Sun represents wood.

TUI: THE JOYOUS

This trigram is made up of one broken Yin line above two unbroken Yang lines. Tui represents joy, happiness, and the youngest daughter. Tui is also the lake, and it is the mouth that manifests joyful feelings. Tui is outwardly weak, but inwardly stubborn. Its element is metal and its direction is west. Its number is 7.

Tui represents the lake.

KEN: THE MOUNTAIN

This trigram represents stillness, a period of waiting and solitude. Ken is made up of one unbroken Yang line above two broken Yin lines. It represents the youngest son. Its element is earth and its direction is northeast. Its number is 8.

Ken is the mountain.

KAN: THE ABYSMAL

This trigram is made up of one unbroken Yang line sandwiched between two broken Yin lines. Kan is the middle son. Its element is water, and its direction is north. Kan suggests toil and hard work. It is not regarded as a happy trigram. Its number is 1.

Kan represents the water.

LI: THE CLINGING

This trigram is made up of one broken Yin line between two unbroken Yang lines. The element of Li is fire, and it represents the middle daughter. Li is also the sun, brightness, lightning, heat, and dryness. It denotes something firm and unyielding on the outside, but weak and hollow within. Its direction is south. Its number is 9.

Li represents fire.

THE EIGHT LIFE ASPIRATIONS OF THE PA KUA

One of the most common uses of the Pa Kua is to enhance the Feng Shui of your home, room, or office by dividing it into eight sectors or corners. These sectors are identified according to compass direction, and each sector is identified with a life aspiration.

The life aspirations are: mentors/helpful people, marriage prospects, family relationships and health, wealth and prosperity, career prospects, recognition and fame, education, and children's luck. According to Feng Shui, it is possible to activate any of these life aspirations to benefit residents.

To divide your area, you first need to purchase a good and accurate compass – investing in a good one is essential, since the compass is used in almost every Feng Shui application. Next, stand in the center of the house, room, or office and draw a rough plan of the area, identifying each corner according to its compass direction. There are eight directions in all, the four cardinal ones (north, south, east, and west) and the four secondary ones (southeast and southwest, northeast, and finally the northwest).

With the corners and sectors of your home, room, or office identified, you can then ascertain which corner of your room is associated with which life aspiration. To do this, you need to look at each of the trigrams of the Pa Kua as they are arranged in the Later Heaven arrangement. Each trigram is associated with a life aspiration and also with a compass direction. The corner of your room associated with family relationships would, therefore, be the eastern corner. The Pa Kua can be superimposed onto a plan of your home to identify the sectors.

The Later Heaven arrangement of the Pa Kua is used to identify which corner of the home is associated with which of the eight life aspirations.

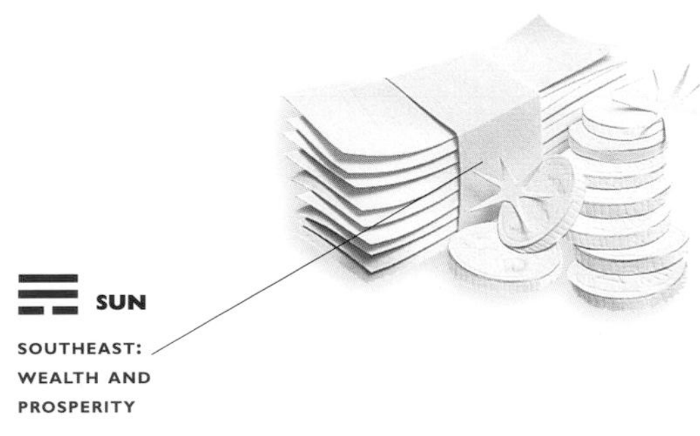

SUN

SOUTHEAST: WEALTH AND PROSPERITY

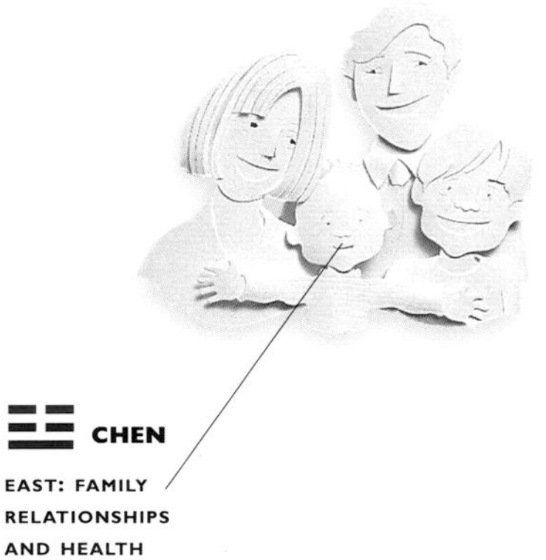

CHEN

EAST: FAMILY RELATIONSHIPS AND HEALTH

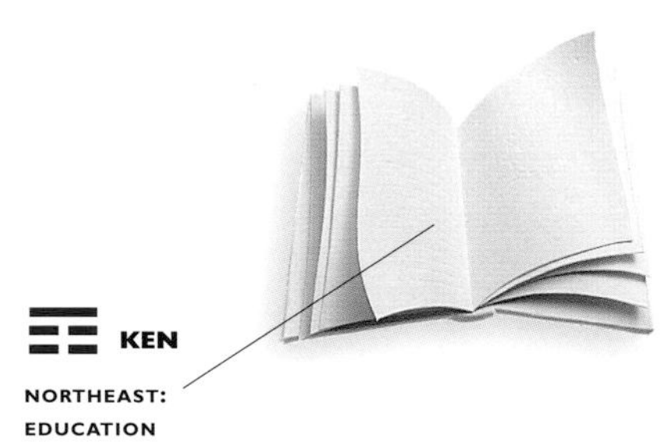

KEN

NORTHEAST: EDUCATION

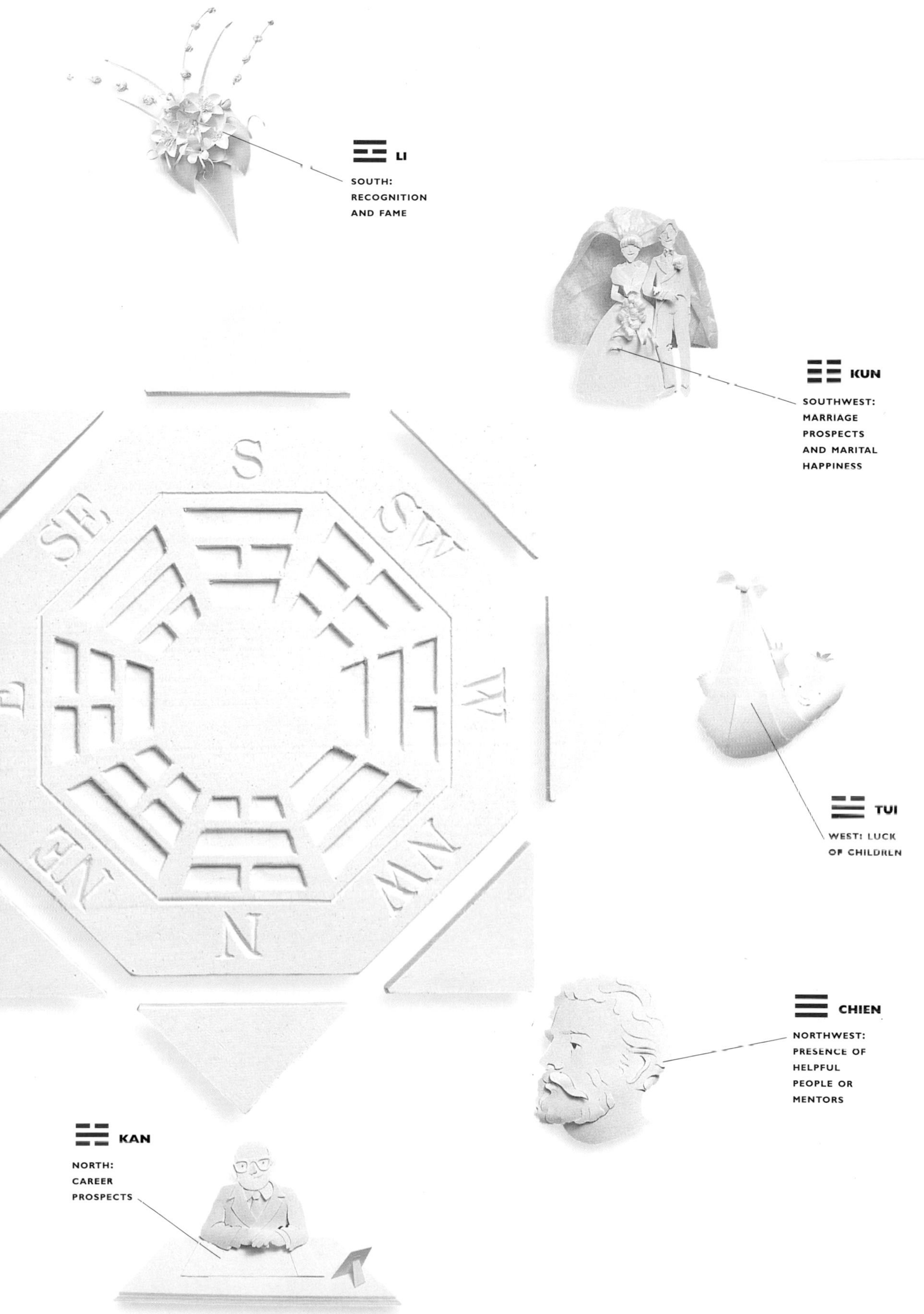
LI
SOUTH: RECOGNITION AND FAME
KUN
SOUTHWEST: MARRIAGE PROSPECTS AND MARITAL HAPPINESS
S
SE
SW
E
W
NE
NW
N
TUI
WEST: LUCK OF CHILDREN
CHIEN
NORTHWEST: PRESENCE OF HELPFUL PEOPLE OR MENTORS
KAN
NORTH: CAREER PROSPECTS

ACTIVATING THE SECTORS

Extracting the most from Feng Shui principles is essentially an individual pursuit. For maximum success, you need to define and be clear about your own objectives, deciding whether you desire wealth, health, fame, or status, for instance. To activate better fortune, you need to create good Chi flows into the sector you wish to activate. Creating good Chi serves to enhance the luck of the corners and, by extension, the life aspiration that it represents. Thus, if you want your children to do better at exams, be more obedient, and so forth, you must activate the western part of your house or the western part of your room. In the same way, if money is what you want, do something about your southeastern corner. If you want to meet the man of your dreams, all you need to do is activate the southwestern part of your house.

There are a couple of potential pitfalls. If you find that the corner that is important to you is occupied by your toilet, it could be bad news indeed. For example, if the toilet is located in the southwestern corner of your house, you will find that your marriage prospects (if you are single) and your marriage happiness (if you are married) are being flushed down the toilet. Stop using that particular toilet immediately. Having the kitchen located there also diminishes the luck of that sector.

Having decided what you want to activate, you can then proceed to energize the relevant corner. These methods are described in Part Three of this book and include using any one of several Feng Shui enhancing objects, such as placing a bright light in the appropriate corner, hanging a wind chime or installing a fish tank. Further investigation of the color and element associations of the Pa Kua will help.

If you wish to stimulate the wealth corner of your house, for example, which according to the Pa Kua's Later Heaven arrangement is the corner represented by the trigram Sun, then you must activate the southeastern side of your house. Place your study, your bedroom or your office in this sector. You can also place a Feng Shui "enhancer" in that corner. You can use plants, crystals, fountains, or an aquarium, for example, but the best object to place in this corner would be a healthy green plant. This is because the southeast is represented by the element wood and plants belong to the element wood. It is not necessary to overdo it, however. Just one object is sufficient. Remember that balance and harmony are vital.

MISSING CORNERS

If you find that when you place your Pa Kua onto the plan of your home you have a missing corner, perhaps due to the shape of your house, you will lack the luck symbolized by that corner. In these cases, you should try to "build in" the corner. This could be done either by extending your home or by using a wall mirror to extend the house into this corner. Alternatively, a light could be placed in the missing corner outside the house. For this reason, Feng Shui practitioners prefer a house to be square or rectangular, but it does not matter, as long as you make sure that each sector is the same size.

Purchasing a good compass is the first step to successful Feng Shui.

THE EIGHT LIFE ASPIRATIONS

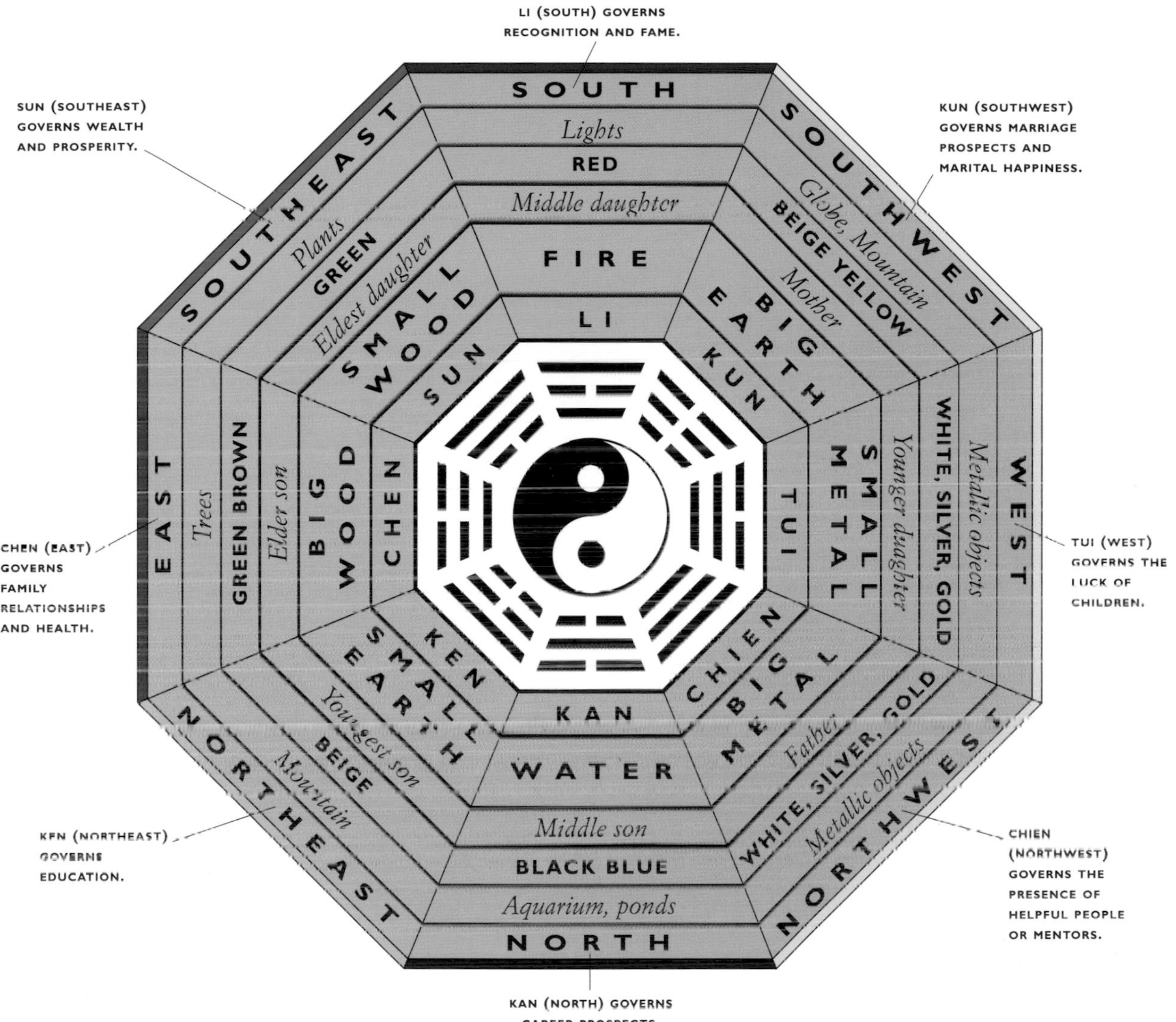

The Pa Kua illustrated on this page sums up the various attributes that have been attached to the eight main directions by different Feng Shui systems. Each of the symbols belonging to each Kua (or side) are said to be in harmony with each other, and are therefore complementary. Use the element relationships to determine productive and destructive cycles and think about how these interact with the plants, colors, and furniture of your house or office.

FENG SHUI ENHANCERS

Kuan Yin, the Goddess of Mercy, assists those in need.

Once you have decided which life aspiration you wish to activate, there are a variety of tools you can use to enhance the corresponding corners of your home. These can be divided into eight categories of remedies:

- bright, reflective objects or objects that reflect – lights, mirrors, lead crystal objects, and crystal balls
- living things or simulations of living things – live plants, fresh flowers, aquarium or pond fish, or artificial imitations
- objects that make pleasant sounds – wind chimes that produce wonderful tinkling sounds each time there is a breeze, bells of all shapes and sizes, gongs, and xylophones
- objects that have a circular movement – mobiles, windmills, revolving doors, miniature water fountains, table and overhead fans
- heavy objects that simulate Yang – boulders, sculptures, stones, and statues
- modern electrical products that can simulate activity and sound – stereo music systems, radios, and televisions
- long, hollow objects – flutes, preferably made of bamboo, and modern wind chimes made with hollow pipes
- colors – especially when used in harmony with the Chinese concept of the five elements.

These remedies can be placed in appropriate corners of your home to activate your life aspirations. Bright lights can be placed in almost any corner, and are one of the most potent tools to enhance your chosen fortunes. Similarly, modern electrical gadgets, placed appropriately, can expand one's career opportunities, bring happiness and life into family relationships and marriage prospects, create golden occasions for generating wealth, expand the help from mentors, bring success to one's children, and

Red roses placed in your marriage, or southwestern sector, will increase your chances of finding the right marriage partner.

increase one's chances of fame and recognition. Other enhancing objects have particular relevance for each of the eight life aspirations.

FAMILY AND WEALTH

Placing plants and flowers in the eastern and southeastern sectors will enhance family relationships and wealth prospects. This is because these two sectors are linked to the wood element, which can be represented by plants. Do make certain, however, that the plants stay healthy and throw away any that are dead. Dead plants create Shar Chi and bring bad luck. Plants with thorns or prickles, such as cacti, should also be avoided – much more appropriate are plants with broad, healthy leaves. A small aquarium placed in these sectors can also do wonders for these life aspirations, but it must be kept clean.

CAREER

Installing a fishbowl in the northern sector of your home or room will activate your career, but avoid going overboard and introducing a very large tank: too much water can drown your prospects. Keep small guppies in the tank, or some goldfish, but avoid predatory fish and angel fish, whose angled bodies deflect benign Chi.

CHILDREN'S LUCK AND MENTORS

Wind chimes hung in the western and in the northwestern sectors will enhance your children's luck and attract support from helpful and influential people. The chimes must be hollow, allowing the Chi to flow through. Fresh flowers are also helpful in the northwestern sector.

MARRIAGE AND EDUCATION

Natural crystals placed in the southwestern and northeastern corners will activate your marriage and education corners. Crystals are wonderful Feng Shui enhancers, especially if they are combined with light in a chandelier.

Fish are excellent wealth enhancers, and should be placed in the southeastern sector of your home.

PERSONAL FAME AND REPUTATION

By installing a bright light in your southern sector you will enhance your personal fame and reputation – the brighter the light the better. Bright lights are wonderful conductors of good Feng Shui and are suitable for southwestern and northeastern sectors as well.

Candles floating in a bowl of water create excellent Yin (water)/Yang (fire) balance. Place this blue arrangement in your northern sector to spark your career prospects.

THE LO SHU MAGIC SQUARE

In the history books of old China, it is written that sometime around 2005 B.C. (or about 4,000 years ago), a noble turtle emerged from the legendary River Lo, carrying on its back nine numbers arranged in a grid. The grid pattern corresponded to the Pa Kua's eight trigrams, centered around a ninth pivotal point.

The nine numbers were arranged in such a way that, when three numbers were added together, whether chosen in a horizontal, vertical, or diagonal line, the result was always 15, which happens to be the number of days it takes for the new moon to become a full moon.

This arrangement of the numbers into a three-by-three grid became known as the Lo Shu square. The square exerted a powerful and mythical influence on Chinese cultural symbolism, and the pattern of numbers soon became irretrievably connected with the trigrams of the Later Heaven arrangement of the Pa Kua. At the same time, the symbolism of the grid was extended to create connections between the numbers and the four celestial animals – the dragon, the tiger, the turtle, and the phoenix. So-called Lo Shu "magic" features strongly in Compass School Feng Shui methods.

THE LO SHU GRID AND THE PA KUA

Some of the most powerful Feng Shui formulas are closely allied to the mysterious secrets of the Lo Shu grid. Correlations between the Lo Shu square and the Pa Kua become apparent when the grid is superimposed onto the Pa Kua using the compass direction as a guide, where south is always equated with the number nine and north is always represented by the number one. With the numbers in place, the Lo Shu grid then unlocks further meanings within the Pa Kua based on the Chinese source books, on the grid, and on numerology (or the meanings of these numbers).

Together, these two symbols have become the cornerstone of Compass School Feng Shui formulas, not only for Feng Shui viewed in a spatial dimension, but also for Feng Shui viewed in a time dimension. This is because every day, every month, every year, and every twenty-year period has its own special Lo Shu number. Based on these Lo Shu numbers, practitioners are able to calculate good days and bad days for various activities. Since these calculations tend to be tedious, these good and bad days for undertaking a variety of activities, such as

According to Chinese legend, the magic square first appeared about 4,000 years ago on the back of a turtle as it emerged from the River Lo.

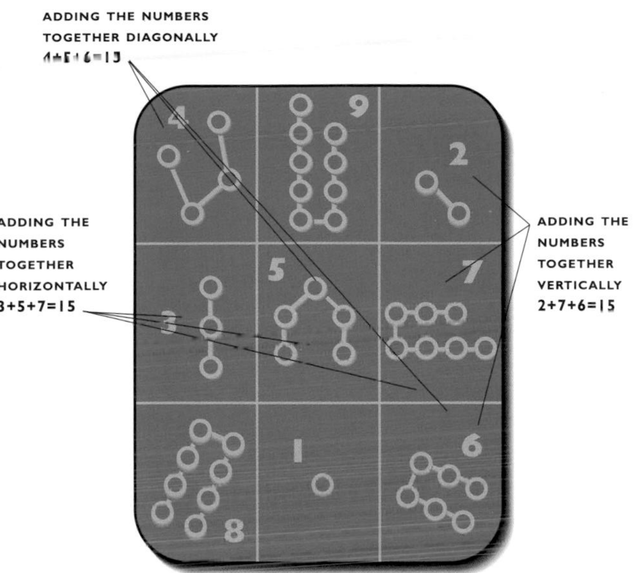

The pattern of dots on the turtle's back represents the numerical configurations of the Lo Shu square. By adding the numbers together in any direction the result is always fifteen.

moving house or changing jobs, are calculated each year and published by the Chinese in their annual almanac, the Tong Shu.

MAGIC PROPERTIES

The Lo Shu square also became the foundation of Taoist magical practice, and many of Taoism's magical rituals continue to be synchronized in accordance with the Lo Shu pattern. Perhaps it is because of this that Feng Shui formulas based on the Lo Shu number grid have been practiced by generations of Chinese people. Perhaps, also, more than the Pa Kua, it is the Lo Shu grid, with its intriguing arrangement of numbers, that holds the real key to the wisdom of the ancients, a wisdom that is both scientific and akin to magic.

MAGIC SQUARE

4	9	2
3	5	7
8	1	6

The ancient Chinese believed that the universe was based on mathematical principles; numbers, therefore, had great significance. They were the key to the invisible forces that governed both heaven and earth.

Scholars studying the origins of the Lo Shu grid have speculated on the striking similarities between the grid's numbers and certain potent symbols from other cultures, especially the ancient Hebrew sign for the planet Saturn, which is similar to the symbol created by the sequence of the numbers in the Lo Shu grid.

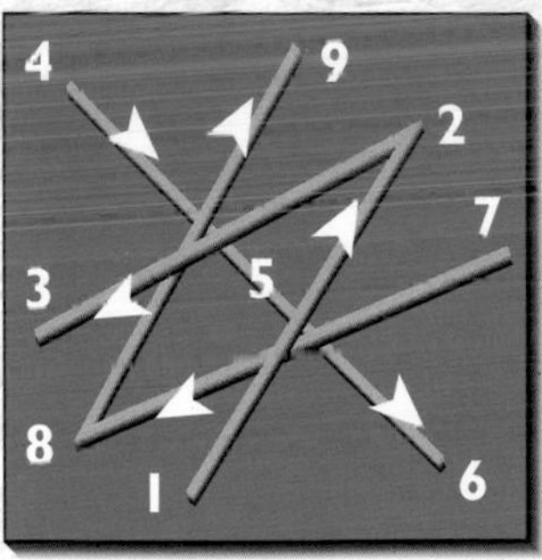

The pattern created by the Lo Shu grid's numbers is remarkably similar to the Hebrew symbol the Sigil of Saturn.

Chapter Five

ADVANCED FORMULAS

The practice of Feng Shui requires an appreciation of Yin and Yang forces, knowledge of the five elements and their productive and destructive cycles, familiarity with the eight-sided Pa Kua symbol, and an ability to discern the meaning of the *I Ching* trigrams. These are the fundamentals of Feng Shui practice. More advanced Feng Shui theories depend on understanding how the intangible forces represented by these symbols interact to create balance or imbalance in the atmosphere. These and other aspects of Feng Shui practice are summarized in this chapter. To those who are as yet unfamiliar with the staples of Chinese cultural knowledge, the explanations that accompany Feng Shui recommendations may, at first, seem alien. Once understood, however, the logic that underlies the practice soon becomes clear.

THE FASCINATION and challenge of Feng Shui practice lies in its many theories, methods, and interpretations. It is more than just village superstition. The philosophy behind its practice – to live in harmony with nature and with the physical landscapes of the earth and to become aware of the subtle energy lines in the environment – deserves further study and serious attention. The prospect of reaping the benefits of good Feng Shui means that applying this ancient practice in a modern context is worthy of a trial. Over the last few years, interest in Feng Shui has certainly increased – indeed, there are over 50 Feng Shui consultants in Malaysia alone and all do a very brisk business.

The Form School of Feng Shui focuses on the contours of physical landscapes – mountains and rivers, and their shapes, sizes, and courses. Auspicious and inauspicious sites are compared to highly symbolic representations of the celestial animals – the dragon, the tiger, the phoenix, and the turtle. Areas of abundance and prosperity are likened to sites that are replete with the dragon's cosmic breath – the vital Chi. Form School Feng Shui depends on one's powers of observation and the creativity of one's imagination.

With the Compass School, the practice takes on more precision. Many of the theories of the Compass School are complex, but because of its more mathematical and scientific basis, it is actually easier to practice.

The techniques and methods of the latter school are generally based on the eight-sided Pa Kua symbol and the nine-sector Lo Shu magic square, with its arrangement of the numbers one to nine set out in a way generally believed to possess a powerful influence over the fortunes of the universe.

Building on these fundamentals, there are many different ways of practicing Feng Shui methods. Some are static and are based on very precise measurements and directions, while others are described by their practitioners as "moving," principally because they introduce the time dimension to the calculation of good and bad luck.

Old formulas that represent a special skill or a closely guarded secret are seldom parted with

There are many intangible forces affecting our homes – the surrounding hills and trees, the direction of the front door, the proportions of the house itself – and many different methods of interpreting these forces.

easily. Usually, these secrets, referred to as special "Kung Fu," are passed on only from master to pupil. Even in the process of teaching, the master almost always holds back some key ingredient, reserving this only for his best and brightest student – someone deemed worthy of taking over the master's mantle when the latter departs this world. This chapter concentrates on highlighting some of the more popular theories used by the Feng Shui masters of today.

EAST-HOUSE/WEST-HOUSE THEORY

This Feng Shui theory suggests that the eight directions of the eight-sided Pa Kua symbol represent eight types of houses. These are divided into two categories of four houses each, known as the east houses and the west houses. The names of the houses, their front and back door directions, and the elements associated with them are summarized on page 89.

To identify the kind of house you have, first check the direction of your front and back doors. Take these directions from the inside looking out. When in doubt, use the back door as the determining factor to identify what type of house it is. For example, if your back door faces northwest while your front door faces southeast, yours is a Chien house. It belongs to the west group and its element is metal. If your back door faces south and your front door faces north, yours is a Li house. It belongs to the east group of houses and its element is fire. If the front door faces north and the back door faces southwest, the back door takes precedence, so it is a Kun house (and not a Li house), belonging to the west group.

East-group houses are associated with the elements water, wood, and fire. The houses are thus in a harmonious relationship with each other, since water produces wood, which produces fire. East-group houses clash with west-group houses because the elements form a destructive relationship (the metal of a west house destroys the wood of an east house, for example).

The Feng Shui of east-group houses can be enhanced with plants, flowers, bright lights, and water structures. Place these enhancers near the front door, or in the corresponding element sectors identified on the Pa Kua *(see pages 80–81)*.

West-group houses are associated with the elements metal and earth. To enhance the Feng Shui of west-group houses, use wind chimes and crystals.

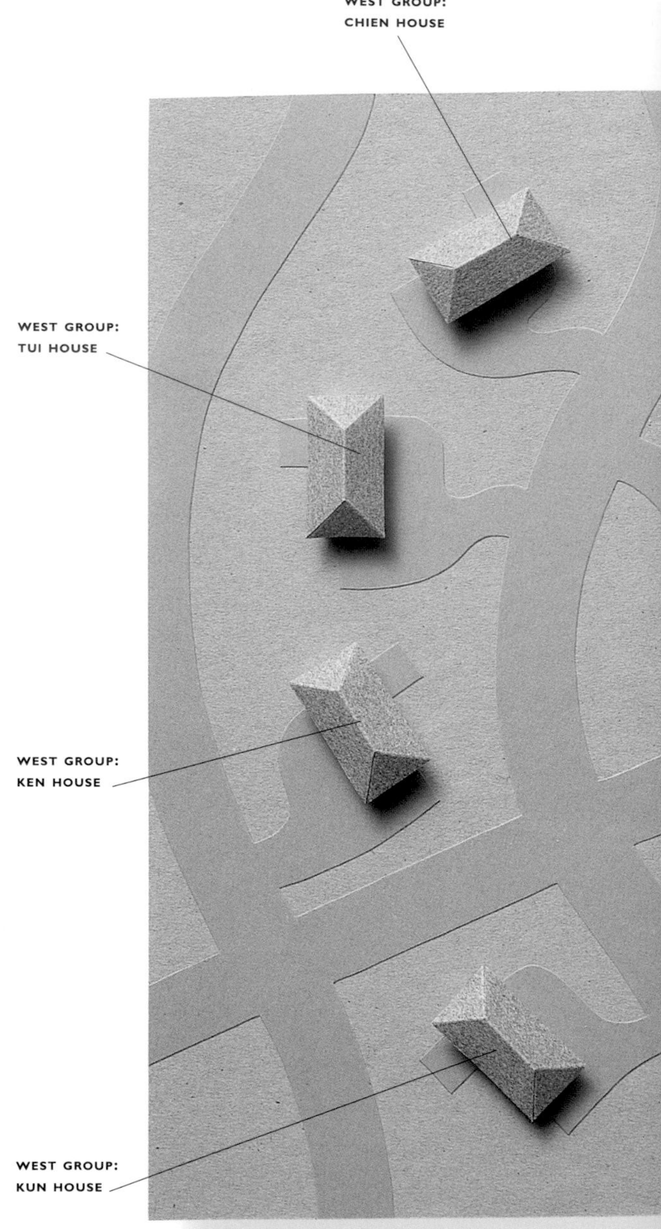

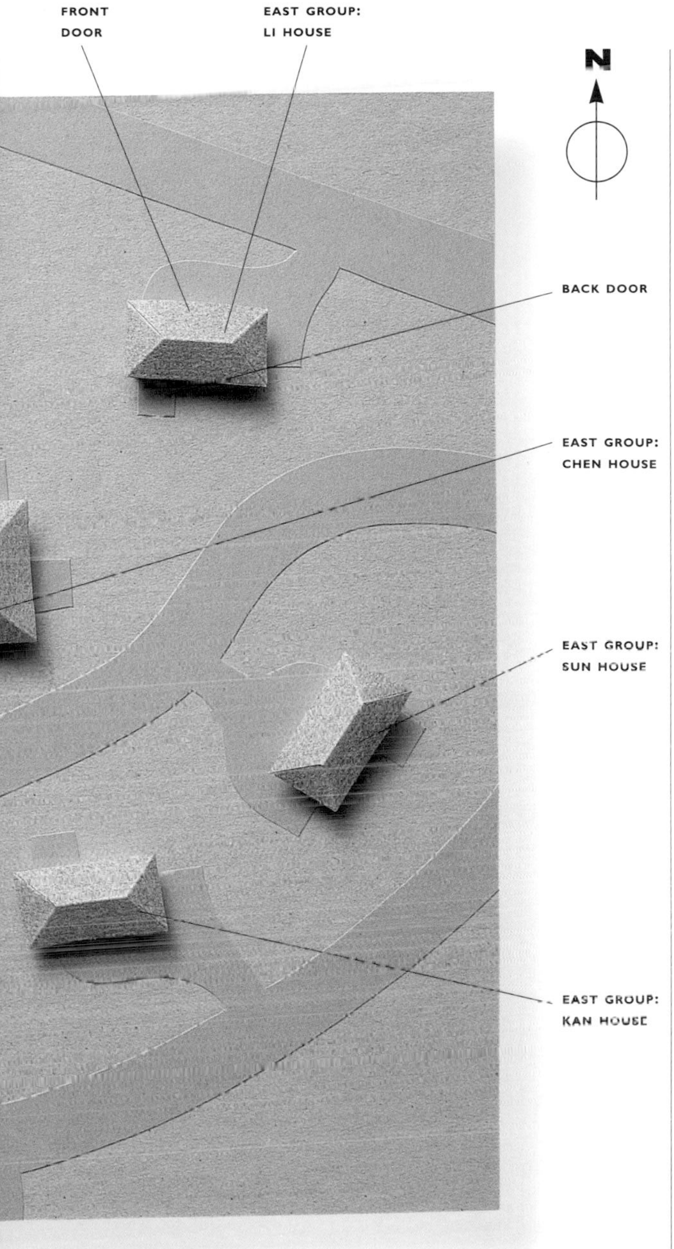

One of the most popular methods practiced by modern Feng Shui masters is the east house/west house theory. The direction of the house is determined by the direction of the front and back doors.

Flowers and plants can enhance the Feng Shui of east-group houses.

THE EAST HOUSES

Name	Front door direction	Back door direction	Element
Li	North	South	Fire
Kan	South	North	Water
Chen	West	East	Wood
Sun	Northwest	Southeast	Wood

THE WEST HOUSES

Name	Front door direction	Back door direction	Element
Chien	Southeast	Northwest	Metal
Kun	Northeast	Southwest	Earth
Ken	Southwest	Northeast	Earth
Tui	East	West	Metal

EAST-GROUP/WEST-GROUP PEOPLE

There is a further dimension to the east house/west house analysis. Like houses, people are also divided into east and west-group types. It is possible to investigate whether your house is good for you by checking whether you are a west or an east-group person using the table on page 91.

This is simply a matter of checking your year of birth against the indicated trigram. From this, you will learn whether you are an east or a west person, and the ideal directions of your front and back doors. East-group people should, of course, live in east-group houses, and west-group people should live in west-group houses if they are to be successful in maximizing their luck.

It follows that if you are a west-group person living in an east-group house, your fortune is not going to be very auspicious. The best arrangement is to have a perfect match, so that if you are a Kan person you live in a Kan house and if you are a Chien person you live in a Chien house.

OVERCOMING A MISMATCH

If your door directions do not suit you, try to change their position to improve your Feng Shui. If your front door faces a direction belonging to a west house and your back door faces a direction belonging to an east house, decide which type of house is better for you and make the changes accordingly.

A WEST-GROUP HOUSE FOR A WEST-GROUP PERSON

TOILET AND BATHROOM IN NORTH

SECOND BEDROOM IN NORTHEAST

MAIN BEDROOM IN WEST

STOREROOM IN SOUTH EAST

A west-group person's good locations are northwest, northeast, southwest and west. Place bedrooms and studies here and avoid siting toilets in these areas.

A WEST-GROUP HOUSE FOR AN EAST-GROUP PERSON

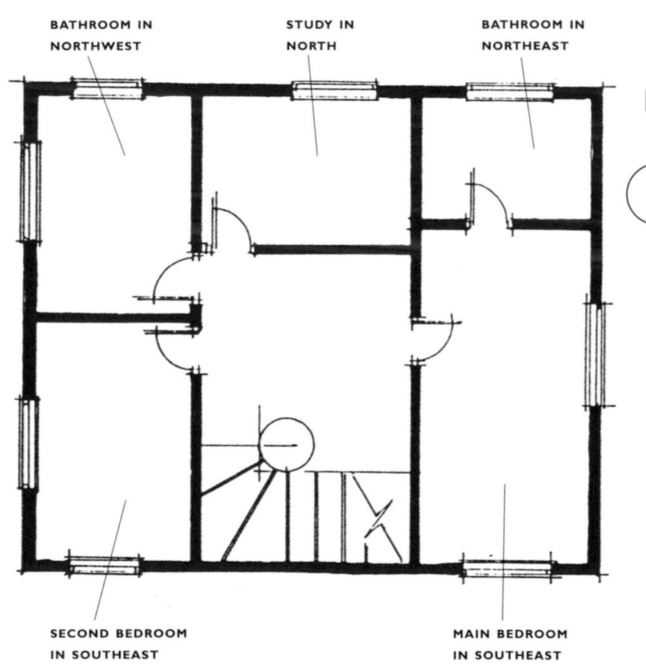

An east-group person's good locations are south, east, north and southeast. If you are an east-group person, try to sleep in the south or southeast.

Having said that, it is acknowledged that it is not always easy or possible to change an east house into a west house and vice versa. So, what should you do if you are an east-group person and you have to live in a west-group house? The answer is, that although the house will not be auspicious for you, you can improve your Feng Shui by rearranging the room layouts. You will need to identify your four good locations and your four bad locations, and use only the good ones for your important rooms and work areas *(further details are contained in the Eight Locations theory on pages 92–95).*

ARE YOU AN EAST-GROUP OR A WEST-GROUP PERSON?

From the table below, match the year of your birth to the trigram to determine what kind of house is best suited to you. Do not forget that the Chinese lunar new year begins in early February. If you were born in January or early February, your Chinese year of birth is therefore the preceding year from the one in which you were born in the Western calendar (someone born in January 1956 should use 1955 as their year of birth, for example).

WEST GROUP			**MALE**						**FEMALE**	
CHIEN	1904	1913	1922	1931	1940	1901	1910	1919	1928	1937
	1949	1958	1967	1976	1985	1946	1955	1964	1973	1982
KUN	1905	1908	1914	1917	1923	1906	1915	1924	1933	1942
	1926	1932	1935	1941	1944	1951	1960	1969	1978	1987
	1950	1953	1959	1962	1968					
	1971	1977	1980	1986	1989					
KEN	1902	1911	1920	1929	1938	1900	1903	1909	1912	1918
	1947	1956	1965	1974	1983	1921	1927	1930	1936	1939
						1945	1948	1954	1957	1963
						1966	1972	1975	1981	1984
TUI	1903	1912	1921	1930	1939	1902	1911	1920	1929	1938
	1948	1957	1966	1975	1984	1947	1956	1965	1974	1983
EAST GROUP										
LI	1901	1910	1919	1928	1937	1904	1913	1922	1931	1940
	1946	1955	1964	1973	1982	1949	1958	1967	1976	1985
KAN	1900	1909	1918	1927	1936	1905	1914	1923	1932	1941
	1945	1954	1963	1972	1981	1950	1959	1968	1977	1986
CHEN	1907	1916	1925	1934	1943	1907	1916	1925	1934	1943
	1952	1961	1970	1979	1988	1952	1961	1970	1979	1988
SUN	1906	1915	1924	1933	1942	1908	1917	1926	1935	1944
	1951	1960	1969	1978	1987	1953	1962	1971	1980	1989

EIGHT LOCATIONS THEORY

This Feng Shui method focuses on the interiors of houses. According to this theory, every house can be divided into eight locations, with each one of the locations corresponding to one of the eight sides (or directions) of the Pa Kua. Each of the eight locations has certain characteristics that may be auspicious or inauspicious.

THE GOOD LOCATIONS

The major location: is suitable for bedrooms (pious Chinese people also consider it a good site for an altar). The stove should be placed in a area directly opposite the best location.

The health location: this part of the house brings good health and energy. This is the best location for dining rooms and for the bedrooms of family members who may be ill.

The longevity location: needless to say, this is good for older members of the family.

The prosperity location: this is the prime location for creating wealth and for bringing prosperity to the household. This is the most auspicious location for the front door, master bedroom, the study, or any area associated with your work or business, and it should be kept well-lit, clean, and vibrant. You must not place your toilet or kitchen in this prosperity location.

THE BAD LOCATIONS

The difficulties location: this signifies the area of the house that causes legal entanglements, disputes, quarrels, anger, and irritation. Do not locate any of the important rooms, such as bedrooms or studies, here. It is, however, suitable for toilets and storerooms.

The loss and scandal location: this signifies an area that generates laziness, listlessness, and loss of energy. It is also suitable for the toilet, the storerooms, or the kitchen.

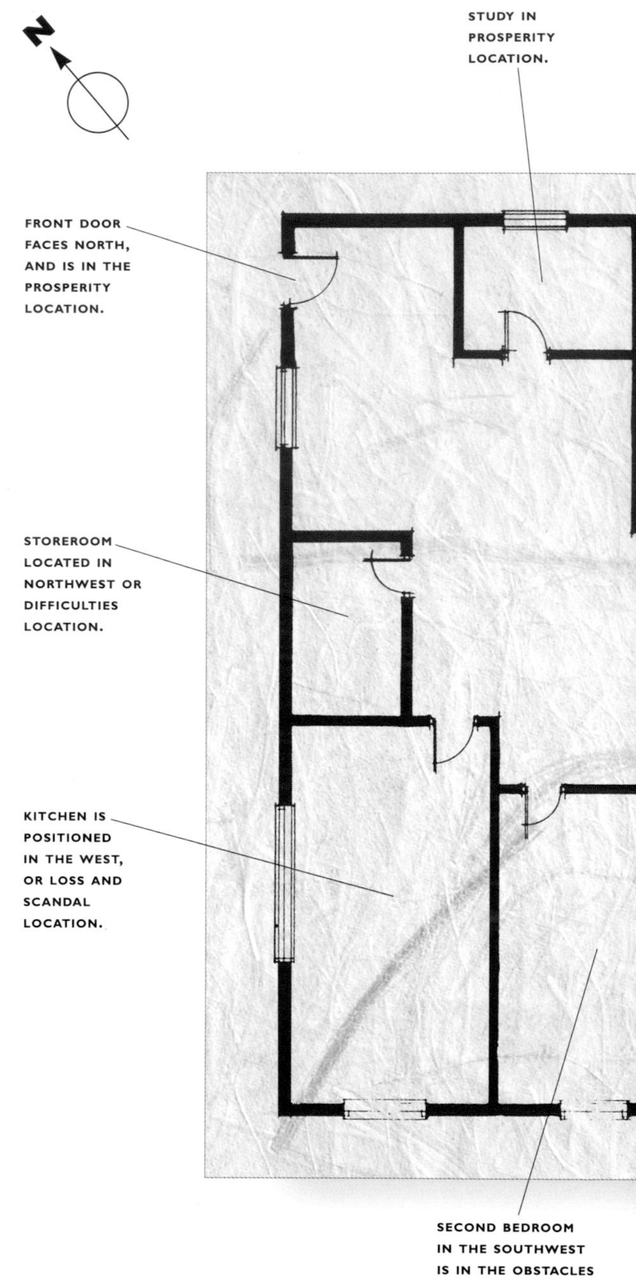

This house plan shows the four good and the four bad locations belonging to the east group; more specifically, a Sun house.

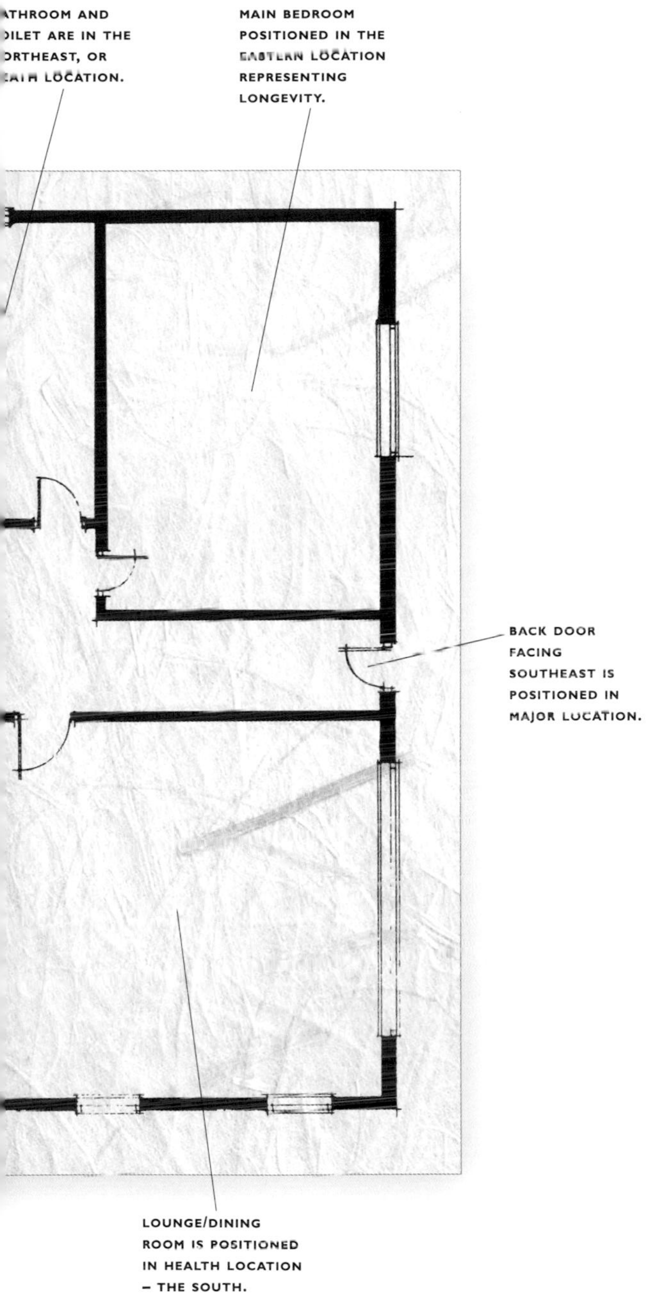

The obstacles location: this symbolizes loss, theft, burglary, being cheated, being betrayed, legal entanglements, and financial loss, and is suitable only for toilets and kitchens.

The death location: this signifies accidents, poor health, fatal illness, disease, misfortunes of a grave nature, loss, and death.

ANALYZING LOCATIONS IN THE HOME

The good and bad locations differ according to the kind of house you are analyzing. Here, "kind of house" means a west-group or an east group house, and, more specifically, which trigram rules the house. We know, from the east-house/west-house theory *(see pages 88–91)*, that this depends on the location of the back door. Before analyzing the quality of the eight locations of your house, you must first determine what kind of house it is that you live in.

It is then possible to identify the good and bad locations of your home using the details given on pages 94–95. From these you will see that good locations and bad locations follow their east and west characteristics. The east directions – south, north, east, and southeast – are all good for you if you live in an east-group house; equally, the west-group directions – northwest, southwest, west, and northeast – are all good for you if you live in a west-group house. If you live in a Sun house your major location will be the southeast, while your death location is the northeast. You will, therefore, need to avoid placing your toilet in the southeastern corner of your home or your bedroom in the northeastern.

Once you have mastered the theory behind this particular method, you will find it easy to make the correlations and – based on the Feng Shui enhancing tips and tools presented in the later chapters of this book – you will eventually be able to enhance each of your good locations.

USING GOOD AND BAD LOCATIONS

Once you have succeeded in identifying the good and bad locations, it is a simple matter to arrange the layout of your rooms and work areas to ensure that you get maximum benefits from Feng Shui forces. If your house is a west-group Tui house, then you should place your bedroom in the west location, your major location, or, if you wish to enhance your wealth, in your prosperity location, which is northwest.

This works if you happen to be lucky enough to be a west-group person living in this west-group house. If, however, you are an east-group person living in a west-group house, you can improve your Feng Shui by rearranging the room layouts to suit you and ignore the type of house it is. Identify your good and bad locations and then proceed to use the good locations for your important rooms and work areas. If you are an east-group Chen person, for example, your excellent locations are south, east, north, and southeast, and your luck will improve if you sleep in the south sector, even if yours is a west-group house. A west-group person, whose good locations are northwest, northeast, southwest, and west, should try to sleep in the west or southwest sectors.

Once you have identified the good and bad locations of your particular house, do not fret or worry unduly if you find that you have a toilet, say, in the prosperity location, or a bedroom in the difficulties location. These things can be modified and the effects of locations can be reduced or enhanced. If your toilet is located in the prosperity area, try not to use that particular toilet. Keep the toilet door closed. If your bedroom is located in the difficulties location, change your bedroom, or, if this is not possible, then make certain that you are at least sleeping in a way that allows your head to be pointed in the prosperity direction, so as to draw on the good Feng Shui of that location.

CHEN (BACK DOOR: EAST)

MAJOR LOCATION:	EAST
HEALTH LOCATION:	NORTH
LONGEVITY LOCATION:	SOUTHEAST
PROSPERITY LOCATION:	SOUTH
DIFFICULTIES LOCATION:	SOUTHWEST
LOSS AND SCANDAL LOCATION:	NORTHEAST
OBSTACLES LOCATION:	NORTHWEST
DEATH LOCATION:	WEST

SUN (BACK DOOR: SOUTHEAST)

MAJOR LOCATION:	SOUTHEAST
HEALTH LOCATION:	SOUTH
LONGEVITY LOCATION:	EAST
PROSPERITY LOCATION:	NORTH
DIFFICULTIES LOCATION:	NORTHWEST
LOSS AND SCANDAL LOCATION:	WEST
OBSTACLES LOCATION:	SOUTHWEST
DEATH LOCATION:	NORTHEAST

KAN (BACK DOOR: NORTH)

MAJOR LOCATION:	NORTH
HEALTH LOCATION:	EAST
LONGEVITY LOCATION:	SOUTH
PROSPERITY LOCATION:	SOUTHEAST
DIFFICULTIES LOCATION:	WEST
LOSS AND SCANDAL LOCATION:	NORTHWEST
OBSTACLES LOCATION:	NORTHEAST
DEATH LOCATION:	SOUTHWEST

CHIEN (BACK DOOR: NORTHWEST)

MAJOR LOCATION:	NORTHWEST
HEALTH LOCATION:	NORTHEAST
LONGEVITY LOCATION:	SOUTHWEST
PROSPERITY LOCATION:	WEST
DIFFICULTIES LOCATION:	SOUTHEAST
LOSS AND SCANDAL LOCATION:	NORTH
OBSTACLES LOCATION:	EAST
DEATH LOCATION:	SOUTH

KUN (BACK DOOR: SOUTHWEST)

MAJOR LOCATION:	SOUTHWEST
HEALTH LOCATION:	WEST
LONGEVITY LOCATION:	NORTHWEST
PROSPERITY LOCATION:	NORTHEAST
DIFFICULTIES LOCATION:	EAST
LOSS AND SCANDAL LOCATION:	SOUTH
OBSTACLES LOCATION:	SOUTHEAST
DEATH LOCATION:	NORTH

KEN (BACK DOOR: NORTHEAST)

MAJOR LOCATION:	NORTHEAST
HEALTH LOCATION:	NORTHWEST
LONGEVITY LOCATION:	WEST
PROSPERITY LOCATION:	SOUTHWEST
DIFFICULTIES LOCATION:	SOUTH
LOSS AND SCANDAL LOCATION:	EAST
OBSTACLES LOCATION:	NORTH
DEATH LOCATION:	SOUTHEAST

TUI (BACK DOOR: WEST)

MAJOR LOCATION:	WEST
HEALTH LOCATION:	SOUTHWEST
LONGEVITY LOCATION:	NORTHEAST
PROSPERITY LOCATION:	NORTHWEST
DIFFICULTIES LOCATION:	NORTH
LOSS AND SCANDAL LOCATION:	SOUTHEAST
OBSTACLES LOCATION:	SOUTH
DEATH LOCATION:	EAST

LI (BACK DOOR: SOUTH)

MAJOR LOCATION:	SOUTH
HEALTH LOCATION:	SOUTHEAST
LONGEVITY LOCATION:	NORTH
PROSPERITY LOCATION:	EAST
DIFFICULTIES LOCATION:	NORTHEAST
LOSS AND SCANDAL LOCATION:	SOUTHWEST
OBSTACLES LOCATION:	WEST
DEATH LOCATION:	NORTHWEST

COMPARING THE FORMULAS

Please note that the Eight Locations theory is one of the compass formulas used by practicing Feng Shui masters. It is similar to, but not exactly the same as, the Pa-Kua Lo-Shu formula which is more potent. *(See pages 98–103 for details of the Pa-Kua Lo-Shu formula.)*

PRACTICAL TIPS FOR IDENTIFYING HOUSES AND LOCATIONS

When defining the eight locations of a house or building, the first thing you need is a floor plan of the house. This must be drawn to scale, as measurements must be very exact. Next, find the center of the house, draw a circle around the center and divide the circle into eight equal sectors. Place a compass on the plan to position it, then mark each of the sectors according to the compass reading in order to identify the eight directions and locations.

This analysis need not only be undertaken for a house, it can also be used for a building, an entire shopping complex, a whole country, or a small room. There are no space limitations in the application of Feng Shui, because the influences of Feng Shui are directional. They apply equally to small areas and to large areas.

The position of the cooking stove is vital for Feng Shui calculations. If it faces the front or back doors, positive Chi will quickly disappear. If it is too close to the refrigerator or sink, there will be a clash between the elements of fire and water.

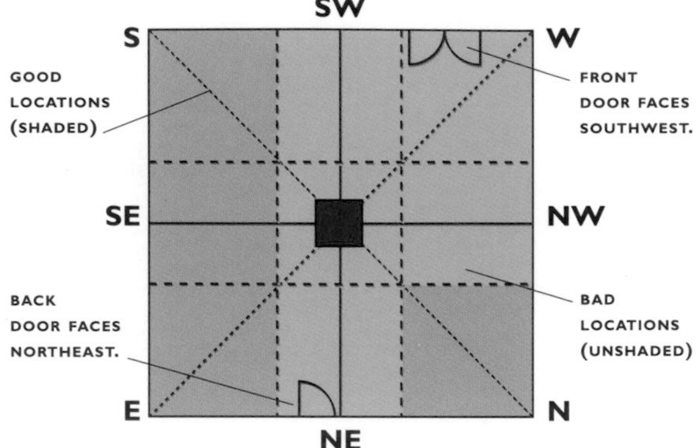

Dividing a house into its eight good and bad sectors is achieved by identifying the compass directions. This is a Ken house because its back door faces northeast.

The key to identifying houses, and from there, determining locations, depends on correct identification of the front and back doors. With modern house design, however, it can sometimes be tricky trying to pinpoint exactly which is the front and which is the back door, especially since some buildings have as many as four doors, and some houses have several secondary doors, such as patio doors or doors leading from a sunroom.

In ancient times, properly-sited houses were backed by mountains and faced rivers. Modern Feng Shui masters substitute big buildings for mountains and roads for rivers – so that the direction of the house or building facing the main road is then regarded as the front of the house and the opposite side considered its back. Even if there is a main door on the side of the house facing onto a side street, that cannot always be regarded as the front of the house.

It is also believed that the true front of the house is where most of the favorable Chi can concentrate and gather. This is the side of the building that faces either a main road or a broad expanse of undeveloped land, such as a park, open space, a children's playground, or a pedestrian area. The side of your house facing such a space is considered the front of the house, and the back is then the opposite side.

In rare instances, where the house has an irregular or unusual shape (for example, L-shaped, cross- or butterfly-shaped), the house is regarded as having no single front and back door. Each wing or arm of the building is considered to be an independent entity that has to be examined separately. Such houses are not considered auspicious, because they suffer from a lack of focus. Without there being a clearly defined front door, the house suffers, mainly because favorable Chi coming in is easily dispersed and thus lost to the house.

Finally, it is necessary to address the practical difficulties associated with the realities of rooms and floor plans. Clearly, it is not possible to limit your use of the house just to the good locations. One cannot place all the beds and all the doors of the house in the four good locations and site only toilets and storerooms in the bad locations. The entire exercise becomes even more complicated and impossible if there are equal members of the household belonging to both east and west groups. Somewhere, it is vital to compromise.

Compromise is best achieved by defining what it is that the family most desires. Is it wealth, health, family harmony, or a good marriage? Depending on the result, you can plan your positions accordingly.

If the house is not symmetrical, and the so called "center" lies outside the building itself, or is not clearly defined, as in the L- or U-shaped house, demarcate the buildings into two or more separate parts before attempting to centralize and identify the eight locations.

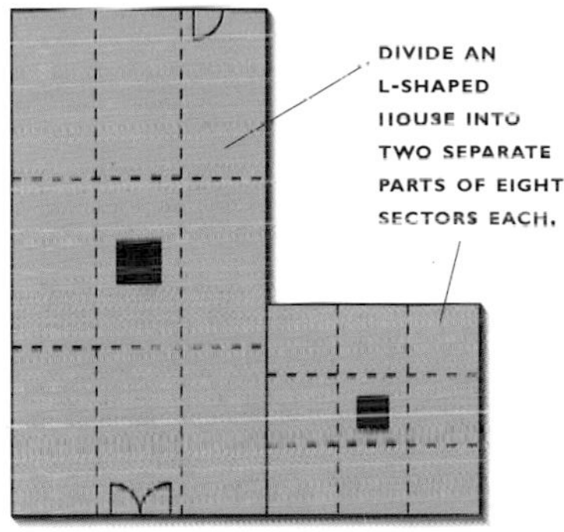

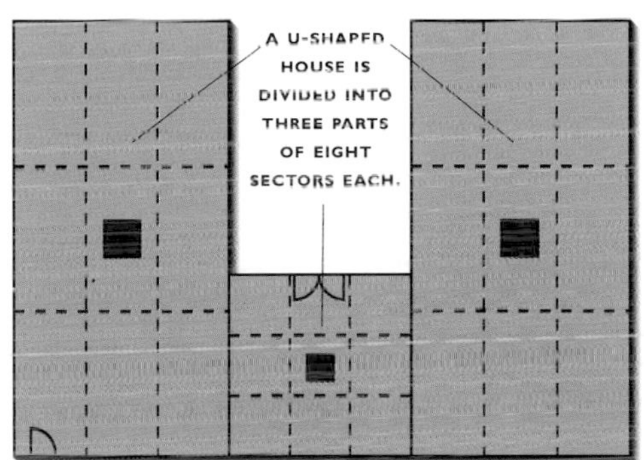

Not all rooms or doors have equal importance in Feng Shui. It is possible to rank structures and furnishings according to the influence they exert on one's fortune. However, for Feng Shui purposes, there are three things that must be sorted out satisfactorily, and they are the location and direction of the main doors (front and back), the bedrooms, and the cooking stove.

If there is a conflict of interest between the husband and the wife – because each belongs to a different group – then the main doors and the stove should be positioned to benefit the husband, and the bedroom to benefit the wife.

THE PA-KUA LO-SHU THEORY

The Pa-Kua Lo-Shu theory, as the name suggests, is based on the two premier symbols of Chinese Feng Shui practice – the eight-sided Pa Kua and the nine-sector Lo Shu magic square. By combining the potencies of these two symbols, Feng Shui masters have developed formulas that are believed to be extremely powerful if accurately followed. According to these detailed formulas, it is possible for every individual to identify his or her four auspicious and four inauspicious directions. In this respect, the theory is very similar to the two theories already discussed in this chapter.

Following the Pa-Kua Lo-Shu theory, every abode can be divided into nine sectors, eight of which correspond to the eight directions of the compass and the eight sides of the Pa Kua, the ninth being the one in the center. Each of the sectors represents one of eight auspicious or inauspicious situations *(the eight sectors are described in detail on pages 102–103)*. It is necessary to differentiate between locations and directions – rooms should be sited in an auspicious location and face an auspicious direction. However, the direction is taken from the inside of the house or room, looking out.

According to Feng Shui practitioners, once you have successfully identified the good and bad Feng Shui characteristics of the various sectors and corners of your house, you are then in a position to allocate the rooms and design their layout in ways that are most beneficial to you and to the other members of your family.

As with all Feng Shui theories, application of the results must be practical, and nobody should set

Activating the Sheng Chi corner of your house will bring success in examinations.

Sheng Chi is the best location for generating wealth and prosperity.

about large-scale reconstruction of rooms and front doors. Usually, there are simple and pragmatic solutions to all Feng Shui formulas – ranging from the addition of a plant to the placing of a mirror – as we will see in later chapters, when interior design is discussed in greater detail.

Activating the Nien Yen, the longevity location of the home, is particularly beneficial for enhancing the quality of life.

CASE STUDY

Mr. Loh was a popular businessman who lived just outside Canton. He had a successful business buying and selling a variety of household and wooden products. His Kua number was 4, and he had married a woman whose Kua number was 1 (which corresponded to his very best Lo Shu number). They were happily married with five children, all sons.

When Mr. Loh decided to enlarge his house, however, his problems started. Inadvertently, Mr. Loh shifted the position of his oven, and in doing so turned his oven's fire mouth to face southwest (or Lo Shu number 2). This was his Wu Kuei or Five Ghosts direction. Worse still, it was also his wife's Chueh Ming (worst) direction. As if that were not bad enough, Mr. Loh also changed the direction of his main door to the Wu Kuei direction.

The outcome was a major tragedy. Mr. and Mrs. Loh lost all five sons. It was quite by chance that Mr. Loh met up with Master Qi, a local Feng Shui master who was well-schooled in the Pa-Kua Lo-Shu theory. Upon arriving at the house, he immediately diagnosed the problem, and proceeded to make several changes.

First, the master relocated the kitchen to the southwest sector of the house, the Wu Kuei sector, to "press" on the five ghosts. Next, he turned the oven so that its fire mouth faced the Nien Yen direction, or north. Then he changed the main door so that it faced the Tien Yi direction, or south.

Within a few months, Mr. Loh's wife became pregnant and delivered a son the following year.

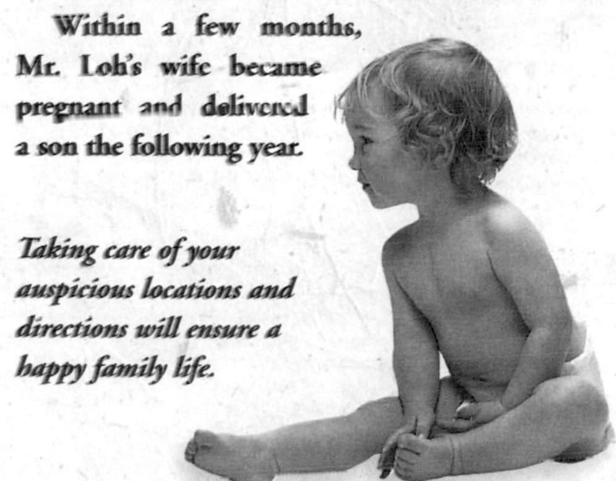

Taking care of your auspicious locations and directions will ensure a happy family life.

THE RELATIONSHIP BETWEEN KUA NUMBERS AND LOCATIONS

Under the Pa-Kua Lo-Shu theory, each of the auspicious and inauspicious locations differ from person to person. To identify the four auspicious locations that will bring you different kinds of good fortune and the four inauspicious locations that must strenuously be avoided, you first need to calculate your Kua number. There are two different formulas for working out your Kua number, one for males and another for females; these are described on page 101. You will find frequent reference to Kua numbers in subsequent sections of this book. It is, therefore, a good idea to work out your Kua number now and make a note of it.

Each Kua number is linked to specific auspicious and inauspicious locations, and these are traditionally represented, for ease of reference, in the form of the circular patterns shown at the foot of this page. (Here the patterns show north at the top for ease of reference.) In these, the favorable and unfavorable locations are named according to their meanings *(see the descriptions of these meanings on pages 102–103),* and colored following the key below. (There is no Kua number 5 in this Feng Shui system, males who have a Kua number of 5 should instead use the number 2, and females with the Kua number 5 should use the number 8.)

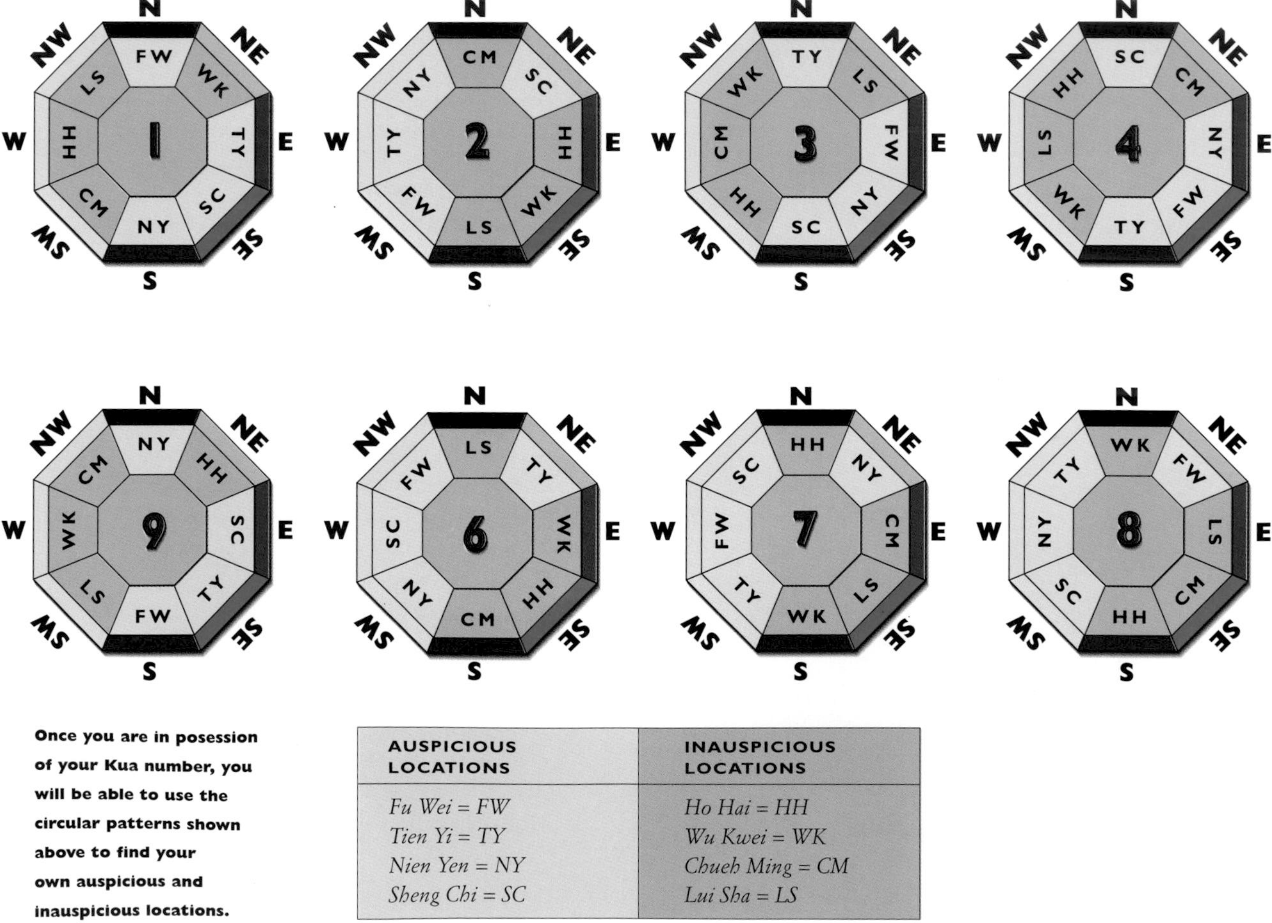

Once you are in posession of your Kua number, you will be able to use the circular patterns shown above to find your own auspicious and inauspicious locations.

AUSPICIOUS LOCATIONS	INAUSPICIOUS LOCATIONS
Fu Wei = FW	*Ho Hai = HH*
Tien Yi = TY	*Wu Kwei = WK*
Nien Yen = NY	*Chueh Ming = CM*
Sheng Chi = SC	*Lui Sha = LS*

CALCULATING YOUR KUA NUMBER

KUA NUMBERS FOR MALES

Take the year of your birth and add together the last two digits; if the result is 10 or more, add the two digits to reduce them to a single number, deduct the result from 10 and the answer is your Kua number.

KUA NUMBERS FOR FEMALES

Take the year of your birth, add together the last two digits; if the result is 10 or more, add the two digits to reduce them to a single number, then add 5. If the result is 10 or more, add the two digits to reduce them to a single number and the answer is your Kua number.

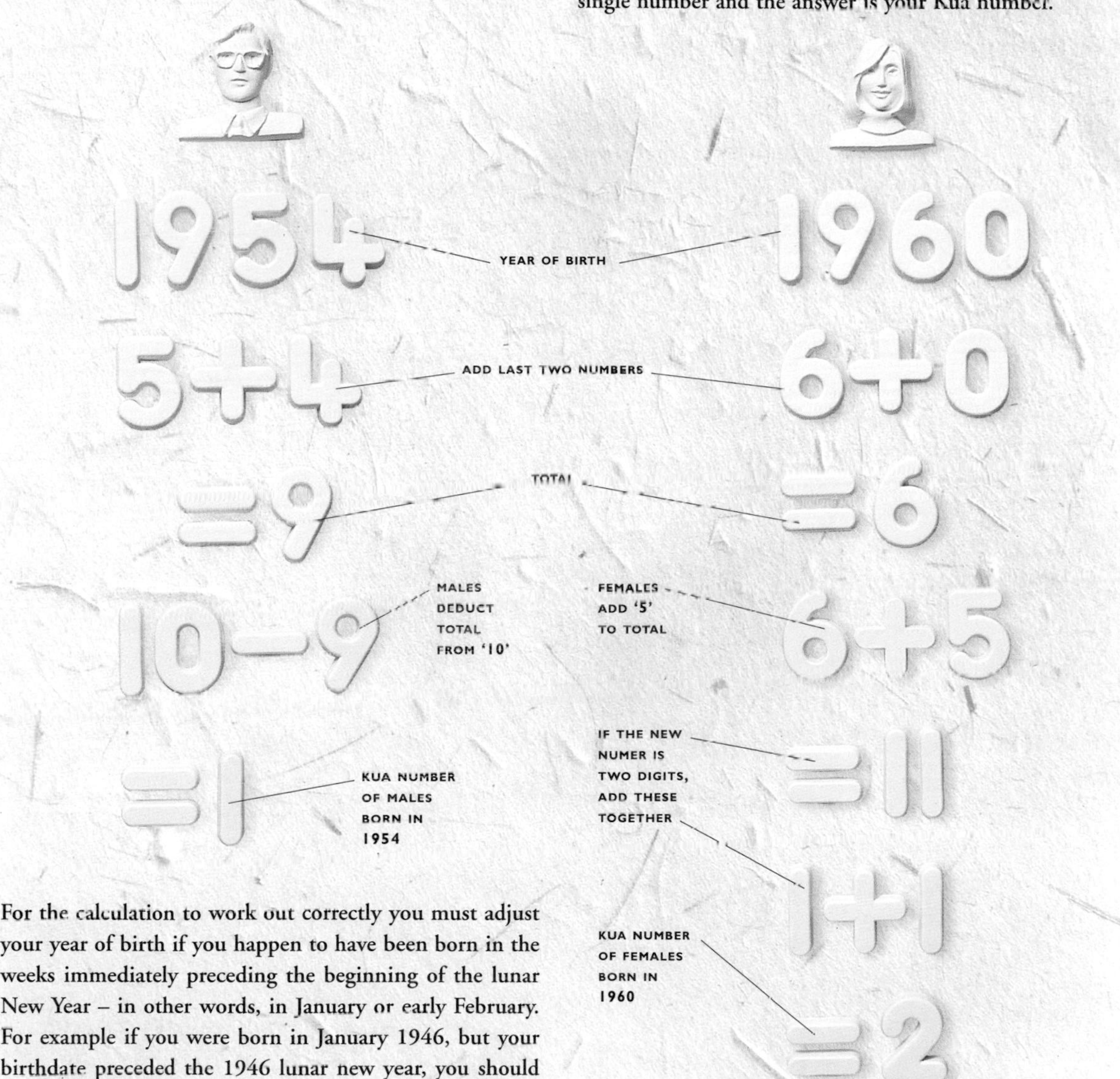

For the calculation to work out correctly you must adjust your year of birth if you happen to have been born in the weeks immediately preceding the beginning of the lunar New Year – in other words, in January or early February. For example if you were born in January 1946, but your birthdate preceded the 1946 lunar new year, you should use 1945 as your year of birth.

THE AUSPICIOUS LOCATIONS

SHENG CHI

meaning "generating breath"

This is the best location for attracting great prosperity. If you are a politician, activating or tapping your Sheng Chi location will bring you a high and honorable position. If you are a student, it will bring success in examinations and scholarship applications. If you are a businessman, it will bring great wealth. To tap the Sheng Chi, put your bedroom, study and/or front door, in this location and position your front door to face this direction.

If you seek prosperity in any form, place your front door in your Sheng Chi location.

TIEN YI

meaning "doctor from heaven"

This is the best location for members of the household who are sick or suffering from health problems. Tien Yi is exceptionally potent in curing prolonged and inexplicable illnesses. The best method of tapping the Tien Yi location is through the siting of the family stove. Position the stove with its source of energy (the "fire mouth") facing the Tien Yi direction.

Siting the stove in the Tien Yi sector will prove to be auspicious for the family's health.

NIEN YEN

meaning "longevity with rich descendants"

This is the location for enhancing the quality of your home life and family relationships – between husbands and wives, parents and children, and between siblings. The Nien Yen location should be tapped if the members of the family argue too much, or are unable to have children. It is also favorable if grown up children are finding it difficult to attract suitable marriage partners. It is also an excellent location for siting the master bedroom if the husband and wife are growing apart. Indeed, the Nien Yen is excellent as a cure-all for all manner of family problems and difficulties.

Alleviate marriage problems by situating the master bedroom in the Nien Yen sector.

FU WEI

meaning "overall harmony"

This is the location for achieving peace. It is favorable for maintaining general good fortune and for enjoying a comfortable life, though not achieving anything spectacular in terms of abundant wealth or business success. Fu Wei offers better-than-average luck – a most favorable livelihood, more boys than girls in the family (previous generations considered sons to be a manifestation of good luck), and strong protection against unfavorable luck.

THE INAUSPICIOUS LOCATIONS

HO HAI

meaning "accidents and mishaps"

This location leads to financial loss and all kinds of intermittent difficulty and frustration. However, it is the least unlucky of the four inauspicious locations. A storeroom in this location would be quite acceptable.

A storeroom would be safe in the Ho Hai location.

WU KWEI

meaning "five ghosts"

This location generates the kind of bad luck which results in fires, burglary, loss of income, and loss of employment. It also causes quarrels and misunderstandings between family members and between you and your friends and colleagues. Wu Kwei causes mischief at home and at work. You can suppress the five ghosts by having your toilet sited in this location and flushing them down the toilet.

Locating the toilet in the Wu Kwei sector would be acceptable.

LUI SHA

meaning "six killings"

As the name implies, this location represents grievous harm to you and your family. It also symbolizes missed opportunities at work and in business. Lui Sha causes legal entanglements, illness, accidents, and, in a worst case scenario, actual death. Again, toilets can be placed in this sector to suppress the evil Feng Shui. You can also render the sector totally ineffective by locating your storeroom here.

CHUEH MING

meaning "total loss of descendants"

To the Chinese mind, this location represents the worst possible kind of disaster or bad luck that can befall any family. This is the worst of the eight locations, and Feng Shui practitioners should make every effort not to locate the main door (or master bedroom) in this sector. Bad luck comes in its most severe forms – symptoms are the loss of children, loss of wealth, bankruptcy, and/or very severe and chronic illness. Every effort must be made to suppress it by locating a toilet or bathroom in this sector. It can also be suppressed by having the kitchen here, although the stove or oven should face a favorable direction.

Locating the kitchen in the Chueh Ming sector will alleviate the bad luck associated with this sector.

CHOOSING BETWEEN THE DIFFERENT THEORIES

The source philosophy and symbolism for much of the science of Feng Shui is derived from ancient texts, principally the *I Ching* (known in the West as the *Book of Changes*). Thus, as we have seen, the principal symbol of Feng Shui practice is the eight-sided Pa Kua, with its trigram arrangement. The ways of using and interpreting different formulas are all based on the Pa Kua, so that all the theories are variations and extensions of each other.

Inevitably, the similarity between these different formulas will cause some confusion to those approaching the subject for the first time, and it is easy to become uncertain about which theory to follow. The best approach is to be as pragmatic as possible (pragmatism is the great Chinese virtue) and try each method in turn to find out which one works best for you. Better still, try to understand all the methods as facets of one complete system, and adopt what might be called the "holistic approach" of marrying the different theories together and adopting the parts that are most suited to your situation (this is, after all, what many professional Feng Shui practitioners do).

Feng Shui influences have both time and space dimensions. The detailed investigation of time Feng Shui is known as "Flying Star Feng Shui."

Feng Shui is extremely effective for romance and marriage if the correct corners of the home are activated.

Perhaps the best way of summing up the Feng Shui approach is to say that it is all about achieving harmony and balance. These are the fundamental principles that should always be borne in mind.

It is also important to recognize that almost all Feng Shui practice is symbolic, not literal. Hence, the eight sides of the Pa Kua and their associated trigrams can symbolize many different things, including colors, directions, objects, elements, human character traits, seasons and planets, virtues and vices, landscape features, and rooms within a house. In this book, it is only possible to hint at the scope of the Pa Kua as it has been developed by Chinese sages over the centuries. Those wishing to delve deeper into the science of Feng Shui should study the *I Ching* in greater depth.

MORE ADVANCED THEORIES

In addition to the formulas given in this book, there are also other more complex formulas. These are generally more specialized and address more aspects of Feng Shui practice. For example, there are very specialized formulas that deal with the time dimension of Feng Shui, where the significance of changing forces during different periods, months, and days is taken into account. This process highlights the intangible influence of numbers, both individually and in combination, and is based on the pattern of Lo Shu numbers as they move in a time cycle in the lunar calendar. The formula and method for determining these good and bad influences for homes and buildings is collectively referred to as "Flying Star Feng Shui."

There are also formulas devoted exclusively to the flow of water. As a symbol of wealth, water plays a vital role in the creation of good Feng Shui and one of the most potent formulas is the Water Dragon Classic. This formula offers twelve water flow and exit directions across a plot of land, based on twelve categories of houses. The method for determining the category of your house is contained within the formula.

These specialized formulas are for the most part extremely technical and should be investigated only by those who are already thoroughly familiar with the basic principles of the practice of Feng Shui.

In a controlled way, Feng Shui can have a beneficial effect on wealth and lifestyles.

Feng Shui can be used to great effect for the well-being of children. To achieve this, activate the child's knowledge corner.

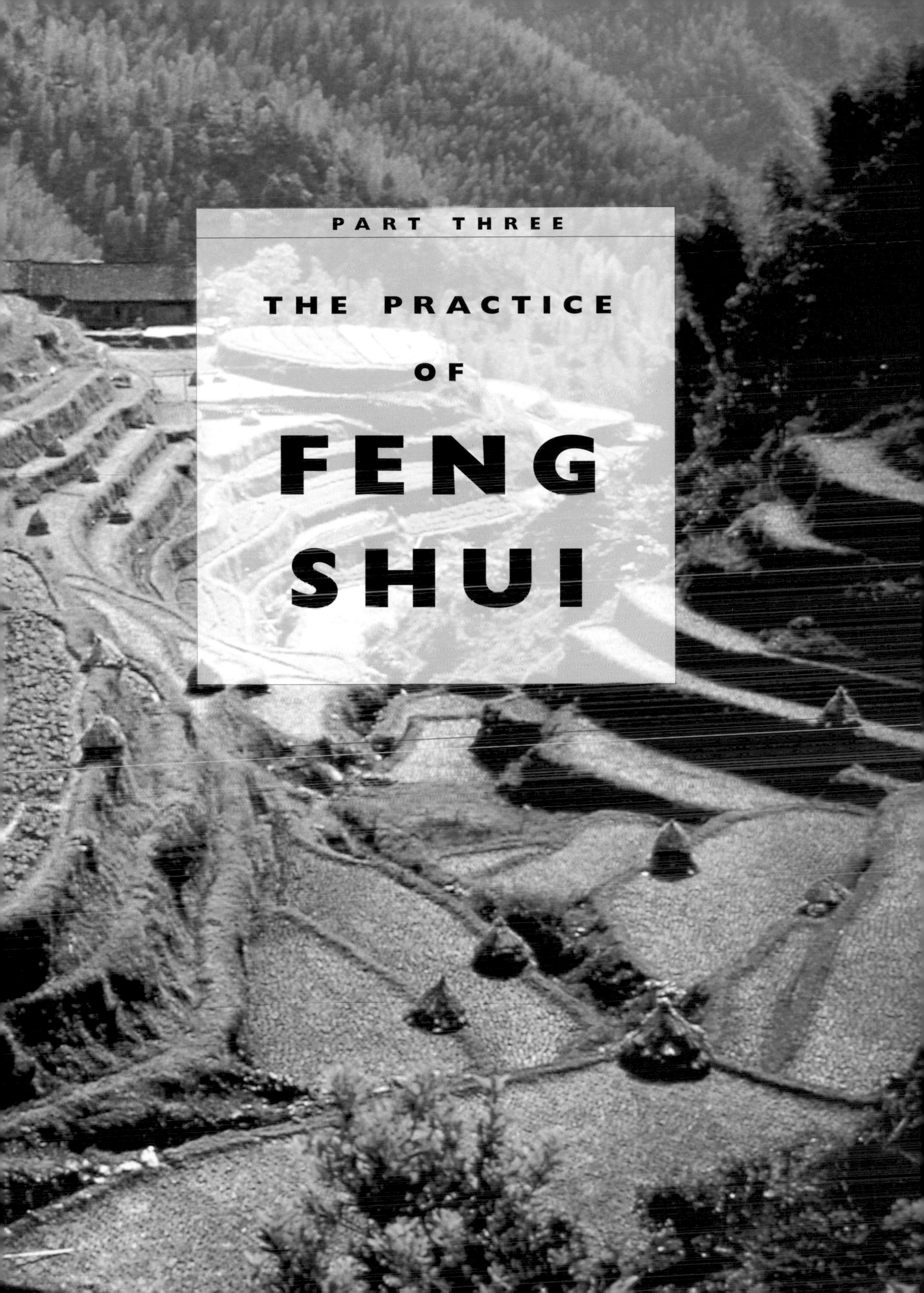

PART THREE

THE PRACTICE OF FENG SHUI

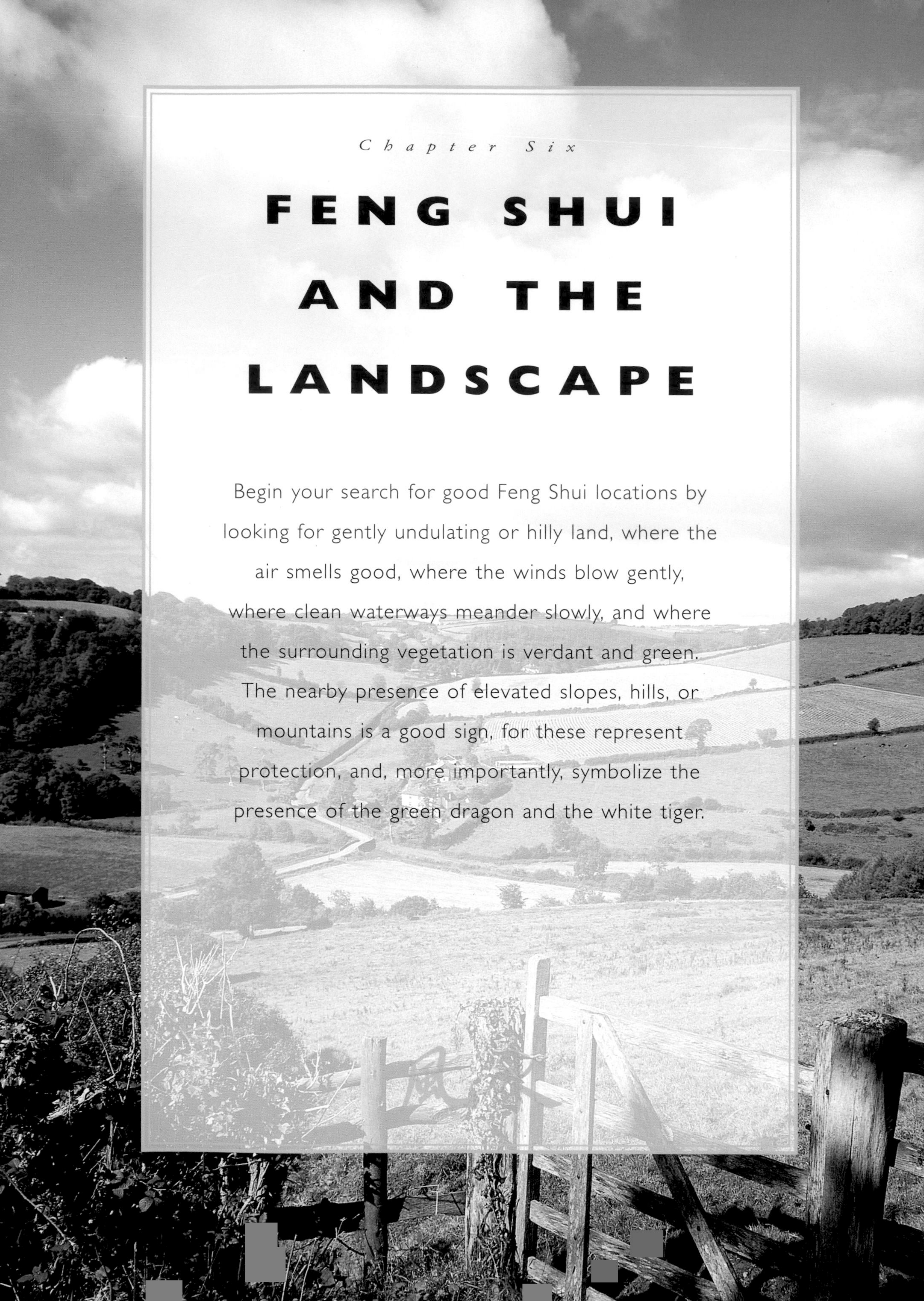

Chapter Six

FENG SHUI AND THE LANDSCAPE

Begin your search for good Feng Shui locations by looking for gently undulating or hilly land, where the air smells good, where the winds blow gently, where clean waterways meander slowly, and where the surrounding vegetation is verdant and green. The nearby presence of elevated slopes, hills, or mountains is a good sign, for these represent protection, and, more importantly, symbolize the presence of the green dragon and the white tiger.

THE ANCIENT Feng Shui masters of China understood that human destiny is enhanced if we live in harmony with nature, thereby tapping into its auspicious influences. Nature is likened to a living organism and its breath pervades everything. It thereby produces the varied conditions that modern practitioners term good and bad luck. The landscapes surrounding our homes or places of work must reflect this harmonious interface with nature for there to be good Feng Shui.

Harmony with nature is more easily achieved if your dwelling is situated in a place that has auspicious influences of terrain, including any nearby mountains, rivers, and lakes; a place where the quality of the air and wind suggests an abundant presence of the benign "breath" of nature.

In the Feng Shui tradition, auspicious locations are usually slightly elevated places where "the green dragon of the east" nestles gently with "the white tiger of the west," with their bodies curving gently towards each other to form a horseshoe, or armchair shape. At the same time, the site should be protected from the north winds by a range of hills, symbolically known as "the black turtle." In the south, the presence of "the vermillion phoenix" considerably enhances the site, and if there is also a view of meandering or slow-moving water, and if the vegetation in the area is green and luscious, then you have found the classic Feng Shui site. Placing your dwelling place here ensures an abundance of wealth, comfort, and good fortune.

By contrast, certain types of terrain can never be auspicious. Feng Shui masters advise that land that is completely flat cannot house dragons, nor can places where the air is stale, where plants cannot flourish, where the winds are harsh and threatening, or where hills are sharp and pointed.

This beautiful setting in the Austrian Alps reflects the natural balance of Yin – the flat water – and Yang – the towering mountains.

PREHISTORIC SITES

The symbolism of the dragon and tiger, turtle and phoenix can also be interpreted in man-made structures. A prehistoric mound, for example, can be interpreted as an exquisite turtle-shaped hill. If your home is protected at the back by such a hill, then you will always have support. But if you confront the hill, by having your main door opening onto it, you risk continuous bad luck.

Silbury Hill, a turtle-shaped prehistoric mound in Wiltshire, England.

THE SYMBOLS OF LANDSCAPE FENG SHUI

For practical purposes, the would-be Feng Shui practitioner must understand that all references to celestial animals are purely symbolic. Dragons and tigers are, in reality, hills and mountains, or contours in the undulating landscape, as are the turtle and the phoenix. In the modern context, practicing masters say that neighboring buildings and houses can also represent dragons and tigers. It is, however, essential to note that the dragon "hills" must always be slightly higher than the tiger "hills," and that the dragon must always be to the left of you (or in the east), while the tiger must be on your right (or in the west).

The landscape must also exhibit the dragon's cosmic breath, the Chi that plays such a central and pivotal role in the practice of Feng Shui. These are energy flows – invisible yet powerfully potent. Auspicious Chi is usually referred to as Sheng Chi ("benign breath"). Feng Shui is all about capturing this Chi and, wherever possible, harnessing it for the benefit of your dwelling or place of work.

Such places are not easy to find, and the Feng Shui practitioner must use a little imagination in the search. If you cannot find the perfect green dragon/white tiger configuration, gently undulating land can also be auspicious. But pay very special attention to the relative heights and distances of surrounding mountains (or buildings). You do not want to be hemmed in by soaring mountainsides (or tall buildings), nor do you want to be forced to site your front door facing a sharply inclined slope. Look for homes built on land positioned to make the most of pleasant views. If possible, the view should be of meandering waterways or the distant sea. It is most important that the view from your home should not be blocked.

Royal Crescent in Bath, England.
Houses with front doors that overlook a park enjoy good Feng Shui because Chi has a chance to accumulate in the open space before entering the home. The houses here are all approximately the same size and shape, encouraging Chi to flow smoothly among them.

The ideal landscape location – with hills exhibiting dragon-, tiger-, turtle-, and phoenix-shaped contours.

THE BRIGHT HALL

One of the most important features of auspicious landscape Feng Shui is to have a "bright hall" or empty, unencumbered land in front of the main door – like a park or football field, or just empty land. If the grass is green and verdant, the result will be auspicious luck for the residents of dwellings facing it.

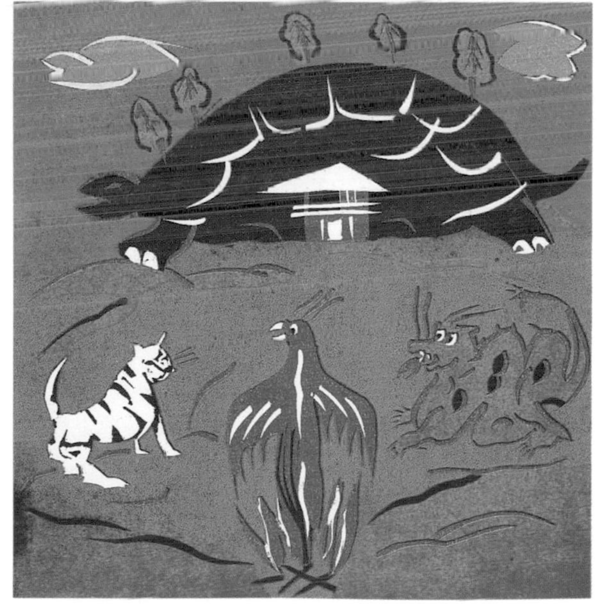

The four celestial animals should all be positioned correctly, relative to each other, in the ideal landscape.

GOOD FENG SHUI LOCATIONS

Not all of us are in the enviable position of successful businessmen and film stars – able to afford to pick and choose the location of their homes anywhere in the world. Even so, we can try to select a home that is well-sited, from a Feng Shui point of view, and avoid those properties built in bad locations.

When studying Feng Shui principles, it also quickly becomes apparent that ancient Chinese wisdom makes sound common sense in modern property terms. Looking for a house with a good view, sheltered from winds, and not overshadowed by neighboring buildings, nor sited alongside major highways may be good Feng Shui practice, but it also makes very sound sense in anyone's terms. As estate agents never tire of telling us, only three things matter when buying property (whether residential or commercial), and they are location, location, and location.

Houses protected by clumps of trees or gently undulating hills also receive support during troublesome times.

So, let us assume you are in the market to buy some land on which to build a house, or that you are looking for a new home and are considering the respective merits of the developments on offer. What characteristics would you look for from the Feng Shui point of view?

AUSPICIOUS WATER

First, look for gently sloping land that faces water. The presence of slow-moving rivers or gentle streams is always indicative of good Feng Shui. The best locations are those that seem to be embraced by water *(see page 120)*. Symbolically, the auspicious Chi wraps around the house situated there, bringing good fortune to its residents.

If your house is situated near a river, or even a little stream, it has exciting Feng Shui potential, but you must check that the water will always be kept clean and unpolluted, and that the waterway is not likely to get choked up or blocked by garbage. Stagnant, polluted water creates pernicious breath, which brings illness and bad luck.

PROTECTION FROM HILLS

Where you can, try to locate a piece of land that allows the back of your house to be protected by a range of hills, another building, a clump of trees, or some form of gently elevated land. This represents the black turtle hills, which support you and your family through difficult times. In simple terms, it protects your back.

If natural protection is not available, you must gauge whether you can create such protection artificially by, for instance, planting a row of trees. For this reason, you should avoid buying property sited on a ridge with a drop at the rear of the house. This exposes you to danger. Nearby buildings can also symbolize protection, provided that they are not so large in comparison with your house that they overwhelm you. Pervading all Feng Shui practice is the notion of balance. Select the kind of property that merges naturally with the surrounding landscape and with neighboring houses.

SIGNS OF BALANCE IN VEGETATION

When checking out a neighborhood, observe how the plants and trees grow on neighboring pieces of land or in the immediate vicinity of your property. If the grass on your land is especially green and lush, it is a place of good Feng Shui. Vegetation is considered to thrive where Sheng Chi accumulates because of the good Yin/Yang balance, represented by sunlight and shade, wind and moisture. In a word, fertile land is good Feng Shui; dry, arid, rocky land is not.

This chair incorporates the auspicious horseshoe shape that is so synonymous with the ideal living location.

It is best to avoid locating a house near a road that has been cut into a hillside, particularly if red earth has been exposed, indicating an injured dragon.

You should also observe how the various elements of nature – rocks, boulders, soil types, water, and the quality and type of vegetation – co-exist with one another. When they are in balance, no single element overwhelms the others. Instead, they complement each other and enhance the area's aesthetics. Balance at all times is the key to finding places with good Feng Shui.

EXPOSURE TO THE ELEMENTS

Finally, it is vital that you avoid places that are completely exposed to the elements – particularly to the wind, water, rain, and storms. Land on top of hills, on the edges of cliffs, or too near the sea, for instance, can be inauspicious.

LOOKING FOR GOOD LOCATIONS – TIME AND WEATHER

In the search for good Feng Shui locations, most Feng Shui masters are extremely particular about the time of day when they conduct their site investigations. They believe that certain times of day are more auspicious than others for viewing and analyzing land or homes.

Feng Shui masters do, however, differ in their opinions on the matter. The general consensus seems to be that the early hours of the morning, just after sunrise, are good for site investigation, and that it is best not to view land in the evening, when the sun is on the wane. This, they say, is because it is important to see how the rising sun affects, or shines on, your site in order for you to assess the mix and balance of Yin and Yang.

The sun and sunlight are Yang, while shade and darkness are Yin. As the sun rises, you can gage the impact of Yang on the land as it replaces the Yin that prevailed through the night. If the balance is good, you will get a good feeling about the land. If it is unbalanced, the feelings generated will be discordant, and hence inauspicious.

In countries where seasonal weather changes are very marked, Feng Shui consultants advise that site analyses should be conducted at or around noon in winter and at daybreak in the summer.

Several ancient texts also place great emphasis on the weather conditions prevailing on the day you go out to view a piece of land. Rain is regarded as auspicious, and if it starts to rain even as you view the land, this is a sign that the land has good Feng Shui. If the rain develops into a major downpour or a storm, however, the day has become unbalanced. It is not a good sign.

It is important to stress that this particular piece of advice is based as much on superstition and cultural folklore as on the authority of the classical masters. The Chinese have always believed that

A dry landscape with harsh winds, like that of the Grand Canyon, does not house dragons and can, therefore, never be auspicious.

In contrast, this hilly, verdant landscape is the perfect home for the dragon and will be full of promising and supportive energy.

Deciding the time of day at which to conduct the site investigation is a very important part of Feng Shui. A potentially stormy day (left) is inauspicious, while the bright sunlight (below) indicates that the day is too far advanced to judge the Yin/Yang balance.

light rain is an auspicious sign for almost anything – they believe it signifies a happy sky dragon and symbolizes plenty, money, and wealth. No doubt such beliefs have their origin in the seasonal cycle: light rain is important for irrigating the fields and also for ensuring a good harvest.

THE INFLUENCE OF WIND PATTERNS

It is important to think about the direction and strength of the winds to which your plot will be exposed, because light breezes are auspicious, but strong winds buffeting your house will scatter benign Chi and prevent it from settling. Sites that are protected from the prevailing wind are excellent, as are sites that face the direction of warm breezes, with their backs protected from the cold.

In Hong Kong and in China, it was always standard practice to plant a sheltering belt of trees to the north of a house or village to provide protection from the coldest winds. This example can always be followed by builders planning new developments. Again, it makes sense to shelter the home, and ensure a more pleasant environment.

In modern city contexts, the strictures about wind are even more important, because apartments in high buildings are vulnerable to air turbulence – you do not want to buy an apartment that has a balcony so windy that you cannot safely sit out on it or leave your plants out on it. At ground level, too, gaps between very tall buildings have the effect of concentrating and accelerating the wind, creating a wind tunnel effect.

HILLS AND THE ELEMENTS

If you are fortunate enough to have a choice of land, it is advisable to avoid certain types of locations. Hilltops are inauspicious locations because water, and Chi, flows away from the property, so that good fortune cannot accumulate. There is also little protection from enemies if the land is totally exposed. If, however, there is higher ground within view and you can locate your home with its back to the higher ground, then the Feng Shui will be considerably improved.

There is a further dimension to landscape Feng Shui that involves the association between different elements and different hill shapes. Thus, hills with sharp and pointed peaks represent the element fire. Hills with gently rounded tops represent metal or gold. Wood is represented by hills that rise steeply, or that have steep, cliff-like sides. If the top resembles a plateau, the element represented is earth. Finally, if the plateau has an irregular surface, it represents the element water.

Very often even expert Feng Shui practitioners may disagree about the precise shape of a hill and the element represented. Experience is usually required to identify hill shapes. Even so, there are other clues that might help. Soggy ground indicates the prevalence of the water element, while barren rocks and boulders that are not cemented together with clay denote fire, and an abundance of trees denotes the element wood.

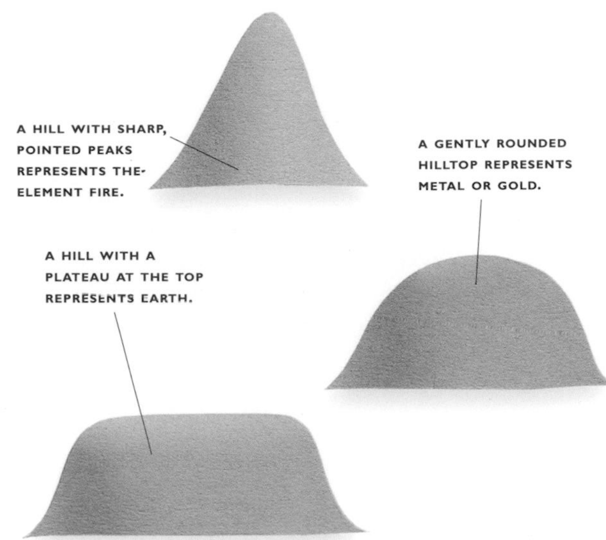

To practice landscape Feng Shui, it is necessary to interpret the meaning of hill shapes, for they can influence the surrounding land. For example, hills representing fire and water will upset the harmony of the land, as water destroys fire.

The next step is to consider whether the elements you have identified are in harmonious relationship with each other *(see pages 70–71 on the productive and destructive elemental cycles),* and, just as importantly, whether they are in harmonious relationship with your own element. *(Everyone's year of birth is ruled by one of the five elements: you can check your own element in the table on pages 214–215.)* It is highly detrimental, for instance, if hills or boulders representing both fire and wood are in close proximity to homes, as this renders the residents prone to quarreling. On the other hand, where the element combinations are beneficial, good luck prevails.

A swimming pool on the top of a hill or apartment is inauspicious – the water above spells danger.

MAN-MADE ADJUSTMENTS TO THE LANDSCAPE

When the natural contours of the landscape are lacking, or where there is an insufficient balance of the forces or elements, bringing disharmony to a location, Feng Shui advocates that thoughtful altering of the landscape is advisable. The effect of straight rivers, and hills that threaten life and prosperity, for example, can and should be modified by growing clumps of trees that provide protection and shelter.

Man-made adjustments to the landscape are not, however, always auspicious. When assessing a site, one must also look for, and be conscious of, the presence of existing or potential development that may be made to the landscape, thereby affecting the Feng Shui of the area. Tunneling through hills and mountains to construct straight roads cannot be good, as such roads bring Shar Chi and poison arrows. Roads and construction work can upset the balance of Yin and Yang and the currents of wind and water. Worse still, they can injure the dragon.

When the Emperor Shih Huang Ti ordered the building of the Great Wall of China, the Feng Shui of the country was believed to have been affected drastically – and, indeed, millions of China's men died at the wall. Since then, of course, the wall has come to symbolize a structure of great sorrow for the Chinese, and there are any number of heart-rending legends associated with its history.

ABOVE *The Great Wall of China, originally built as a defensive measure, has ultimately brought tragedy.*

BELOW *Many man made interventions in the landscape serve to carve up potentially auspicious locations.*

ROCK FORMATIONS

The practice of Feng Shui has always reflected the influence of symbols, and the spectrum of auspicious and inauspicious symbols is so broad as to leave room for the imagination to run riot. Hong Kong Feng Shui masters are especially imaginative in their interpretations of rock, boulder, or hill formations.

Buildings on top of Huangshan Mountain, China. Living at the top of an exposed mountain can be very hazardous because the Chi is quickly dispersed and drained away.

If there is a prominent rock formation, boulder, or hill near the land you are assessing, you are advised to gage its shape and possible impact. Try to imagine yourself confronting it each day as you go in and out of your home. If it feels threatening in some way, perhaps it is better to avoid the land. On the other hand, if it makes you feel good each time you look at it, the energy that flows from it may very well be positive.

Wonderful stories abound in Feng Shui folklore of whole villages in China benefiting from a benevolent phoenix-, or turtle-shaped rock which was seen to be watching benignly over their fortunes. Yet other stories relate how several seasons' worth of wheat harvests were destroyed year after year until a small hillock overlooking the village, which appeared to represent a greedy rat, was finally flattened.

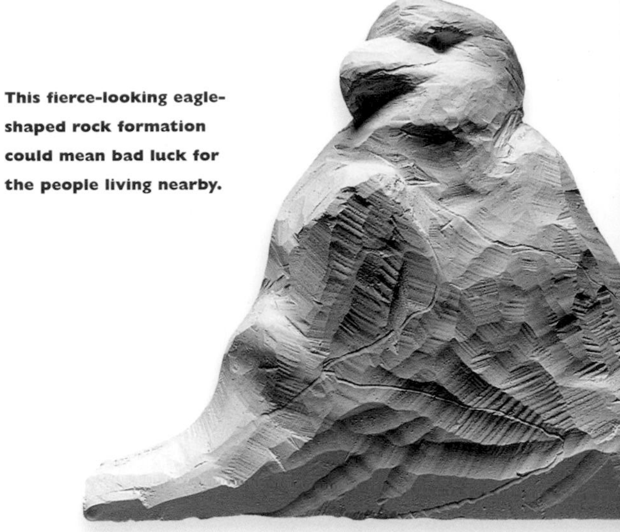

This fierce-looking eagle-shaped rock formation could mean bad luck for the people living nearby.

Look for hill formations or sloping ledges that remind you of some good fortune symbol (such as the head of a snake or a dragon, especially if either seems to be coughing out a pearl). If your property has a view of such a symbol, living there will make you very rich. Three small peaks within view promise great academic honors for your children,

while hills and boulders that represent malevolent or fierce animals (tigers, rats, or eagles) could bring ill-fortune in the form of bad health or poverty.

Avoid locations that lie anywhere below a hill topped by a large boulder or rock outcrop. Such a boulder could crush the fortunes of people living in the vicinity, resulting in grave misfortune and poverty. This is one of the most potent recommendations of Feng Shui masters, because the presence of inauspicious rock formations can negate good Feng Shui, even that of classic dragon and tiger sites. Good Feng Shui features cannot overcome the pernicious effect of such bad landscape structures, unless some way can be found to diffuse, deflect, or destroy the threatening structure.

This pleasant English landscape offers good Feng Shui. The undulating countryside is not monotonously flat or too threateningly steep; the clumps of trees provide a balance of sunlight and shade.

THE MID-LEVELS LANDSLIP

An outcrop of rock resembled a malevolent frog waiting to swallow up the surroundings.

In Hong Kong during the severe rains of 1974, a large condominium complex on Po Shan Road, situated in the island's luxury Mid-Levels district, collapsed in the middle of the night, sliding down the hillside and killing over 300 people. Feng Shui masters had repeatedly warned residents of the imminent danger caused by an outcrop of rock located just above the apartment block, whose shape resembled that of a malevolent frog with its mouth wide open, as if waiting to swallow up all those below it. Those who heeded the Feng Shui masters' warning moved out and escaped the terrible fate of the residents who stayed on. Since that time, no new tower blocks have been constructed in the vicinity of the frog.

FENG SHUI AND WATER

Water almost always symbolizes wealth and prosperity. This is because water is believed to be an excellent purveyor of Chi, especially if it is a meandering, clean, and slow-flowing river. These characteristics allow the Chi to settle, thereby bringing good luck. Straight rivers and fast-moving waterways are not considered to be auspicious, because the Chi is rapidly washed away even as it is created.

The presence of water can also be artificially created, and this can be just as effective for Feng Shui. The size of a pool of lake that is created for such purposes should reflect balance and harmony. The nearer the water is to the land or dwelling place, the smaller it should be, so as not to overwhelm the house with Chi that is too strong. The farther away it is, the larger the body of water can be.

Land that nestles against hillsides, with a distant view of the sea, is preferable to land that is close to the sea. The same reasoning can be applied to lakes and pools, particularly if they are very large in size. Remember that too much of anything is unbalancing. Too much water can drown you.

Dirty water creates Shar Chi, or poisonous breath, which brings unlucky vibrations, especially ill-health. It is worse if the water is foul, smelling of decaying materials, or is muddy and polluted. Genuinely healthy Feng Shui can can only be created in the presence of clean water that is allowed to flow freely.

Buildings, like this cottage in Scotland, with a view of peaceful water in front and protective hills behind, have excellent Feng Shui.

WATER DRAGON CLASSIC

It is useful to consider the advice given in the famous book known as the *Water Dragon Classic* when assessing the relative merits of waterways. According to this work: "If water flows rapidly away from a site, it drains off – how can wealth and abundance accumulate? If it comes in straight, and it goes off straight, surely it will injure man? Darting left, the eldest son meets with misfortune, and darting right, the youngest meets with calamity."

When watercourses meet or meander, the productive and destructive cycles of the elements also come into play. Thus, although water is, as a general rule, extremely auspicious, the way the watercourses meet is equally vital and important. Sometimes, certain configurations, instead of bringing good luck, could very well bring misfortune, as when a fire-shaped water or a wood-shaped water meet with a metal-shaped water. This is because fire destroys metal and metal destroys wood. Watercourses representing metal meander in wide, gentle curves, while those representing fire zig-zag across the river bed. Earth-shaped water changes course abruptly. (In urban Feng Shui, roads can be substituted for watercourses.)

In the *Water Dragon Classic*, an ideal location is one that nestles among watercourses, so it is protected in the belly of the dragon. Chi flows through watercourses, and the branches that immediately surround a site and protect it are known as the inner Chi, whereas the main trunk of the river that surrounds the site at the outermost point carries the outer Chi. Outer Chi has the ability to nourish the inner Chi, which in turn then penetrates the household. The sketches reproduced on this page show auspicious sites for houses in relation to various types of watercourses, taking into account the shape of the watercourse, how it branches, and how it joins the flow of other rivers.

In the sites illustrated here, the dot represents a dwelling in a favorable location, from which the inhabitants stand to gain prosperity, wealth, and fame.

The shapes made by rivers and streams as they meander, branch, and meet are also of significance in Feng Shui terms. Different shapes are associated with different elements, and it is important to ensure that the element relationships are harmonious and blend with your personal year element to produce good Chi.

A house embraced by the protective, auspicious arms of a slow-flowing stream is in one of the best Feng Shui positions.

MAN-MADE STRUCTURES

In modern Feng Shui practice, buildings and roads can stand in for the hills, mountains, and roads of the ancient masters. There are, however, many pitfalls to avoid, and man-made structures need to be analyzed with care, for many represent more of a threat than a benefit.

Do not, for example, buy property that is hemmed in by tall buildings, or land that faces or is close to huge man-made structures such as electricity pylons, transmission towers, power stations, or water tanks. Also avoid land facing straight roads (especially at the end of a cul-de-sac), railroad tracks, and T-junctions. These bring poison Chi, which is difficult to correct, as do buildings with crosses or steeples. In Feng Shui, anything straight that is pointed at the land or home should be avoided.

Likewise, Feng Shui masters do not like land that is situated too close to churches and graveyards, cemeteries, crematoriums, and hospitals. These places, the abodes of the dead, emanate strong Yin vibrations that overwhelm the breath of life. Dragons are also seldom found residing near such buildings.

Just as hills that symbolize malevolent animals are to be avoided, so one should steer clear of man-made buildings that resemble threatening objects or inauspicious characters. Flyovers that look like knives and scythes cutting into your property or plot of land are also inauspicious. Be wary of such structures and buildings, and scrupulously avoid buying a piece of land that is near or adjacent to them, or worse, facing directly onto them.

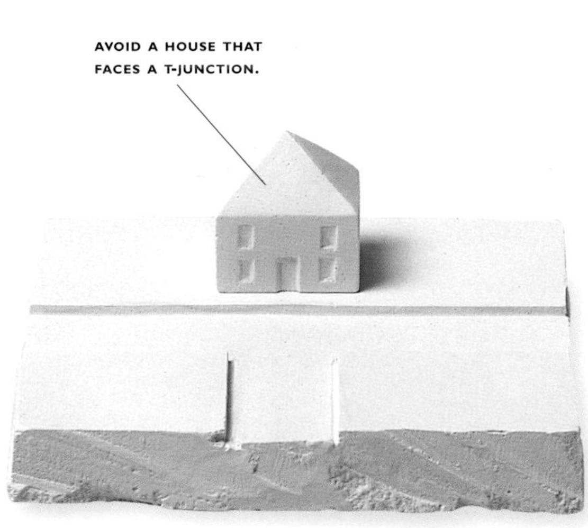

A house placed directly opposite a T-junction suffers from having a poison arrow aimed at it.

Tall buildings and similar man-made structures should not be built close to smaller-scale houses.

THE ADVERSE EFFECT OF FLYOVERS

One of the most damaging of man-made structures from a Feng Shui point of view is perhaps the road flyover. If you find that one is built in front of your home or apartment, or that one is planned, and that it would seem to be positioned so that it cuts into the building, you would be strongly advised to try to move out as soon as possible, since the "killing breath" caused by flyovers is extremely difficult to counteract.

In the mid 1980s in Hong Kong, one very influential and wealthy man was given just such a warning, which he did not act upon – a decision that was to cause him a great deal of grief. When a new flyover was built next to his luxury home, his Feng Shui master strongly advised him to move out quickly, and at any rate to move out before the New Year. Because of his busy schedule, he was unable to find time to make the necessary arrangements and eventually forgot to do so.

Later that same year he made a number of business decisions that were to have a drastic effect on the fortunes of the Hong Kong stock exchange at a time when the stock markets of the world were in a state of collapse. They were also to have grave consequences for his own career.

Early in the following year, he was arrested and charged with corruption, an arrest that shook the establishment of Hong Kong to its core. It was to take a long time and a great deal of financial outlay in expensive legal fees for him to sort out his problems. Had he heeded the advice of his Feng Shui man, his fortunes could well have been different.

Poison Chi is present if a house is facing a tall cross or if the shadow from the cross falls on to the house.

Yang dwellings (of the living) should not be overwhelmed with brutal, alien architecture.

CHOOSING HOUSE PLOTS

If you are planning to buy a house on a new development, it is advisable to investigate first whether the land being offered for sale is reclaimed or filled land, since the earth Chi in such land is often unstable, and hence not very auspicious.

When selecting small plots of land within estates or developments, it is advisable to ensure that all the plots offered for sale are about the same size, so that the houses eventually built will contribute to a regular and balanced development, without danger of the dimensions of any house creating intimidating Chi for the rest of its neighbors. Balance will encourage Chi to flow smoothly from one house to the next. You should also check the design and position of the rooflines of the houses to be built on neighboring plots to ensure that you will not be hurt by pointed roof lines ("poison arrows").

Check the proposed internal road systems within the housing estate to ensure that the plot you are looking at is not inadvertently facing a straight road. Feng Shui masters usually advise against purchasing land located in a dead end, especially if the property itself stands at the very end of the road. Not only does such land theoretically face a poison arrow directed straight at it, it also symbolically represents being placed in a tight corner. For people in business, especially, living in a cul-de-sac suggests that solutions or escape routes will be hard to find if they find themselves confronted with difficulties.

Finally, check the timing of the construction of phases of the development project so that freshly-cut, exposed land does not adversely affect you. Where the terrain has been cut or badly scarred by development, and soil is exposed (especially soil that is red in color), superstitious practitioners believe that the exposed earth symbolizes the blood of an injured dragon, which is bad Feng Shui.

Until the situation is remedied by replanting or the regrowth of vegetation, it is advisable to avoid living in or near such locations. It is best to avoid buying property too close to land that is still being developed, especially if the hills being cut are just above your land. Injured dragons hovering above you will create bad Feng Shui.

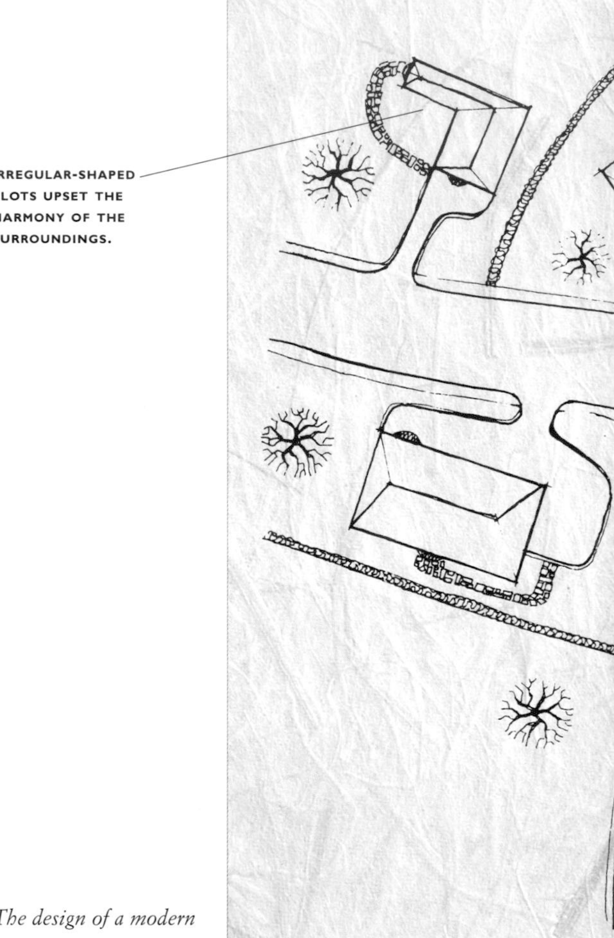

The design of a modern housing estate can result in energy forces interacting with each other to create bad Feng Shui.

Trees are a sign that there is plenty of healthy Chi in the earth, and they bring good luck to the land. They can also be used to block the flow of harmful Chi.

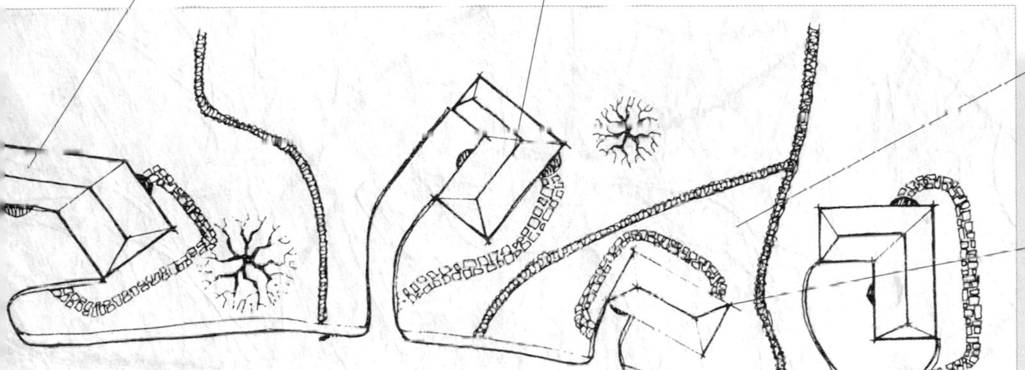

HOUSE FACES A ROAD BRINGING SHAR CHI DIRECTLY TO THE FRONT DOOR.

L-OR U-SHAPED HOUSES HAVE "MISSING CORNERS" AND ARE INAUSPICIOUS.

A TRIANGULAR PLOT IS VERY INAUSPICIOUS.

POISON ARROWS FROM ROOFLINE ARE DIRECTED AT A NEIGHBORING HOUSE.

ROOF LINES DO NOT CREATE POISON ARROWS FOR THEIR NEIGHBORS.

PLOTS OF LAND ARE REGULAR IN SHAPE AND THE OVERALL DESIGN IS BALANCED.

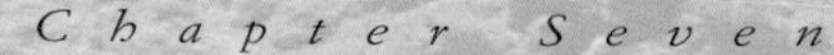

Chapter Seven

FENG SHUI AND YOUR HOME

Auspicious Feng Shui in the home is vital to the tapping of earth luck. It does not matter if the home is a palace or a small rented room. Your place of abode, the place where you sleep and seek shelter, where you eat your meals, and where you bring up your family, represents the most important place for trying to ensure the best possible Feng Shui.

Once your home is comfortable and balanced, the harmonious flows of Chi will be of great benefit to you and your family, and problems and obstacles will be more easily overcome. Work at the office will also be less stressful, and during good times (when your heaven luck is particularly favorable), you will enjoy good fortune.

THE LAST CHAPTER concluded with guidelines on the choice of site for your home considered in the broadest terms – in particular, whether the site was well situated within the overall landscape. Having satisfied yourself on this score, it is then necessary to work down to the next level of detail and look at the merits of individual housing plots, and the siting of the dwelling within that plot.

Regularly-shaped land is always preferable to irregularly-shaped land, and the best shapes are squares and rectangles. Shapes to avoid are triangles, L, T, or U shapes, and any plot where the sides are not parallel or are of different dimensions. Irregularly-shaped land often implies that a corner is missing, and this has serious implications in Pa Kua analysis, where every corner represents a favorable or auspicious life situation. The eight-sided Pa Kua and the Lo Shu magic square, two vastly important tools of Feng Shui practice, always work best – and are less ambiguous in their implications – when they are applied to regularly-shaped plots of land.

Whether your home is a grand palace (below) or a humble cottage (right), you and your family can benefit from the application of Feng Shui guidelines.

BALANCE AND HARMONIOUS DESIGN

When designing your house, give adequate consideration to the notion of balance. Good Feng Shui is all about creating and maintaining balance between the various elements of the environment. This means keeping an eye on the dimensions of the house itself relative to the surrounding environment – the size of doors and windows, the size of rooms, and the number of doors and windows. It also means keeping a balance of sunny and shady areas, of greenery and concrete, of colors, and of Yin and Yang.

PROPORTION

Balance creates harmony, which in turn creates good Sheng Chi for the house. If your house is so large as to overwhelm the neighborhood, and worse still, overpower your land, make sure you have compensating features designed into the house plan. The use of outdoor lights has the effect of "extending" the yard, while dark color schemes can be used to balance out the Yang force of a house that is too big for its site.

Ideally, your house or plot should be similar in size to those of your neighbors, thus ensuring an even and continuous flow of benign Chi from one to the other. Plots with generous amounts of land around the house are excellent, and conducive to the free circulation of benign Chi, whereas the opposite – mean and cramped dwellings – will stifle the flow of Chi.

Balance should also be reflected in the ratio of the windows to the doors (three to one), and in the size and height of rooms. Large, airy rooms are better than small rooms, but they should not be so large, nor so high, as to overwhelm the balance.

COLOR

If possible, let the elements – represented by the color schemes of walls, roof tiles, and floors – be

SITING THE HOUSE WITHIN THE PLOT

Site the house in the center of the plot, so that neither the front nor the back yard is disproportionately large or small. Placing the house too far to the front or too far to the back creates a state of imbalance.

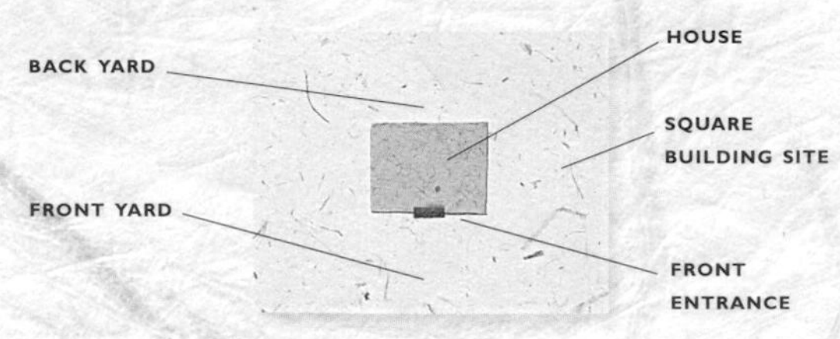

A house should be positioned in the center of the building plot; however, the back yard can be slightly larger than the front to offer protection to your home.

If the land on which a house is to be built is irregularly shaped, you can "cure" the problem using garden lights to brighten "missing corners" thereby "regularizing" the overall shape. Trees may also be planted to camouflage irregularities. A common problem with small land plots in housing developments is that the house is too big for the scale of the site, leaving insufficient room for a yard. In such cases, enhance the corners of the land with lights.

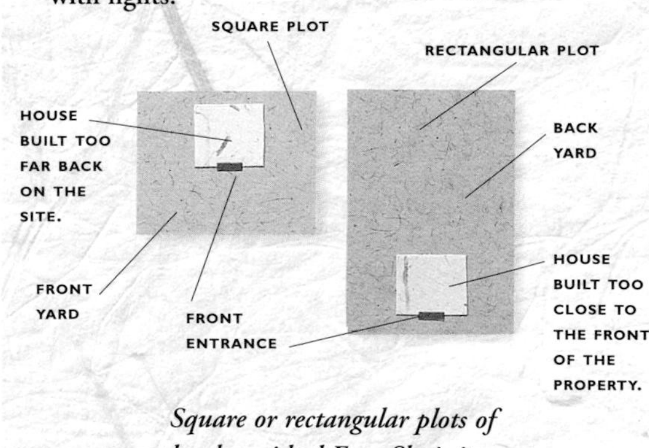

Square or rectangular plots of land are ideal Feng Shui sites.

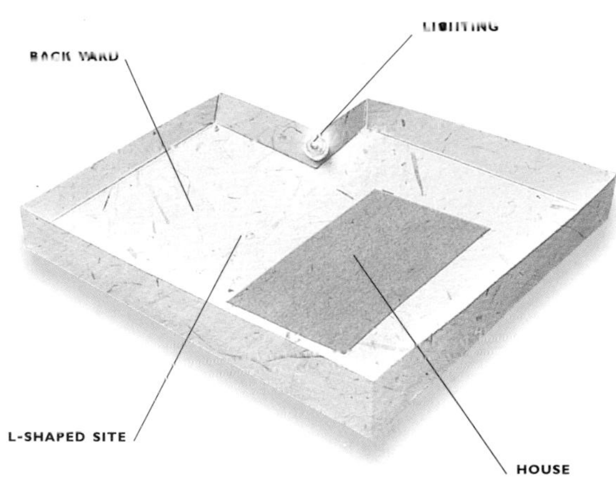

The weak corner of an L-shaped plot could bring illness or an increase in accidents to the occupants of the house. This potentially harmful feature of your property can be overcome by installing garden lights.

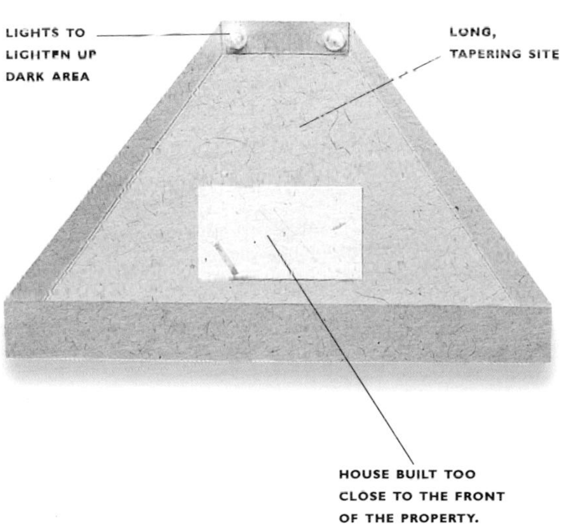

This long, tapering plot of land could create problems for the residents unless efforts are made to brighten up the narrow, inauspicious area at the foot of the garden.

harmonious by checking the element relationships and their productive/destructive cycles. The rooms used by the sons of the ruling classes in ancient China were almost always placed in the eastern sector of the house. This sector represents growth, according to the Pa Kua, and is also represented by the element wood. In order to enhance the Feng Shui of this sector, green tiles were used on the roof, representing wood.

In Feng Shui terms, balance is also maintained by the use of symmetry in preference to asymmetry.

BAD WINDS

If you are in doubt about which way to position your house, look for land that allows you to face south. Many Feng Shui masters advocate this, based on the widely-held belief that the south is the source of warmth and wealth. The south is regarded as auspicious because it holds out the promise of warm summer sunshine and good harvests, while the north is considered the source of ill winds. Some Feng Shui practitioners maintain that the worst direction is northeast, because, they say, this is the way to the gateway of hell, so that main doors facing this direction will receive the pernicious breath of hell!

The best example given to support this view was the repositioning of the entrance doors of the Hyatt Hotel in Singapore. Business was very poor until the positioning of the doors was changed. The hotel's business immediately improved, and it has been doing a roaring trade ever since. The exact rationale for the repositioning of its front doors has never been revealed, and this in itself is not unusual – business leaders who consult Feng Shui practitioners regard the results as commercially secret in case their competitors do the same. I am not entirely convinced, however, about the northeast being the "gateway to hell."

HOUSE SHAPES

In general, square or rectangular homes are much more conducive to good Feng Shui than those that have protruding extensions, or which are L-shaped, U-shaped, or wedge-shaped. Regular-shaped houses are deemed to be balanced and complete, and lend themselves more easily to Feng Shui enhancement.

Avoid houses with too many corners. The angles created give off unfortunate Shar Chi and are not conducive to the attraction of good Chi flows. In the same way, L-shaped houses are to be avoided because this shape resembles a meat cleaver and this is highly inauspicious, suggesting the severance of vital connections and injury to the occupants. L shapes also suggest missing corners, thereby creating imbalance. The residents of a U-shaped house face equally bad fortune, and can expect to be plagued by frequent quarrels, or to be caught up in an unhappy marriage.

An L-shaped house resembles a meat cleaver or knife, and is very inauspicious.

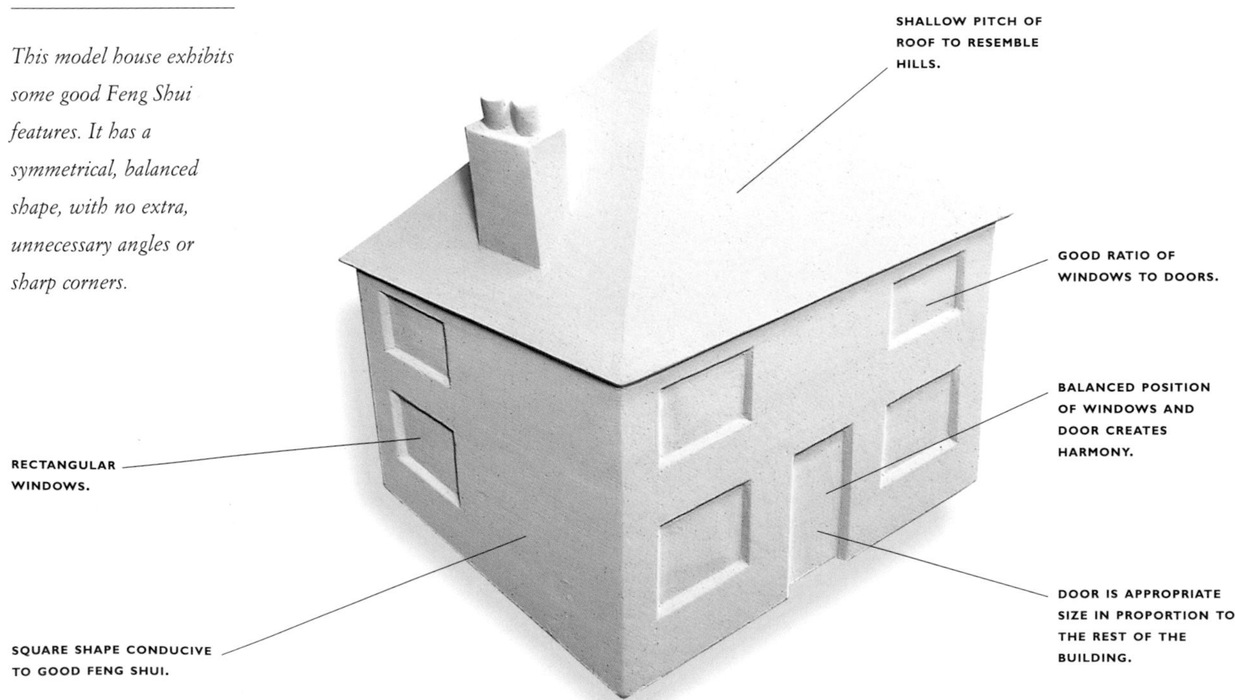

This model house exhibits some good Feng Shui features. It has a symmetrical, balanced shape, with no extra, unnecessary angles or sharp corners.

A U-shaped house is another unlucky configuration; it creates a great deal of unhappiness.

Avoid triangle-shaped houses or houses with too many corners. The angles created give off unfortunate Shar Chi and do not attract good Chi flows.

ROOF LINES

As for the appearance of the house, try to avoid large or numerous angled roof lines that cause harm to neighboring properties. The poison arrow effect of such ridges could harm you if your neighbors adopted Feng Shui "cures" that bounce the bad luck back.

In symbolic terms, roof lines can be compared to hill shapes and to their elemental associations. Once again, therefore, it is advisable to check the productive and destructive cycles of the elements. Roofs that have a shallow pitch resemble hills which are linked to the earth element and are auspicious. Steeply-pitched roofs represent the fire element, and Feng Shui masters usually advise that buildings with such roof lines are inauspicious. Pyramid-shaped roofs are more complex to assess. To the Chinese Feng Shui master, pyramid shapes are favorable as they are usually balanced with a gentle pitch. However, it should not be forgotten that pyramids are associated with the tombs of the pharoahs and are, therefore, considered to be a house for the dead – a Yin dwelling.

Apartment blocks with flat roofs suggest hills with flat plateaux, and these are not very favorable. The ideal is to have a gentle, sloping roof line, which represents the gentle, undulating mountain shapes that are so popular in Form School Feng Shui.

APARTMENT SHAPES

The same rules apply to apartment shapes as to house shapes. Square or rectangular layouts are preferable. As this is seldom possible, it is advisable to try to do something about correcting an irregular shape. Mirrors can be used to extend missing walls in L-shaped apartments. A bank of lights can be placed along the long wall of an elongated apartment to expand its shape.

DRIVEWAYS

The driveway leading to your house should be friendly and non-threatening. Circular and semicircular driveways are the most conducive to attracting good luck Chi flows, as Chi moves in a circular fashion. If there is insufficient space for a circular drive, try to achieve some kind of curved, or indirect, meandering approach.

If the driveway has to be straight, it can be softened with landscaping plants – bushes or flowering shrubs – that break up and camouflage the sharpness and harshness of the straight lines. Above all, make sure that the driveway does not point directly at the front door of the house. Try, instead, to have your driveway at a right angle to the door. If it is aimed at the door, it becomes a poison arrow, and the effect is even worse if the driveway gets narrower as it approaches the house.

Your driveway should be of even width throughout. Driveways that taper in or out suggest constriction, and this has a limiting effect on your career or on your business and financial

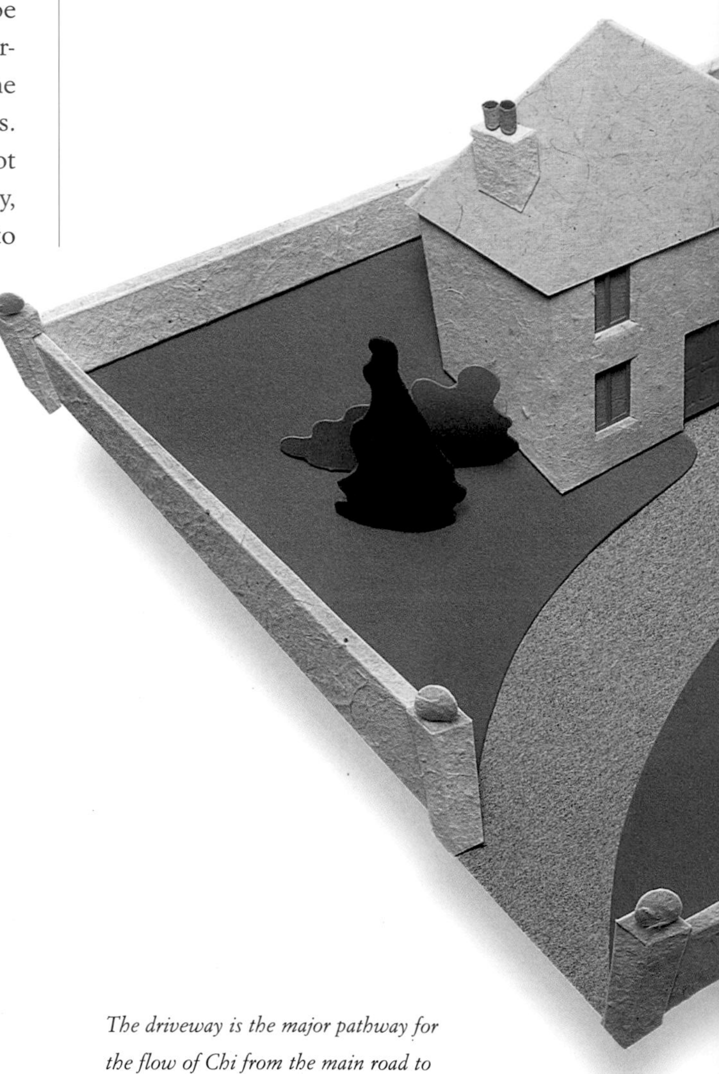

The driveway is the major pathway for the flow of Chi from the main road to your house. If your driveway is too wide, Chi quickly flows away. If it is too narrow, the Chi becomes constricted.

THIS DRIVEWAY FACES DIRECTLY AT THE FRONT DOOR, ACTING AS A POISON ARROW FOR THE FLOW OF NEGATIVE ENERGY.

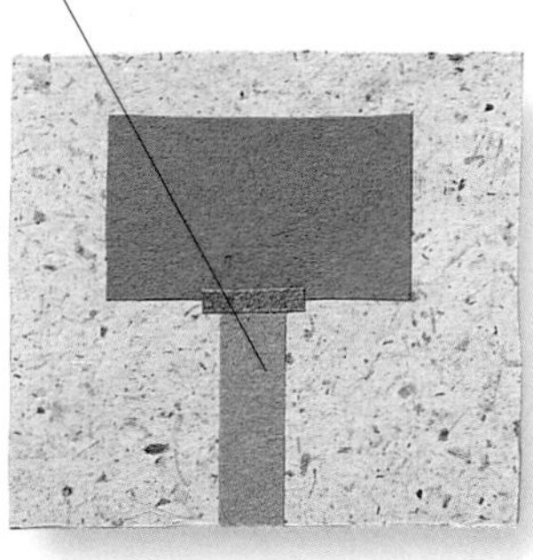

A DRIVEWAY THAT TAPERS IN, AS THIS ONE DOES, MAY HAVE A CONSTRICTING EFFECT ON YOUR BUSINESS AND CAREER OPPORTUNITIES.

opportunities. Lights placed at the narrow ends will help to cure this inauspicious Feng Shui if a tapering driveway is unavoidable. Try to create a design that blends with the dimensions of the house.

Driveways should be broad and level, and never slope downwards, away from the house. Such drives allow Chi to flow out, draining money luck away.

This curved driveway is both aesthetically pleasing and auspicious. It is an example of a very good flow of Chi into the house.

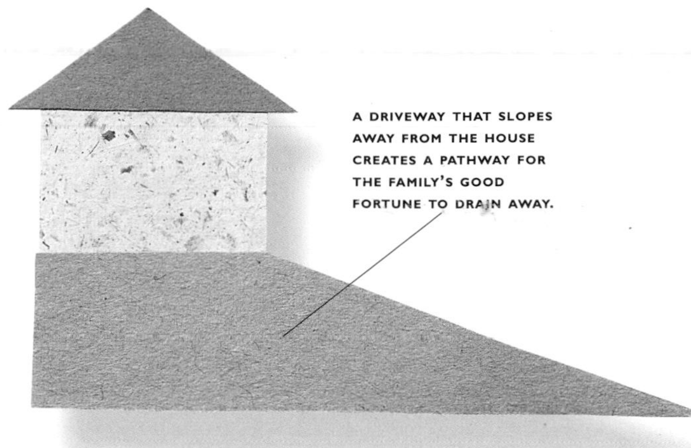

Sloping driveways are inauspicious, whether they are angled up to or down from the house. Flat driveways represent the best Feng Shui.

AVOIDING STRAIGHT ROADS

Feng Shui masters strongly warn against living in a house that faces directly onto a straight road, as can happen if a house is sited at the end of a T-junction. At night, car headlights that resemble fierce tigers aim their ferocity at the house. The effect of this circumstance is deadly. To verify this, just drive into any housing development, and look for houses whose front doors directly face a straight road. You will find that these homes often look sick, that plants there do not flourish and that the house itself looks bad and very unhealthy.

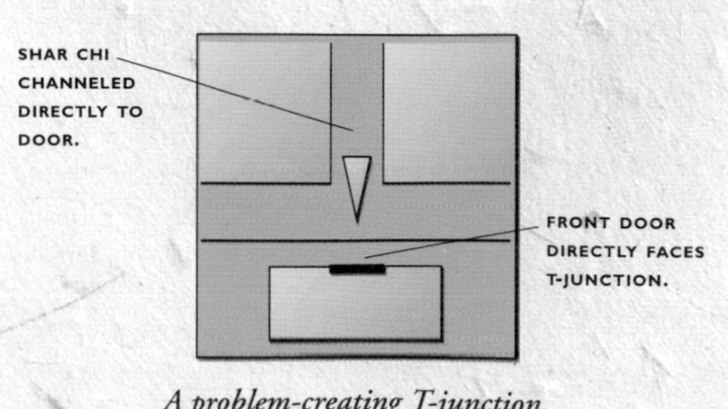

A problem-creating T-junction.

THE POSITION OF DOORS AND WINDOWS

Ideally, all the doors of your home should be aligned to face the direction that is most auspicious for you personally (taken from the inside of the house looking out). There are several methods of determining the best compass directions to follow *(see Chapter Five),* though the East House/ West House formula, based on analysis of the elements, is much favored by Hong Kong masters, and many have also found the Pa-Kua Lo-Shu formula to be extremely potent.

Alternatively, you can follow the recommendations contained in the classic Feng Shui manuscript known as the *Yang Dwelling Classic*, a manual much-favored by Feng Shui masters which lays down guidelines on house and room positions. According to this work, the most important rooms in the house, such as the the master bedroom and the study, as well as the main door to the house, should face south.

Kitchens, it says, should face east, and never southwest. The older members of the family should sleep facing southeast. If the family is in business, then the business premises should also face south, and never northeast or southwest.

BAD VIEWS

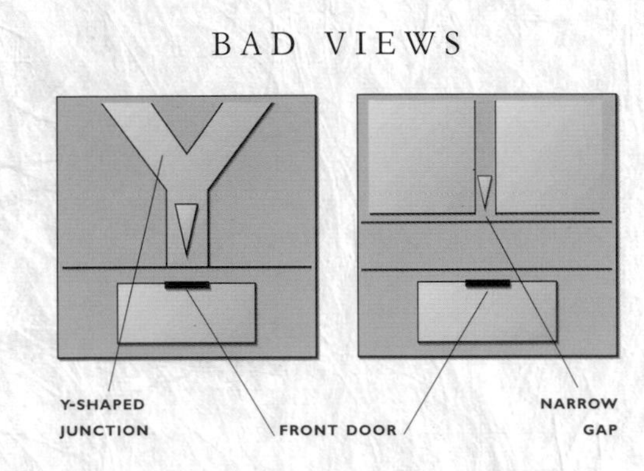

Doors should not face Y-shaped junctions or narrow gaps between buildings.

The Chinese do not like windows that slide up or down, nor do they like windows that look onto poison arrows. Glare from the afternoon sun and car headlights are also considered malign. In such cases, Feng Shui recommends completely blocking out the window with the offending view. The view from your main door should also be directed away from such offending structures and harmful forces.

Small panes of glass ensure that incoming Chi is not overwhelming.

The Chinese do not like windows that move up and down.

Windows that open inward are harmful to careers and money-making opportunities.

Windows that open outward maximize the amount of good Chi that enters the room.

RE-POSITION YOUR FRONT DOOR

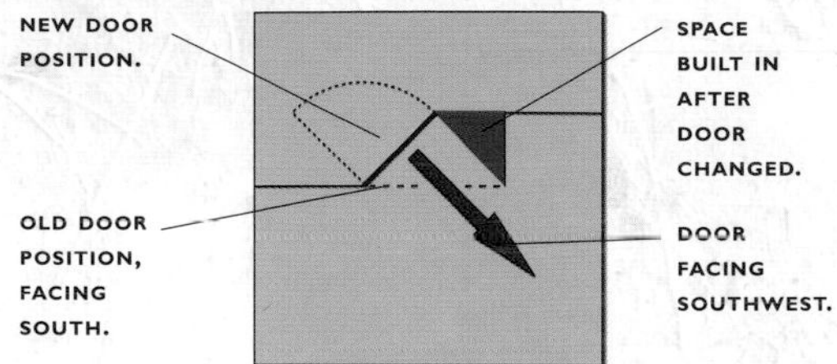

Changing a door direction from south to southwest.

The direction of the main door has a crucial and pivotal role in determining the excellence of your Feng Shui. This is because the main door is considered the point where Chi enters the house. It should, therefore, be positioned to attract good Chi. If there are several people living in the same house, the main door should be positioned according to the birth date of the chief breadwinner in the household.

In addition, main doors should never open onto a solid wall or other obstructions, such as a retaining wall, flyover, a steep hillside, an over-powering building, a huge water tank, or any other massive structure. These all block the flow of good Chi. Position your door so that buildings or steep hillsides protect your side or back, rather than cause you difficulty.

Do not let your main door face a narrow gap between two buildings. This causes the family savings to be squandered away. Small back lanes, situated between two buildings and directly facing your main door, also cause poor health and business loss. Be sure that the main door never directly faces a bend in the road, a bend in a river, or the edge of a flyover. This symbolizes the house being cut by a knife or blade – symptomatic of acute health and financial problems.

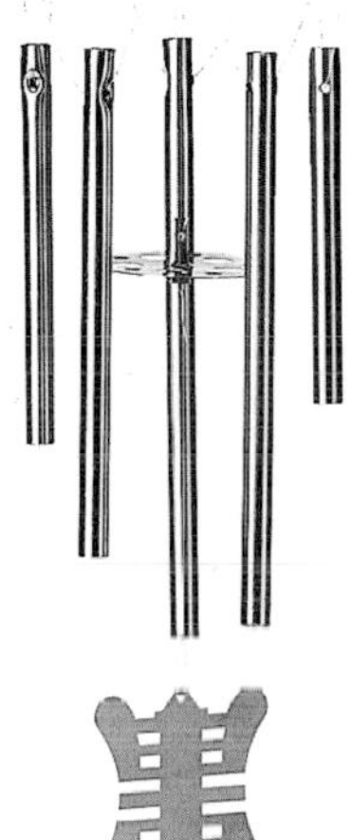

Wind chimes hung above or near a door frighten away unlucky Chi. They should be used in houses with too many windows; otherwise, there will be dissent between parents and children.

The placement and dimensions of windows can also affect the Feng Shui of a house. Windows should ideally be rectangular in shape and it should be possible to open the whole window, preferably outwards. This brings in the good luck Chi and opens up opportunities for the residents of the household. Inward-opening windows are generally considered harmful to careers, and money-making opportunities will be lacking. If there are too many windows in a house, discord is caused between parents and children. In such instances, hanging wind chimes or using crystals will cure the problem.

POISON ARROWS

The main door must be protected against poison arrows, which create bad Shar Chi. This is one of the most crucial aspects of Feng Shui practice. Even if the rest of your house has excellent Feng Shui features, a poison arrow hitting your main door negates everything. This rule takes precedence over compass directions, so that, if there is a sharp angle facing your front door, you must give it a new postition, even if it is your best, most auspicious direction.

The negative effects of secret or hidden poison arrows are so dreadful that Feng Shui masters always look out for these first when asked to investigate a house. Many different features, natural and man-made, can constitute poison arrows. Some are more obvious than others. The practice of Feng Shui involves learning to be alert to these arrows, and developing your powers of observation.

Anything sharp, angled, pointed, or straight, such as telephone poles or a single tall tree, contains secret poison arrows that create Shar Chi.

What are these poison arrows and how do they work? Basically, anything sharp, angled, pointed, or straight, contains poison arrows, and, when directed at your front door, they cause misfortune, ill-health, loss of opportunity, severe business difficulties, quarrels, and loss of money. Poison arrows create Shar Chi, lyrically referred to in the old texts as "pernicious, noxious breath," the antithesis of Sheng Chi, the "benign cosmic breath." Under this

Steep, angled roof lines are dangerous forms of poison arrows, and are especially dangerous when facing your front door. The sharper the angle the more powerful the Shar Chi.

category are angled roof lines, straight roads, railroad lines, tall trees, telegraph poles, street lamps, flagpoles, crosses, towers, the edges of neighboring houses or buildings, a ridge of hills, straight rivers or canals, and drains among many other examples.

A steep, angled roof line facing your front door is the commonest form of poison arrow, and it can bring severe bad luck, causing illness in your children and family members or creating problems with your career and business. Pitched roofs are the most problematical when the angles are very sharp, because the Shar Chi created is more powerful. The best solution is to position your door so that the effects of the bad Chi are deflected away from it.

Trees can be a problem, but only a single tree whose trunk appears threatening falls into this category. If there are several trees in a clump, they do not constitute poison arrows.

POISON ARROWS AND LANDSCAPE FENG SHUI

Straight lines and angles are so dangerous that, even in the ideal green dragon/white tiger configuration, if there are ridges running in straight lines that point at the site of your home, or any man-made constructions that threaten the site in any way, it is considered to be a dangerous location that must be avoided. This is because the poison arrow would wound the dragon, thereby creating massive quantities of poisonous Shar Chi.

If it is not possible to do anything about poison arrows that are already pointed at your home, Feng Shui does offer practical remedies. Bearing in mind that the practice of Feng Shui subscribes to the principle that it is what one sees that makes the difference, all varieties of poison arrow can be screened off by growing trees with thick foliage. This disperses the killing Chi with great efficiency, especially if the leaves of the tree are broad.

Spires and crosses on churches and gravestones create harmful poison arrows. Houses overlooking a graveyard can suffer from damaging Feng Shui forces.

Chapter Eight

FENG SHUI AND INTERIOR DESIGN

Houses must be planned to maximize good Feng Shui for all the members of the household. This chapter will examine specific methods for allocating different corners of the house to different members of the family. We will also look at the various Feng Shui guidelines for positioning rooms with different functions – bedrooms, kitchens, dining rooms, and toilets. We will also see what Feng Shui masters have to say about the design of doors, corridors, corners, beams, split-levels, and staircases, and their relationship to each other.

風水

THE FIRST STEP in Feng Shui house design is to segment the house into nine sectors corresponding to the eight compass directions, leaving one in the center. Each of the sectors corresponds to one of the compass directions – either the primary directions (north, south, east, and west) or one of the secondary directions (northeast, southeast, northwest, and southwest). This is done most easily by using a sketch plan of the house.

With this working diagram, you can proceed to the next step, which is to superimpose the Pa Kua symbol onto the house plan *(see pages 78–79)*. If your house has more than one storey, the same dimensions and corners will apply to all levels. You are now in a position to begin identifying the corners and sectors best suited to each member of your household. You can also identify the characteristics of each sector of your house as well as the most suitable locations for the different function rooms.

The exposed overhead beams and dried flowers in this farmhouse interior are sources of potential misfortune.

HOUSE STYLES

Well-situated main doors should open into wide, bright rooms or lobbies that generate happy and comfortable feelings. Main doors should open inwards and should have a view of as much of the interior of the house as possible.

Nothing should impede the flow of Chi from coming into the house through the main door.

Entry, for instance, into a dark or narrow lobby area stifles the flow of Chi. This can usually be corrected by installing a large mirror on one wall and improving the lighting in the area. The main door should not, however, open into a room that is too large. In these circumstances, a screen can be installed to create a smaller area.

One should also avoid having a main door that opens into a lobby that has a low ceiling, or where there are low, heavy beams. This often causes illness to the residents of the house. Again, installing overhead lights can help alleviate this problem.

This modern interior has lots of dangerous angles, but the negative effects are somewhat softened by the use of lighting and trailing plants.

EXAMPLE OF APARTMENT WITH GOOD LAYOUT FLOOR PLAN

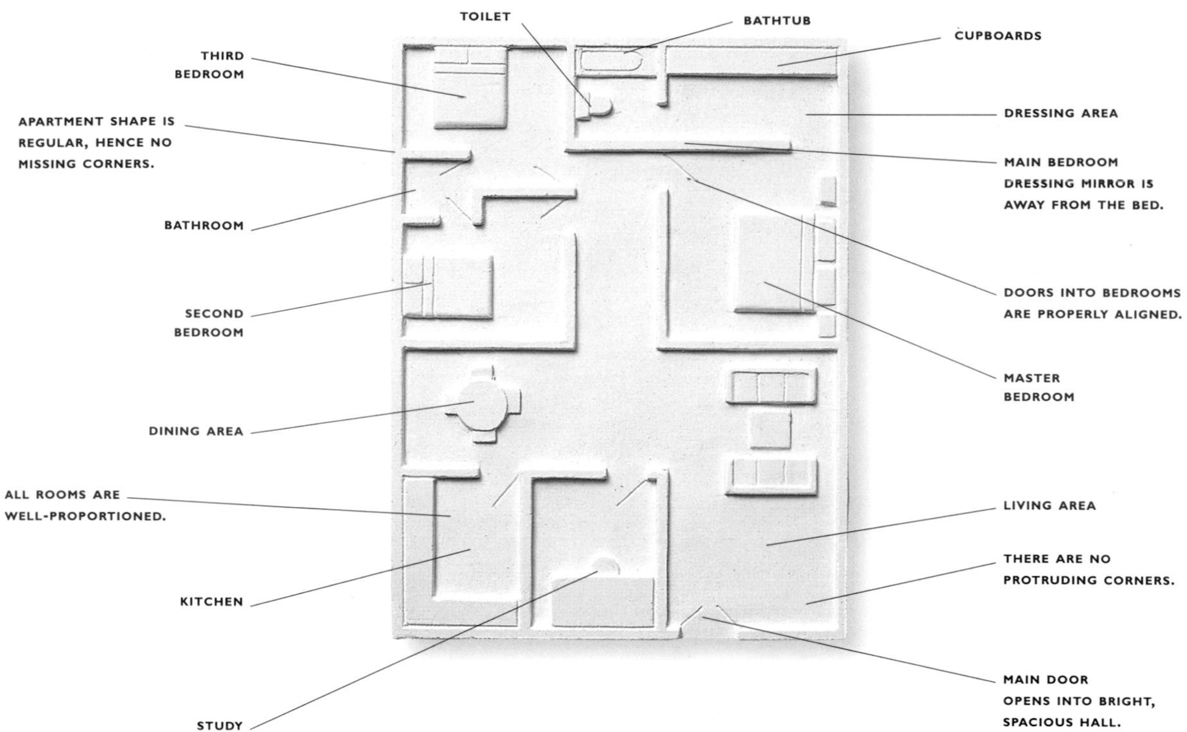

EXAMPLE OF APARTMENT WITH FENG SHUI PROBLEMS

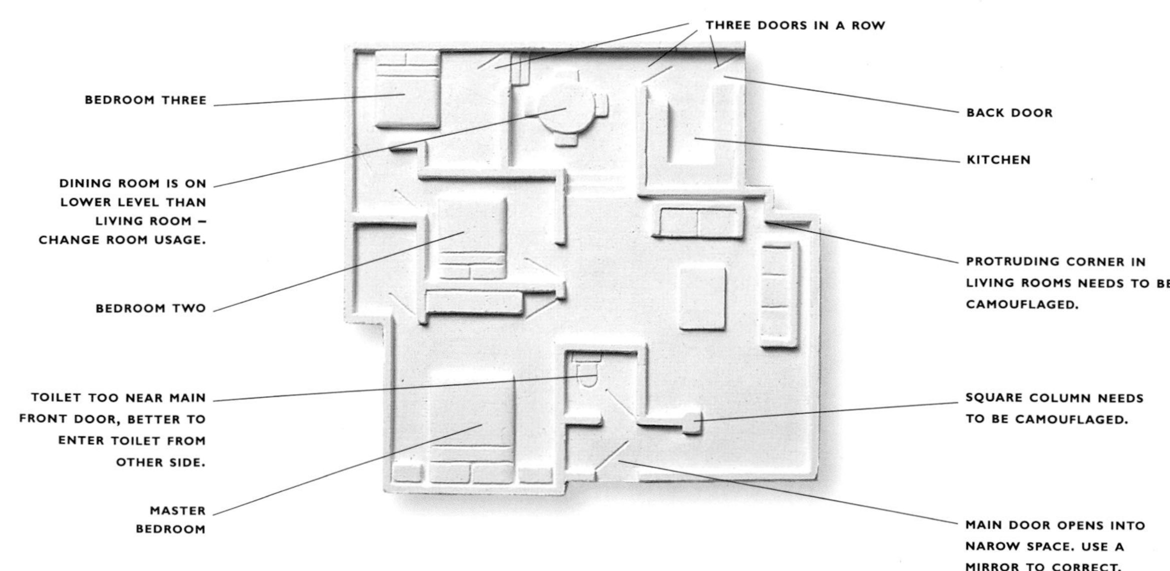

Simple floor plans show the difference between a well-proportioned apartment that has good Feng Shui and an apartment with an irregular shape and layout, creating awkward corners that need attention from the use of Feng Shui tools.

ALLOCATING ROOMS

Once you have superimposed the Pa Kua onto your house plan there are two methods that you can use to allocate your rooms. The first is based on the Eight Life Aspirations theory and the second is based on the use of the Pa Kua trigrams.

EIGHT LIFE ASPIRATIONS METHOD

This is based on a well-tried method, identifying various life aspirations for each of the eight compass directions of the Pa Kua *(see pages 78–79 for a more detailed analysis).* Thus the southeast corner of the home represents wealth and could be used as a study or workroom. The key to allocating rooms with this method is to identify which aspirations you wish to activate. The southwest sector, for example, symbolizes romance and marriage and could be used for a bachelor son or daughter wishing to find a partner. The master bedroom can either be placed in the northwestern or the southwestern sector depending upon who is more important to the family, the father or mother. In conventional Chinese practice, the family patriarch always sleeps in the northwest, unless that sector represents a personally inauspicious direction, based upon their Kua number *(see pages 100–101).*

USING THE TRIGRAMS

Different members of the family can also be allocated rooms according to the Pa Kua trigrams, where each trigram represents a different member of the family. These are summarized below and further examined on pages 76–77.

Each member of the family is represented by a different trigram from the Pa Kua. These can be used to determine the allocation of rooms.

TUI (WEST) REPRESNTS THE YOUNGEST DAUGHTER.

KEN (NORTHEAST) REPRESENTS THE YOUNGEST SON.

LI (SOUTH) REPRESENTS THE MIDDLE DAUGHTER.

KAN (NORTH) REPRESENTS THE MIDDLE SON.

SUN (SOUTHEAST) REPRESENTS THE ELDEST DAUGHTER.

CHEN (EAST) REPRESENTS THE ELDEST SON.

KUN (SOUTHWEST) REPRESENTS THE MOTHER.

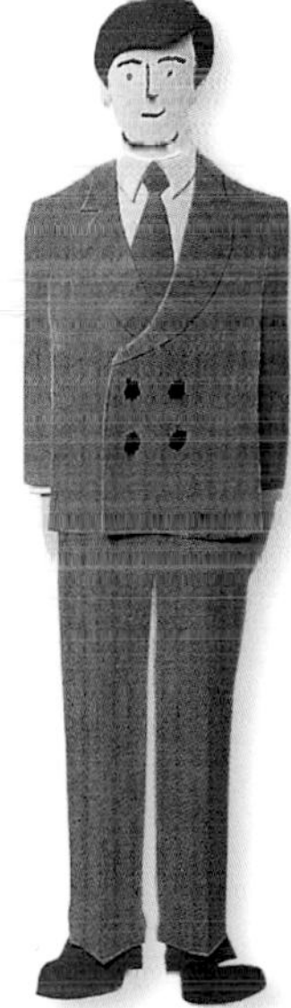

CHIEN (NORTHWEST) REPRESENTS THE FATHER.

COLUMNS AND BEAMS

Having allocated the different rooms in the house to various members of the family, we can now look in more detail at the interior design considerations that apply to all the rooms.

Every house has its fair share of corners, columns and beams, and these are all potential poison arrows that have to be neutralized and prevented from causing harm. As far as possible, overhead beams should not be exposed; nor should they be too low. Beams, when exposed, hurt the Chi of a family and are an obstacle to growth and wealth-accumulation. The modern fashion for exposing structural beams that were never meant to be seen may make your house look older, more rustic, or more cottage-like, but the practice does not make for good Feng Shui.

In fact, beams generally bring oppressive Chi, breeding distrust and dishonesty. When chairs,

BEAMS

A good antidote against an exposed overhead beam is to use the symbolic Pa Kua method. Hang two flutes, each tied with red thread, on the offending beam. They should be hung facing each other with the mouthpiece at the bottom, resembling three sides of a Pa Kua. The Chinese often use two bamboo flutes in this way to overcome the Shar Chi caused by the beam. Hanging a wind chime is also effective, but make sure the wind chime has hollow rods.

Exposed beans and columns are potential poison arrows, and should be neutralized as much as possible.

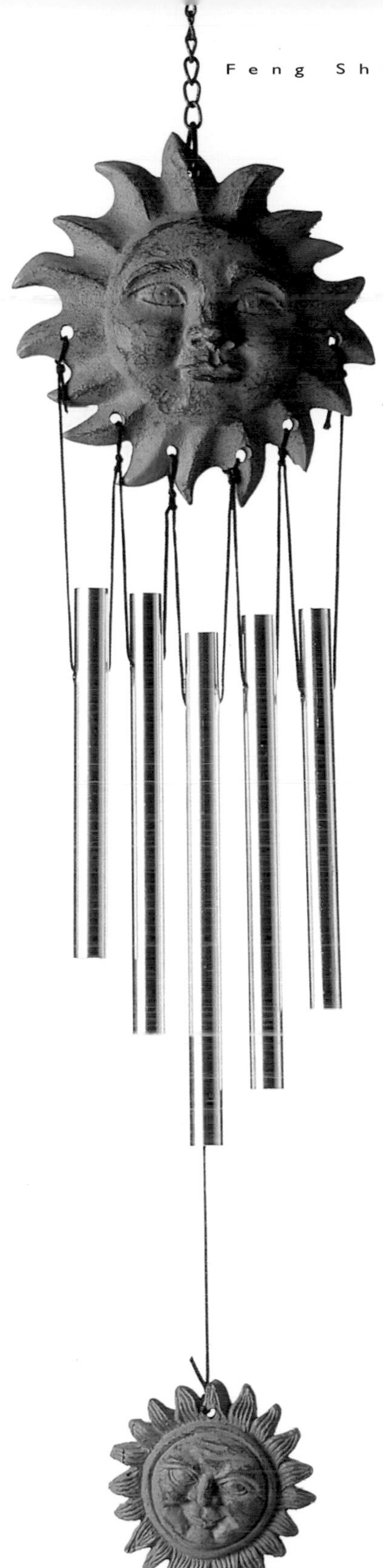

Wind chimes hung from the ceiling will soften the harmful effects of exposed beams.

beds, or sofas are placed below an exposed beam they cause headaches, bad luck, and business problems. If your bedroom has exposed beams, it is advisable to buy a four-poster bed to match the ambience – the canopy will afford you some slight measure of protection.

Fancy plaster ceilings with recessed lighting are another form of sharp overhead beam, causing poison arrows to be created. Ceilings should present a flat surface. Introduce plaster roundels and roses and other such patterns, by all means, but stay away from the sharp, angled designs.

Protruding corners and columns are structural taboos from a Feng Shui viewpoint. Unfortunately, many apartments today contain these features, especially if they have been converted by dividing up a large old house. Fortunately, there are several ways of dealing with the problem.

Firstly, you can use plants to camouflage the edges of a protruding corner or a stand-alone column. The plants (preferably creepers with broad, round leaves) effectively blunt the sharp edge of the corners, thereby diffusing the negative Feng Shui effect. Lighting corners or decorating them with plants encourages Chi to circulate

Secondly, you can hang a wind chime from the ceiling. This also blunts the cutting edge of the corner. Wind chimes should have hollow rods, since this forces Chi to rise through the rods and the tinkling sounds of the wind chime then cause the Chi to become friendly and auspicious. Wind chimes with solid rods are not effective.

Thirdly, wrapping the column with floor-to-ceiling mirrors will help by making the column effectively "disappear."

If the beam is not exposed, the danger is considerably lessened, but if you are aware of where the structural beams are in your apartment, it is best to move away from under them.

STAIRCASES AND MEZZANINES

Split-level rooms and mezzanine floors are not generally advocated by Feng Shui practioners, but if you are faced with no alternative, make sure that your dining area is located on the higher level. This ensures that the Chi of the residents is higher than that of the visitors, who are entertained in the lower-level living room. Bedrooms, family rooms, and studies, should never be located on the lower levels of a house, for the same reason.

Feng Shui guidelines strenuously warn that staircases should never start directly in front of the main door. Ideally, they should even be out of view of the main door. Nor should they end directly in front of an upstairs door. The Chi thus created is too strong and becomes harmful. Gently curving staircases are preferable to those that are straight and long, and they should be neither too narrow, nor too steep. The steps should always be covered, not left exposed, and should be solid. They should not be too narrow, nor have spaces between the steps, as this causes the good luck Chi to escape.

Spiral staircases are not recommended, as their shape resembles that of a corkscrew piercing into the house, and this can cause bad Feng Shui. However, they do no harm if placed in unobtrusive corners. If the staircase is placed in the wealth corner of the house, it will cause financial loss. Spiral staircases are also dangerous if they are placed in the center of the house, since they seem to be boring into the heart of the home. Worst of all is a winding staircase that is carpeted in red; the red carpet can be interpreted as representing the flow of blood from the injury caused by the corkscrew.

APARTMENTS

If you are buying an apartment, you should also pay attention to the communal staircases. These should be located to the sides of the building and should not face the main door; the Shar Chi for everyone in the building will be very damaging. Your own apartment entrance should not face the staircase.

A spiral staircase symbolizes a corkscrew, but is less harmful when located in the corner of a house.

According to Feng Shui principles, the steps of the staircase should not have open backs.

THE ROMANOVS OF RUSSIA

In St. Petersburg, Russia's most beautiful city, it is easy to stand in awe and wonder at the beautiful palaces of the Russian czars. The Winter Palace, in particular, is stunning, with awesome rooms built of malachite, lapis lazuli, and all kinds of marble, and with ceilings hung with hundreds of crystal chandeliers. There are also floor and table designs made into the Pa Kua shape – all spelling tremendously good Feng Shui. In addition, the palaces have fountains in their gardens and face the Neva river. No wonder both Peter and Catherine enjoyed such successful reigns.

The palace of Czar Nicholas, however, is another story. Nicholas and his entire family were murdered during the Russian Revolution in the early part of the 20th century. In Czar Nicholas's palace, there is an enormous straight staircase directly facing the main front door. The first thing you see on entering is the huge staircase rising straight up for three floors. There could scarcely have been a poison arrow more threatening. Is it possible that this staircase caused the Romanov dynasty to die out in Russia?

The Pavilion room in the Winter Palace exhibits good Feng Shui, with its Italianate hanging garden on the right and the River Neva flowing past on the left of this view.

Gently curving, covered stairs are the most beneficial, according to Feng Shui guidelines.

A spiral staircase is particularly dangerous if it is located in the center of the house.

DOORS AND CORRIDORS

We have already seen that doors play an important role in determining the quality of the Feng Shui experienced by any household. They are also one of the easiest things to adjust. When examining the Feng Shui of doors, the most vital thing to do is to make very certain that they are not being hit by anything sharp or angled. Having assured yourself that your doors are free from attack by killing Chi, the other main aspects to consider are their alignment and their relationship to each other.

Fashionable though it is to have a sequence of doors opening one from another to create an enfilade effect (as in London's National Gallery, for example), it is bad Feng Shui practice to have three or more doors in a row, especially if one of them is a back door and one is a front door. When there are doors facing each other, make sure they are of the same width and height, and that they directly face each other. If two doors are at right angles to each other, make sure they each open and shut into the rooms concerned, and do not open out into the corridor or the hallway.

Solid doors are always preferable to see-through doors, and wood is better than glass or steel. The main doors should look like main doors. The grander the main doors, the more auspicious it is for the home, unless the door is deemed to be out of proportion to the home itself, in the sense that it is too grand for the home. It is far better though, that the door appears too grand than too shabby.

If the entrance to your apartment lies at the end of a long corridor, then the Chi flowing towards it will be too fierce. Its effect can be softened with a plant placed halfway down the corridor. However, you should not place the plant too near to your door. The same solution can be used to mitigate the negative effects of long (and narrow) corridors, although it is best not to have long corridors at all in a residential abode, since these represent straight arrows that create Shar Chi. Use bushy plants to slow down the Chi that is flowing through the corridor. Plants also have the effect of forcing the Chi to travel in a meandering fashion, rather than in a straight line, thereby making it auspicious rather than inauspicious.

The beams of this Tudor house have created a poison arrow aimed directly at the front door.

Dublin houses are famous for the elegant doorways – an auspicious Feng Shui symbol.

Elaborately decorated, symmetrical doorways encourage positive Chi to enter the house.

This entrance porch creates extra angles, and the beams above the door form a poison arrow.

DOOR POSITIONS

There are several guidelines on auspicious door directions, the most potent of which is associated with your date of birth. To determine your most auspicious direction, match your Kua number *(see page 101)* to a direction in the table below. When looking for an apartment or house to rent or buy, look for one whose main door faces this direction.

You will also find it beneficial if the doors that lead into your bedroom, study, or office also face your personal auspicious direction.

FOR MALES	
KUA NUMBER 1:	SOUTHEAST
KUA NUMBER 2:	NORTHEAST
KUA NUMBER 3:	SOUTH
KUA NUMBER 4:	NORTH
KUA NUMBER 5:	NORTHEAST
KUA NUMBER 6:	WEST
KUA NUMBER 7:	NORTHWEST
KUA NUMBER 8:	SOUTHWEST
KUA NUMBER 9:	EAST

FOR FEMALES	
KUA NUMBER 1:	SOUTHEAST
KUA NUMBER 2:	NORTHEAST
KUA NUMBER 3:	SOUTH
KUA NUMBER 4:	NORTH
KUA NUMBER 5:	SOUTHWEST
KUA NUMBER 6:	WEST
KUA NUMBER 7:	NORTHWEST
KUA NUMBER 8:	SOUTHWEST
KUA NUMBER 9:	EAST

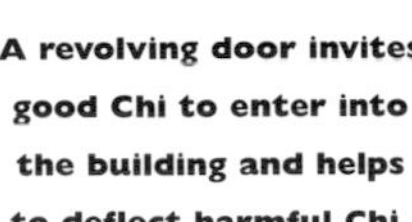

A revolving door invites good Chi to enter into the building and helps to deflect harmful Chi.

These strong double doors act as formidable protectors for the residents of this house.

Energy or Chi becomes auspicious when it is forced through these circular doors.

Red symbolizes Yang energy and brings good fortune if the house is near a Yin hospital or police station.

ROOM SHAPES

Design the shapes of rooms in your home with care. It is much easier to create balance and harmony when rooms are regular in shape and dimension. If possible, therefore, make all your rooms square or rectangular. As with house shapes, so, too, with rooms: L, U, H, or T shapes and triangles all create inauspicious results for the inhabitants. Sloping ceilings are also inauspicious.

Where there are adjuncts to the room, such as dressing areas and adjoining bathrooms or toilets, make sure each of the rooms is regular in shape. Where built-in cupboards are installed, make certain these do not cause any imbalance by leaving small gaps where Shar Chi can accumulate.

L-shaped rooms are deemed "incomplete," as you will see when you attempt to superimpose a Pa Kua onto the room layout. Depending on the position of the room, the missing corner could well represent one of the things you wish for, such as wealth or improved marriage prospects.

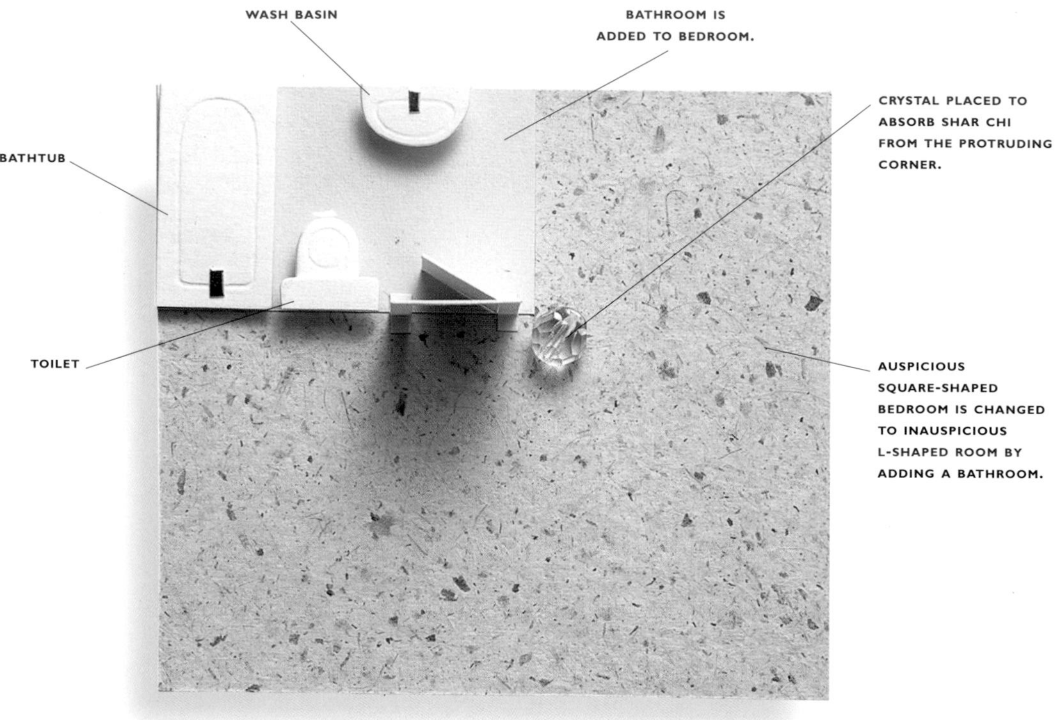

In the example given here, the bedroom has become L-shaped because of the adjoining bathroom. If this also happens to be the southwestern corner of the room, then the marriage corner will house the toilet. Such an arrangement will cause the marriage prospects to be flushed down the toilet. This is, therefore, not a suitable room for a young woman who is hoping to find a husband. The same analysis can be made for other situations. Just imagine all your aspirations, such as your romance, wealth, and family luck being flushed down the toilet every day.

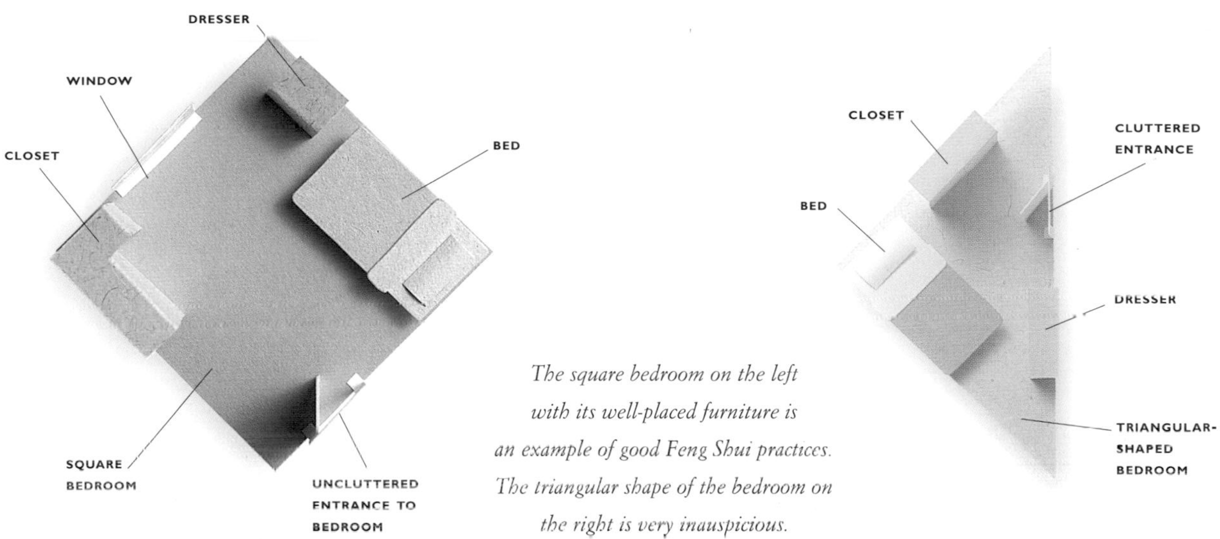

The square bedroom on the left with its well-placed furniture is an example of good Feng Shui practices. The triangular shape of the bedroom on the right is very inauspicious.

LIVING ROOM ARRANGEMENTS

The room layout below represents good Feng Shui. The sofas, chairs, and coffee table are arranged in a Pa Kua shape which is auspicious and balanced. A triangular corner cabinet placed in the top left of the room would be an excellent addition, lending support to the seating arrangement. The paintings on the walls should be representative of good symbolism, or stimulate the element represented by that corner. A painting of plants and flowers could be hung in the wood corner, for example, or a painting of mountains if the corner is represented by the earth element. To complete this room layout, fill the shape marked with dotted lines with decorative items.

This room layout represents the same living room, but with an inauspicious layout of furniture. The sofas, which have been arranged in an L-shape, are unbalanced and inauspicious. All the sharp corners created by protruding corners and tall side cupboards have been left uncamouflaged, causing bad Chi to flow toward people sitting in the sofa area. Finally, the general arrangement of furniture is crowded and seems to obstruct the flow of Chi.

An inauspicious arrangement of furniture can be made auspicious with the help of a few simple devices.

BEDROOMS

Since we spend a substantial part of our lives in the bedroom, it is important that the arrangement of this room is auspicious. In the "before" bedroom arrangement shown opposite, a cluttered entrance into the bedroom blocks the flow of Chi, thereby affecting the occupant's social life. It is also advisable to sleep a little further into the room, as this enhances the balance within the room. In the "after" arrangement, the furniture has been rearranged to facilitate the flow of Chi into the bedroom.

An L-shaped bedroom is inauspicious. Its shape resembles a cleaver and, worse still, it suggests that a corner is missing. If you must sleep in a room shaped like this, it is important to place the beds in the "handle" of the cleaver, since this symbolizes being in control, rather then being the victim of blows. Usually, however, this is just the part of the room that is too narrow for a double bed.

If that is the case, you can improve the Feng Shui of an L-shaped bedroom by placing a wall mirror in the "handle" part of the room. This serves to extend the wall inwards, thereby symbolically getting rid of the L shape effect. Feng Shui masters usually warn against mirrors in bedrooms because the Chi created is too powerful for the resting person. If the bed were to be placed opposite the mirror, the result would be discord between husband and wife. It is acceptable in the case shown below, however, because the mirror is not visible from the bed.

Another option is to neutralize the effects of an L-shaped bedroom by placing a bookshelf across the join, making two rectangular rooms. Normally, bookshelves are not recommended for a bedroom, because they can be seen as symbolic knives, cutting into the occupants, but their effect can be neutralized if they are hidden from view with doors.

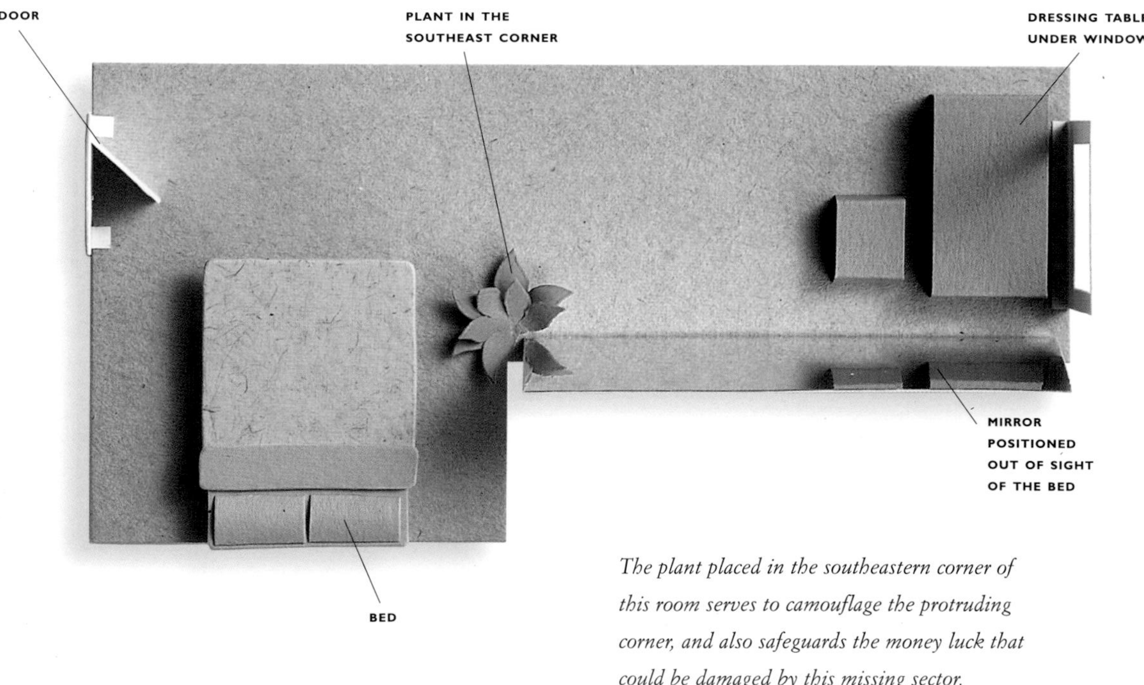

The plant placed in the southeastern corner of this room serves to camouflage the protruding corner, and also safeguards the money luck that could be damaged by this missing sector.

BEFORE

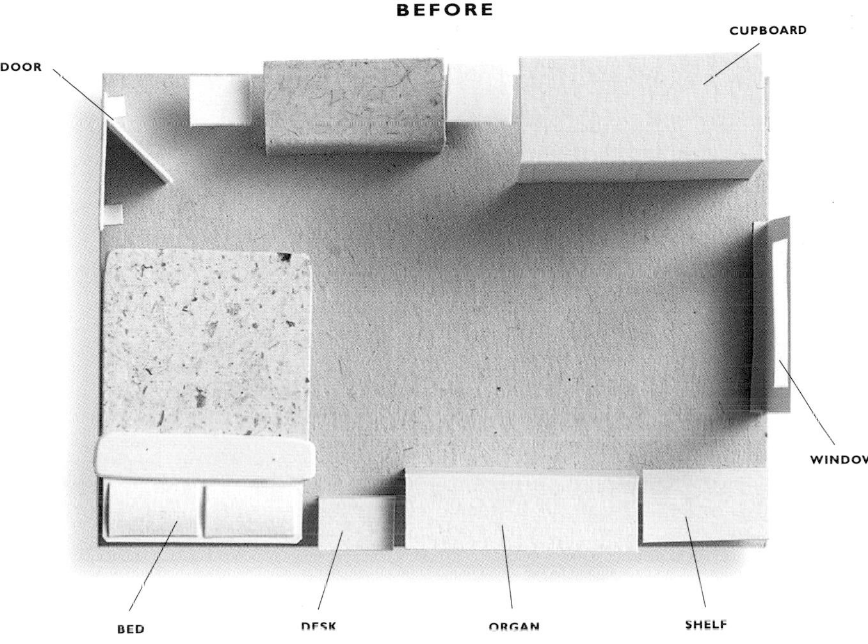

The Feng Shui of the main bedroom is very important because it affects the well-being of the whole household. The arrangement of furniture in this bedroom is cluttered, especially around the door, blocking the smooth flow of Chi into the room. The solution is to remove some items and to rearrange the rest.

AFTER

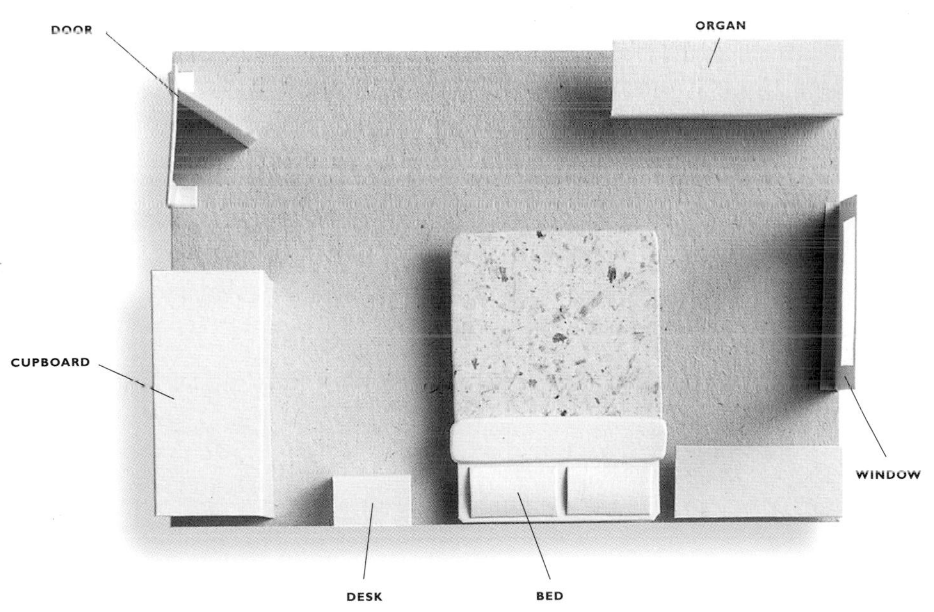

The furniture has now been rearranged so that it no longer overwhelms the sleepers, and the bed has been moved further into the room to enhance the overall balance.

BATHROOMS AND TOILETS

Feng Shui practitioners always recommend that toilets and bathrooms should be tucked away inconspicuously. The toilet should definitely not be located in the vicinity of the main door, since excess Yin energy will be created. This will severely affect the Chi coming through the main door into the house. Toilets should also never be located facing staircases or dining rooms.

Bathrooms or toilets should not be located in any of the important wealth or career sectors of your house. The effect of locating toilets, showers, and baths in auspicious sectors is that you will wash or flush away all prospects of that sector's luck. Toilets should, therefore, never be located at the end of a corridor, or be easily visible from outside the room.

Never locate bathrooms or toilets in the middle of the house, as this spreads bad vibrations out from the center to all parts of the building. Instead, bathrooms and toilets should be sited along the sides of the house. Within the bathroom, the toilet should always be hidden from obvious view.

One of the strongest recommendations made by Feng Shui masters is that toilets should never be conspicuous. That means they should not be too large. If, as is the current trend, you want to have a spacious and luxurious bathroom, make sure that at least the toilet area is nicely tucked away in a corner of the bathroom, ideally hidden behind a half-wall so that it is not visible from the rest of the bathroom. Shutting it away from view deflects the Shar Chi created, thereby reducing its energy.

Badly sited toilets, or toilets that constantly become blocked, will affect the health of the household. Feng Shui practitioners also recommend that doors leading into bathrooms and toilets should be kept closed at all times.

Although this bathroom is too elaborate according to Feng Shui guidelines, it does have the benefit of a separate toilet area that is not visible from the wash basin.

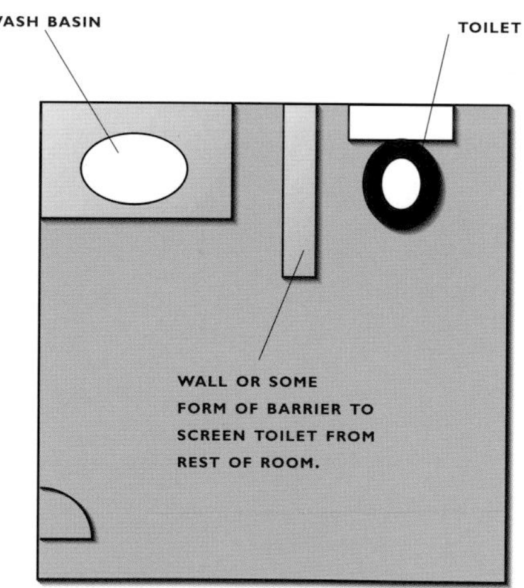

Ancient Chinese homes rarely had bathrooms or toilets. Modern Feng Shui practitioners recommend various "cures", including hiding the toilet from view.

ABOVE **Although a modest bathroom like this is generally preferable, keeping the toilet seat closed is a good idea.**

LEFT **The sharp edge of the marble-topped basin is pointed directly at the toilet. This is not necessarily a bad thing, as it "kills" the Shar Chi emanating from the toilet.**

TOILETS AND MARRIAGE

When toilets are located in the marriage or family corners of the house, problems always result. In fact, toilets give trouble wherever they are located, since every corner of the house represents a desirable life aspiration. Siting toilets is, therefore, a difficult matter, and each individual has to decide which is the least important life situation to them.

It is interesting to note that in the palaces and homes of the wealthy mandarins of imperial China, there were no toilets – nor were there any bathrooms. These are modern creations of Western culture. In imperial times, bathtubs were filled with water by the servants and were then taken away when the master or mistress had finished washing.

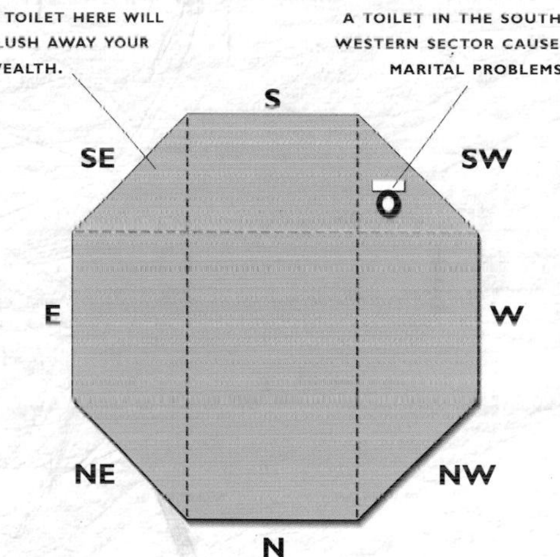

Siting the toilet or bathroom within the home is one of the most problematical aspects of Feng Shui, and few situations are ideal.

KITCHENS AND DINING ROOMS

According to Feng Shui, the kitchen is one of the most important rooms in the home. As such, it must be airy, well-lit, spacious, and regular in shape. The kitchen symbolizes the wealth of the family. It is where the family's food is cooked, and the quality and quantity of food available in a home strongly reflects the family's prosperity, overall health, and well-being. Feng Shui masters believe that kitchens and stoves should not be placed in auspicious locations and that the stove should be correctly positioned. This then brings extreme good fortune, wealth, abundance, and high positions of honor. The position of the stove, or "fire mouth," is also extremely important. The fire mouth should face your auspicious direction, so that your food is cooked with energy that flows from your lucky direction. The fire mouth is the place at which electricity or gas flows *into* the stove. Feng Shui practitioners believe an incorrectly placed fire mouth brings severe misfortune. Kitchen doors should never face the front or back doors; otherwise, the good luck could slowly leak out of the house.

According to the *Yang Dwelling Classic*, the best location for the kitchen is in the south sector of the house, but never in the southwest. In part, this is because of the links between the fire element and the southern sector of the home.

Kitchens are one of the places where it is easy to inadvertently create poison arrows, especially if you have a modern, high-tech kitchen. Jutting corner cupboards create sharp angles that can unintentionally cause unhappiness and ill health. Open shelves can cause Shar Chi to be directed at those working in the kitchen. The solution in this case is to place doors in front of the shelves to hide them from view. Some beautifully designed interiors have created so many problems for friends of mine that they had no choice but to rethink them or redesign them along more sensitive lines – using rounded shelving units instead of square ones.

DINING ROOMS

Dining rooms should never be situated on a lower level than kitchens or living rooms. Round tables are preferable to square or rectangular shapes and sideboards should not be arranged in such a way that the edges point at the dining table. To create good Feng Shui in this room, you can hang a painting of fruits and food. The dining room should also be well-lit at all times to ensure the flow of energy.

MIRRORS IN YOUR DINING ROOM

Mirror walls are excellent for the dining area because it is believed that the doubling of food on the dining table symbolizes abundance for the household. In fact, mirrors are extremely useful Feng Shui tools for all sorts of purposes, such as deflecting poison arrows, "extending" tight corners or "missing" sectors, activating Chi flows, and camouflaging sharp angles caused by columns. Mirrors are also excellent for reflecting good luck symbols and beautiful scenery, such as water, rivers or lakes, thus bringing wealth, which is symbolized by water, into the house.

Certain rules must be observed, however, when mirrors are used, and you must be aware of the bad effects that mirrors can create if positioned incorrectly. Mirrors should never be placed so low as to have the effect of "cutting off" the heads of the tallest residents. They should not reflect staircases, doors, stoves, or toilets, nor should they ever be used to reflect the main door or any other door that opens outside. This has the effect of bouncing the Chi that flows into the house straight out again. Finally, never use mirror tiles.

QUESTIONABLE FENG SHUI

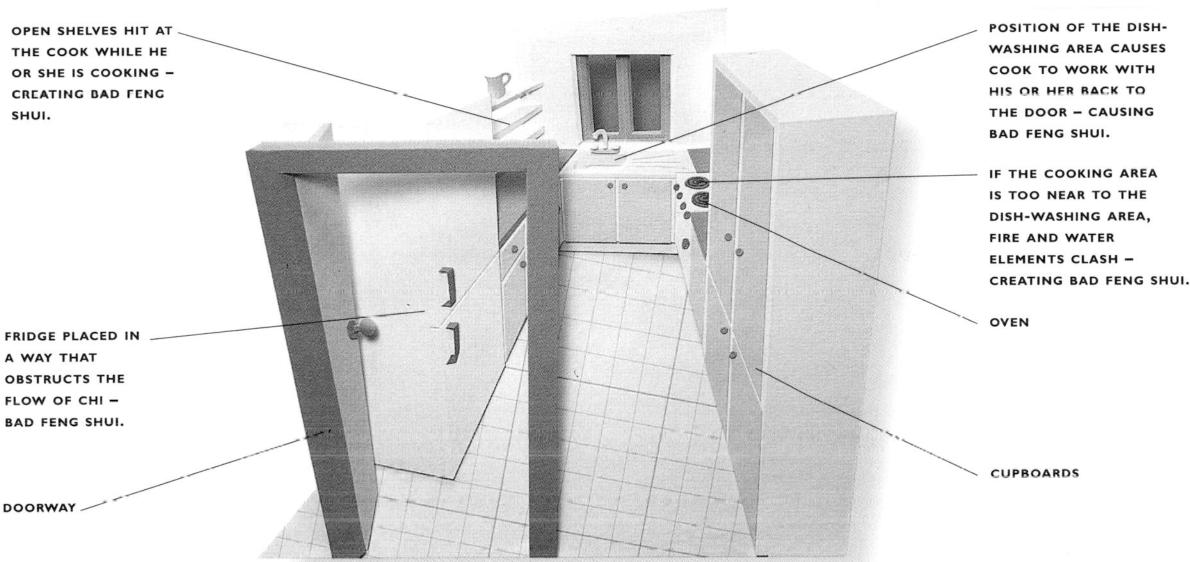

GOOD FENG SHUI

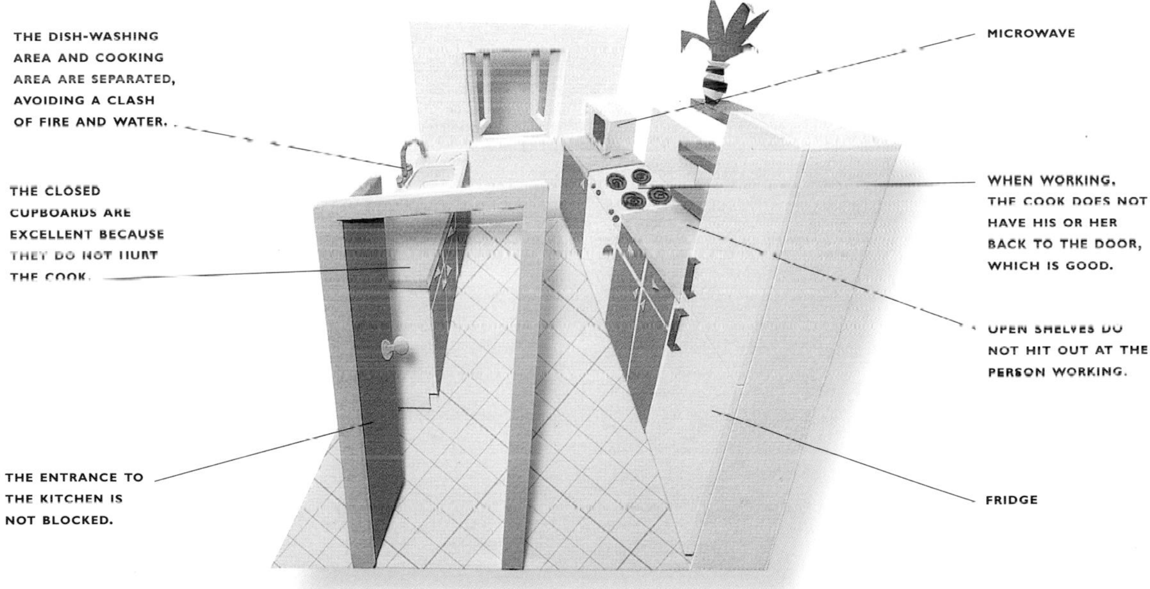

These two kitchen arrangements illustrate how, with a little reorganization, the layout of the kitchen can be changed to encourage good Feng Shui.

SWIMMING POOLS

Gardens are excellent Feng Shui, but modern Feng Shui masters are ambivalent about their attitude toward swimming pools. One group vehemently opposes the idea of having swimming pools altogether, pointing to various examples of family fortunes lost by the second generation and attributing the cause to the presence of large swimming pools in the house. Ironically, these luxury items have often been built as a sign of wealth. Another group of masters maintains that pools can be auspicious if they are in proportion to the house, properly sited with respect to the land, and if they are curved or kidney-shaped and appear to embrace the house, rather than rectangular-shaped.

PONDS

Ponds in a garden are excellent Feng Shui features that enhance wealth luck. If you have a pond, try keeping fish in it to energize the flow of Chi that it creates.

If you are not able to care for your pond properly, however, it is far better to remove it altogether than to let it become murky or muddy through lack of care. Worse still, if the water becomes dark and stagnant, it creates bad luck and causes problems for the business and wealth of residents.

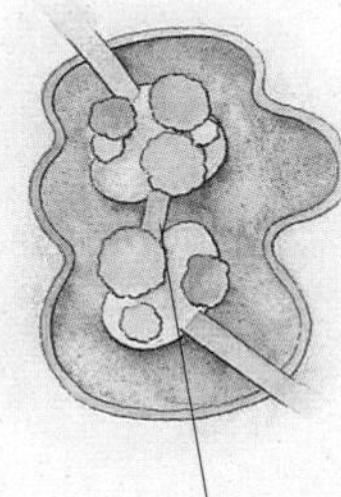

IRREGULAR SHAPES ARE BETTER THAN RECTANGLES.

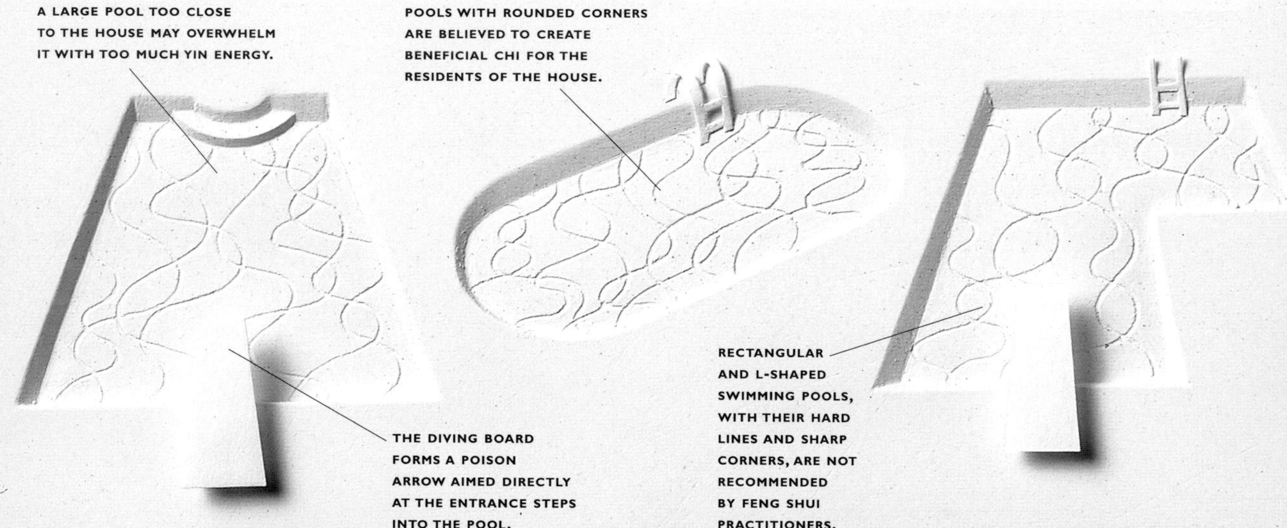

A LARGE POOL TOO CLOSE TO THE HOUSE MAY OVERWHELM IT WITH TOO MUCH YIN ENERGY.

POOLS WITH ROUNDED CORNERS ARE BELIEVED TO CREATE BENEFICIAL CHI FOR THE RESIDENTS OF THE HOUSE.

THE DIVING BOARD FORMS A POISON ARROW AIMED DIRECTLY AT THE ENTRANCE STEPS INTO THE POOL.

RECTANGULAR AND L-SHAPED SWIMMING POOLS, WITH THEIR HARD LINES AND SHARP CORNERS, ARE NOT RECOMMENDED BY FENG SHUI PRACTITIONERS.

Since Feng Shui precepts warn against sharp corners, it stands to reason that rectangular pools of water are inauspicious, especially if they are too large. The Chi created would be too strong if the house itself seems overwhelmed or dominated by the size of the pool. Too much water is said to "drown" residents and is therefore very inauspicious and to be avoided.

But Feng Shui guidelines and philosophy also pronounce at great length about the auspicious influences of water. It therefore seems logical to accept that man-made bodies of water, if designed to blend harmoniously with the environment, should be auspicious. This seems to be the case, since many masters maintain that the good luck features of the landscape that are described in detail in the *Water Dragon Classic*, one of the source texts for Feng Shui practice, can be artificially built to benefit households.

It is my personal experience and belief that water is almost always auspicious, because it is representative of wealth. It is even more so if the water element is deemed good for you according to your horoscope. However, swimming pools should be natural in shape – round like a pond or kidney-shaped, and it does help to landscape the pool and its surroundings so that they blend as naturally as possible with the rest of your garden and with the overall environment.

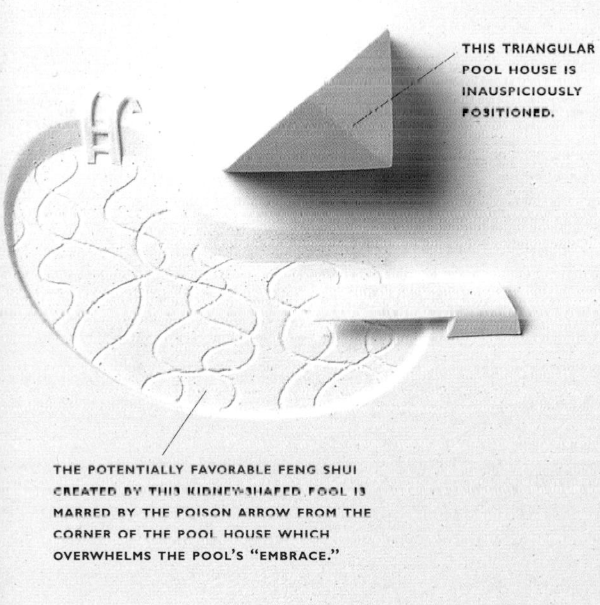

Swimming pools should be natural in shape and not square or rectangular, in contrast to Feng Shui preferences for the shape of homes.

RIGHT **This swimming pool, with its soft, rounded corners and the lush overhanging vegetation, blends in with the landscape and is balanced in terms of the five elements.**

POOLS AND APARTMENTS

A view of water, artificial or natural, enhances the Feng Shui of any apartment building, and many of the principles that apply to swimming pools and ponds in the gardens of houses also apply to apartment blocks. However, pools should not be located within the apartment block, either on the ground floor or on the top floor. Water above or below often spells danger and is never encouraged by Feng Shui masters. Pools should also be balanced in size, and should reflect the harmony of the elements. If your horoscope warns against the presence of the water element in your home (if you are a fire element person, for example), it is advisable to look for an apartment block that does not have a swimming pool.

EXTENSIONS AND LANDSCAPE STRUCTURES

If you plan to enlarge your house, you must first consider the effect the extension will have on the overall shape of the building. Certain shape combinations are auspicious, while others are not. At the same time, you must analyze what effect the extension will have on the overall position of the house and what impact it will have on the directional sector it occupies.

Another method of determining the Feng Shui effects of extensions is to look at the element represented by the sector where the extension is to be built, and then check its impact on the element represented by your main door. Thus, if the extension is to be built on the northern side of the house, it represents the element water. If the main door is located facing the southeast (which represents small wood) then the extension will enhance the door's Feng Shui, since water produces wood.

If, on the other hand, the extension is located in the northwest, representing big metal, then the extension will have a detrimental effect on the door, since metal destroys wood. This method of analysis is highly recommended, since element analysis is one of the fundamental principles of all Feng Shui practice.

This same analysis can be applied to the building of gazebos, stand-alone garages, and other large structures planned for the home.

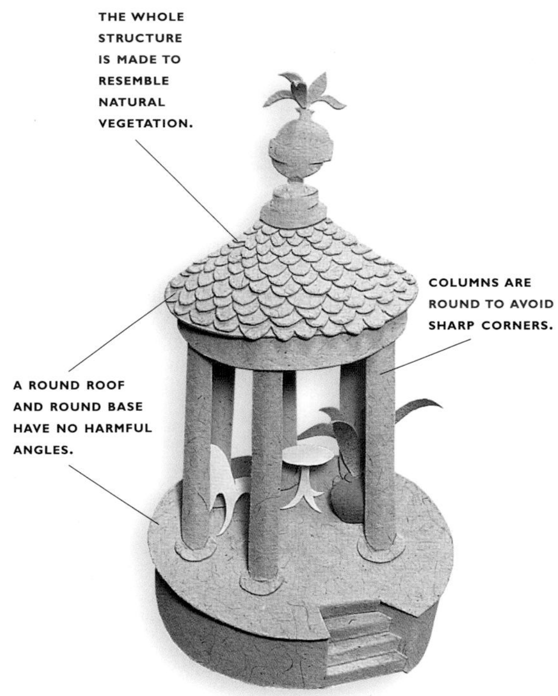

A gazebo set away from the house has the advantage of not adding any unpleasant shapes to the building that may encourage negative Chi flows.

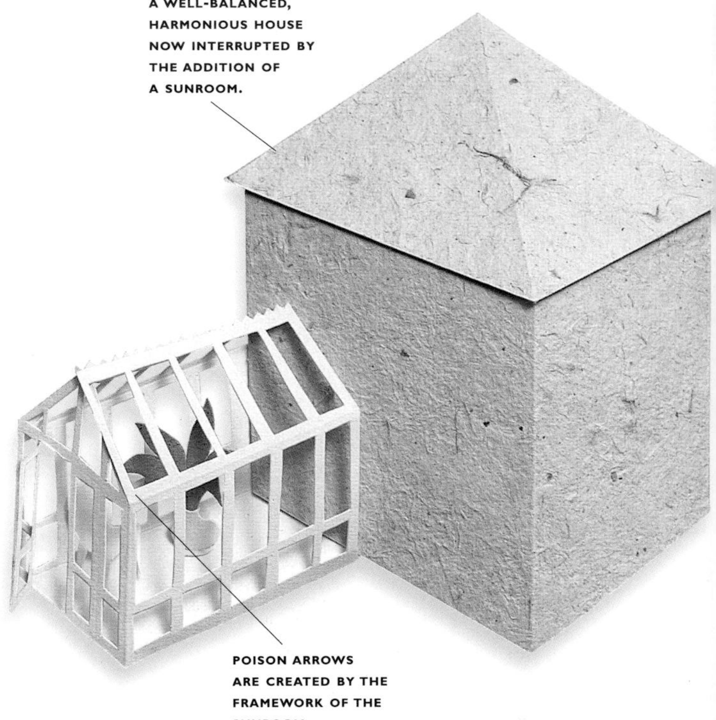

Extensions that result in irregularly-shaped houses, such as L shapes, are not advisable because they change the auspicious shape of the house.

LANDSCAPE PLANNING

In keeping with Feng Shui's central theme of maintaining balance and harmony, gardens can often be landscaped to create good Feng Shui configurations. This can be done by planting lush vegetation and creating elevated hillocks (especially at the back of the house, but never at the front), flowing streams, or rocky waterfalls. By ensuring that there is a good balance of Yin and Yang through the use of boulders, ponds, plants, and various colors, the Feng Shui of homes can be strongly enhanced.

Be sure to maintain balance and harmony in the size and scale of your garden features at all times. Too large a pond, or a hillock that is out of proportion to the garden or the house, will do more harm than good, simply because the Chi generated by, say, an overlarge pond will overwhelm the residents, causing setbacks in their lives.

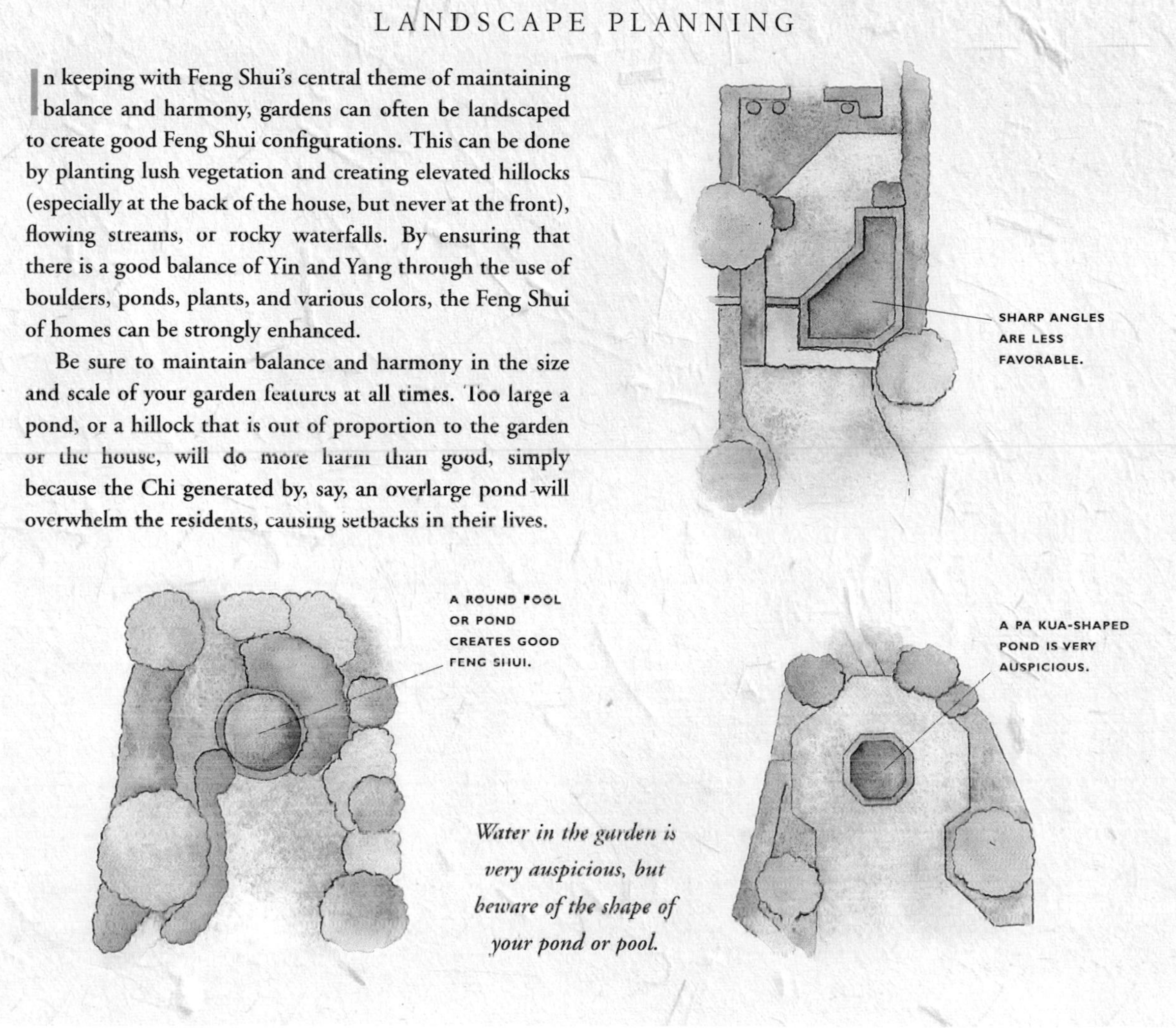

Water in the garden is very auspicious, but beware of the shape of your pond or pool.

FENCES AND WALLS

Fences and walls serve to divide the boundaries of the house from external influences. Walls, for instance, are effective barriers that can block out the effect of harmful objects such as boulders, fast-flowing or clogged up drains, telephone poles, and a whole host of other inauspicious structures. The design of walls should, however, be harmonized with the landscape.

Brick walls and fences should have foliage planted near to them to create a good Yin/Yang balance, where the bricks are Yang and the plants are Yin. Fences made with wrought iron or wood should not be designed with spikes or arrows pointing downwards, as this suggests descent, or with spikes pointed inwards, as these symbolize poison arrows attacking the house. If spikes are pointed upwards, the effect is neutral.

Chapter Nine

DECORATING FOR GOOD FENG SHUI

In Feng Shui practice, a great deal of superstition and symbolism surrounds good fortune objects. These may be special gods believed to attract wealth and longevity into the household, or they may be fruits, flowers, plants, and trees; or they may be special types of animal, either real or mythological.

These objects have a powerful role in attracting benign Chi flows into the home. This chapter, therefore, suggests a number of different ways that works of art, plants, and furnishings can be incorporated into your design plans to add an extra Feng Shui dimension to your living environment.

風水

MUCH OF THE symbolism attached to good fortune objects ensures that they are favorite subjects for artists and artisans, and are, therefore, commonly found on Chinese art objects, including screens, paintings, vases, and sculptures. Such objects are often relatively inexpensive and easy to find in Chinese or Oriental curio shops.

A very favorable and popular symbol, a frog signifies the arrival of wealth and can be discreetly displayed just inside the main door.

FISH FOR SUCCESS

The fish (sometimes with a fisherman) represents success. The fish successfully swimming upstream to be transformed into a dragon is a symbol of the scholar who, having passed examinations, goes on to enjoy wealth and success. Many Chinese people keep real fish in an aquarium or small outdoor pool to enhance their wealth prospects. Displaying the fish symbol as a vase, as a subject in a painting, or on a painted screen should have the same effect. Ideally, the fish should be displayed near the front entrance or on the living room table.

FROGS FOR FORTUNE

The frog bringing gold and silver is an extremely popular symbol, which should be placed just inside the main door to signify the arrival of wealth into the home. It is not necessary to display the frog prominently; put it next to a potted plant so that it is not too obtrusive. If the front door is located in the southwestern or northwestern sector of the home, such a symbol is believed to be even luckier, since these are the directions associated with the metal element, a class to which both gold and silver belong.

Real fish or porcelain ones are extremely beneficial, as they symbolize wealth and prosperity.

THE DRAGON HORSE

Another popular symbol is the unicorn, which is considered to be a fabulous creature of good omen. It symbolizes longevity, grandeur, joy, illustrious offspring, and wisdom. Sometimes referred to as the Dragon Horse, the unicorn is said to possess qualities of gentleness, goodwill, and benevolence towards all living creatures. The Chinese believe that the unicorn is always solitary, and appears only when a particularly benevolent leader sits on the throne, or when a very wise sage is born.

THE DIGNIFIED PEACOCK

The peacock signifies dignity and beauty. For centuries, the brilliant hues of the peacock's tail feathers have made them popular emblems of official rank, and feather fans are often hung in Chinese homes.

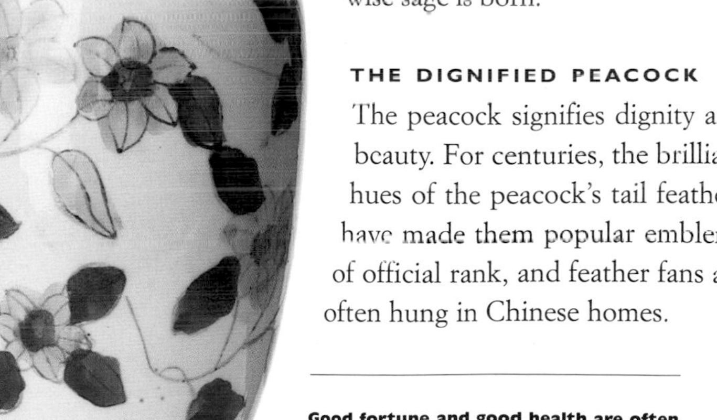

Good fortune and good health are often symbolized by a beautifully crafted Chinese vase. Flowers calm and refresh the Chi that flows around them.

ATTRACTING GOOD FORTUNE

One way of attracting an extremely auspicious Chi flow into the home is to introduce a plum blossom plant, and to place it in either the southeastern or eastern corner of the living room. This has the effect of creating harmonious relationships between the residents, and, more important, it also enhances the money luck of the household. This is because the plum blossom in full bloom signifies great good fortune.

It does not seem to matter whether the plum blossom plant is real or artificial, so if your room is not light or warm enough for the plant, don't worry: a silk, ceramic or painted shrub will do just as well, and has the merit of being in flower at all times, thus greatly improving your prospects of wealth and happiness. But do clean it regularly.

Another plant that works well, especially for enhancing health, is the peach. If someone in the

A display of horses and the color red in the southern corner of the house will invite fame and recognition into your life.

CAREFUL USE OF SYMBOLISM

The horse is one of the Seven Treasures of Buddhism and symbolizes speed and perseverance.

The pantheon of Chinese symbolism includes animals that ensure longevity including the tortoise, unicorn, bat, deer, hare, cicada and crane. Longevity, the ability to live a long and healthy life so that one is able to reap the fruits of a lifetime of respectable living, is one of the most important aspects of good fortune for the Chinese and many homes will contain such symbolism.

The Chinese also take great care to protect their homes, and animals that symbolize such aspirations are the bear, elephant, horse, and leopard. Placing a painting of a bear, for instance, near your main door is believed to be a potent charm against burglars. Care should always be taken, however, when using such symbolism. The tiger, for example, symbolizes military prowess, but the animal is extremely ferocious and some believe it to be capable of "eating up" the inhabitants, while others believe it to be one of the best symbols of protection. Tiger symbols are best placed outside the home, near the front door.

home is ill, it is possible to use paintings of the peach plant to attract good Feng Shui to improve matters. This involves activating the health corner of the room occupied by the sick person. Place the painting (or a jade sculpture of the peach plant in full bloom) in the eastern corner of the room. A real peach plant is obviously ideal for this purpose, but artificial symbols will do just as well. The peach symbolizes longevity and is especially good for attracting a healthy dose of energetic Chi into the room. If the entire family seem to succumb easily to illness, then use this same method, but this time place the peach plant in the eastern corner of the easternmost room of the house.

The academic performance of school children or students in the family can be vastly improved by activating the mind and knowledge corner of the home. This corner corresponds to the northeast, which has earth as its ruling element. Again, this aspiration can either be activated for one child by using enhancers in that individual's own room, or by activating the most northeastern corner of the house if several children are concerned. Placing a geographic globe in that corner promises to enhance the attainment of knowledge. The globe represents the earth, and when twirled daily it creates the movement that stirs up the auspicious Chi.

I have also used just such a globe to activate the business corner of my house (the southeast). My intention was to activate auspicious Chi so that my books would sell all around the world. So far, it seems to have worked.

A good way of activating fame and recognition is to place a collection of horses and some red flowers in the southern corner of any room. South is the direction symbolized by the fire element, and it is a good idea to activate this corner if you are an actor, singer, politician, writer, or anyone involved in any profession that requires public recognition.

CREATING RAINBOWS

Crystals represent the earth element, which is the ruling symbol of the southwest marriage corner. Activating this corner with a crystal will enhance one's social life and marriage prospects.

One of the most attractive methods of enhancing the Feng Shui of any home is to use cut crystals and prisms to catch the morning sunlight coming from the east, or the afternoon sunlight from the west. Hang golf-ball sized cut crystals by the window and, each time the sun shines, watch these crystals create bright rainbows inside the room. This has the effect of energizing the Chi currents, is extremely good Feng Shui, and is particularly potent for creating family harmony and happiness.

USING PLANTS AND FLOWERS

Flowers are excellent purveyors of good Chi flows, especially if they are in full bloom and look healthy. The habit of filling rooms with freshly cut flowers spells good Feng Shui for the household. However, it is important that flowers should be changed immediately when they fade. In fact, it is far better to use artificial or silk flowers – which always look fresh – than to display flowers that have faded. Dying flowers signify illness and bad luck.

For the same reason, it is not advisable to display dried plants or flowers, no matter how beautiful they may look. Dried plants signify death and do not attract good, vibrant, healthy Chi. Besides, they are also too Yin in their effect – belonging to the realm of the dead rather than that of the living.

The *mou tan*, or peony, is excellent for enhancing marriage opportunities. You can activate the marriage corner (the southwestern sector) of any room by displaying a bunch of real or silk peonies. If you cannot find these flowers, a Chinese painting of them will do just as well.

The peony is regarded as the most supreme of all flowers, and the presence of the peony in the home of any traditional Chinese family is usually an indication that there are eligible, unmarried daughters.

One of the best things to introduce into the home are thriving green plants, which bring life into corners and are also superb for deflecting

Blossoming flowers attract good Chi and should be used to activate specific areas or corners of your home.

USING PLANTS TO DIFFUSE A SQUARE PILLAR

Stand-alone square pillars inside homes and offices are highly inauspicious. The sharp edges of such pillars create killing Chi. If the corner is aimed directly at the main door, the bad luck caused can be severe. The sharp, pointed edge of protruding corners also represent harmful Chi lines, and is, therefore, bad Feng Shui.

The best way to neutralize corners like these is to grow a climbing plant up the column, encouraging the leaves and branches to diffuse the ferocity of the edge. Hanging plants can also be attached to a bracket on the column. A fuchsia plant, for example, makes an attractive display.

The vibrant yellow color of these sunflowers adds a dash of Yang energy to a room.

bad Chi created by columns, beams, and other sharp, angled objects. When using plants inside the home, try to select those with broad leaves that resemble the "money plant." Cacti with prickly thorns should be avoided, as should stunted bonsai plants. Succulent cacti, on the other hand, create excellent Feng Shui.

When used in conjunction with analysis of the productive and destructive cycles of the five elements, plants can be very potent Feng Shui enhancers in the home. Green plants are good for those born under the influence of the fire element because wood makes fire, but are not so good for those born under the water and earth elements, as wood destroys earth and exhausts water. In Feng Shui terms, plants can also be used to activate the various corners of your home depending on the life aspirations that you wish to emphasize. Look at the elements associated with each side of the Pa Kua. If you wish to enhance your career prospects, for example, try placing a healthy green plant in the northern sector of your house.

Plants bring good Chi into your home as long as they are healthy and thriving. Choose broad-leaved plants, like the Chinese money plant (above), rather than plants with thorns or prickles like the cactus (left).

ASIA'S "GARDEN CITY"

In Singapore – dubbed Asia's Garden City – plants are used on a huge scale to soften the edges of roads and introduce Yin elements to Yang structures. It is the same with high rise buildings. Well-tended plants and trees line all the thoroughfares of Singapore, and at night, bright lights attract good, vibrant Chi to the island.

Flowers can be used for many Feng Shui purposes. A wedding bouquet, even in silk, can be placed in the southeast or marriage corner to enhance romantic prospects.

WORKS OF ART AND HOUSEHOLD GODS

Fuk, Luk, and Sau, the gods of wealth, high rank, and longevity, respectively, are found in the dining rooms or living rooms of almost every Chinese home around the world. These are the three-star gods, the most important – and the most popular – of the symbolic gods in the Chinese pantheon. They are seldom worshipped. The Chinese believe that merely having their form within the house is sufficient to attract the good fortune that they signify.

Fuk is the god of wealth and happiness.

Fuk, the god of wealth and happiness, stands taller by a head than the other two gods. He is always placed in the center. Luk, the god of high rank and affluence, holds the scepter of power and authority. Sau, the god of longevity, has a domed head and carries a peach in one hand and a walking stick in the other. He is sometimes accompanied by a deer, which is another symbol of longevity.

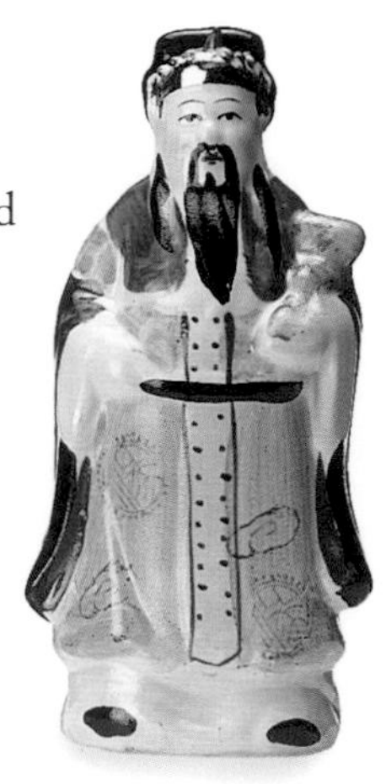

Luk is the god of high rank and affluence.

Fuk, Luk, and Sau represent the three most important aspects of good fortune. They are always displayed together and their presence ensures good health, prosperity, plenty to eat, and successful male offspring. No right-thinking Chinese home would be without these gods, and they come in a variety of sizes and forms. Wealthy families often commission specially crafted giant figurines to display in halls that are designed especially to house them. Middle class families often display them as ceramic figures, beautifully painted in bright colors, or in precious materials such as gold, enamel, or ivory. Wherever they are displayed, Fuk, Luk, and Sau must always be located in a position of honor, and placed higher than any table in the area.

Sau is the god of health and longevity.

Guardian lions are also extremely popular with the Chinese, who use them as symbols of protection. Usually the guardians are placed in pairs high up on gate posts, or on the ground on either side of the main door.

A guardian lion protecting one of the main halls of the Forbidden City. Miniature lions which can be purchased easily must be placed outside the home and never inside.

"LUCKY WESTERN FIGURINES"

Since Feng Shui is a Chinese practice, many of the symbols associated with it are of Chinese origin. However, people from the West can just as easily display other types of objects that symbolize good luck according to their own cultures with the same effect. Horseshoes, for example, are seen as lucky objects when displayed in homes in the West. In Feng Shui terms their shape is auspicious and if displayed in the northwest and western sectors of the home, associated with the element metal, can be very effective enhancing tools.

Crystal chandeliers, Fabergé eggs or paintings of beautiful palaces and scenery can be used in the same way. I am especially fond of paintings of lovers and of mother and daughter bonding as they symbolize family happiness. However, do avoid hanging abstract art that suggests unhappiness, grief or depression, such as prints of Picasso's disturbed faces.

The Kiss, Francesco Hayez (1791–1882). Enhancing tools need not only be of Eastern origin.

These stone lions are believed to protect the home from harmful influences and from people who may be out to harm the residents. Stone lions stand guard at all the main halls of the Forbidden City in Beijing (Peking), and can also be seen in front of Chinese Taoist temples. Some people use a fierce bird to guard the entrance of the house instead of lions.

In Buddhism, the lion is considered a saintly animal – lions are often seen in front of Chinese Taoist temples. The lion dance, complete with loud music, is believed to scare off malign spirits and bad luck, as well as attracting good fortune.

A sculpture with soft contours and symbolizing love and caring is an ideal art work with which to decorate a family home.

LIGHTING EFFECTS

Apart from plants, perhaps the easiest Feng Shui tool to use in decorating and enhancing your home is light. Light symbolizes the fire element, which produces earth, enhances itself, and causes wood to blossom. The fire symbolism of electric lights is thus extremely useful for activating the southern, the southeastern, the eastern, and the northeastern sectors. Light, as Yang, also helps to achieve balance and harmony in the home and attracts good Chi flows. Bright lights are particularly important in the entrance areas of the home. These should ideally be kept switched on if the foyer is dark and cramped.

CHANDELIERS

Crystal chandeliers are excellent for the purpose, though not necessarily the elaborate chandeliers of millionaire's homes. More modest arrangements of cut glass will do just as well. If you have them in your home, do not forget to turn them on – they have little Feng Shui value unless lit up.

Chandeliers are also excellent when hung in the center of the home, which traditionally symbolizes the essence of the household. The center is symbolic of the earth element, and fire produces earth.

This desk lamp is poised like a threatening hammer or cleaver and will produce hostile energy forces.

The sparkling light given off by crystal chandeliers has excellent qualities for enhancing and activating beneficial Chi.

COLOR AND SHAPE

Lights to avoid are the modern, angular, high-tech designs, any lamp that has a hostile or pointed shape, and any lamp that resembles a sharp instrument. Sharp angles direct killing Chi, and pointed shapes are best avoided.

When selecting lamps, think about using color – as well as light – to complement the relevant element of the corner being lit. For example, a lamp colored dark blue will be suitable for the northern sector, since blue equates with water; you could also use a blue-colored light bulb to activate the northern corner, which symbolizes career success.

AUSPICIOUS COLORS

The Feng Shui approach to the use of color differs depending upon who one talks to. The color black, for example, is generally avoided because it is the opposite of light, which is customarily considered the epitomy of good Feng Shui. Yet black also represents water, which, in turn, represents money. Black can, therefore, also be considered to be a good color.

White symbolizes death to the Chinese and is a color of mourning. Yet white is also symbolic of light, which is good Feng Shui.

In researching the definitive Feng Shui statement on color, I have discovered that the best approach is to go back to the basics of harmony and of Yin/Yang balance, and also to apply the philosophy of the elements, the latter involving an investigation of one's own element (depending upon one's year of birth), and then to select colors that complement it.

Thus, black represents water, red is fire, green is wood, white is metal, and yellow is earth.

For general Feng Shui purposes, it is safe to say that any color that does not seem out of harmony is acceptable. If you were born in the wood element year, for example, then you could use black as your dominant color. On the other hand, if you were born in a fire element year, then black could literally be deadly for you and you should avoid it. This is because water nourishes plants (wood), but extinguishes fire.

A knowledge of the traditional connotations of colors is also useful, as long as you also bear in mind the "elements approach" outlined above. Red, for instance, symbolizes happiness and is traditionally used at Chinese weddings. It is, therefore, a "safe" color to use to attract good fortune, but people whose element clashes with fire should not have too much of this color around them.

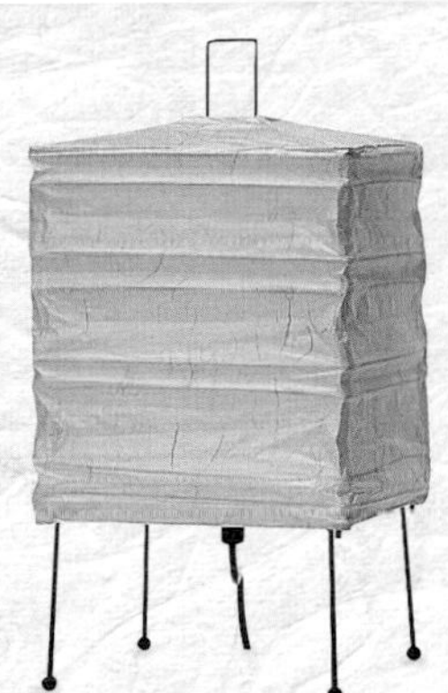

A soft, neutral lampshade gives an air of peace and tranquillity to a room.

Choose lamps with soft, pleasing colors that complement the corner of a room. A dark blue lamp is ideal for a north corner, because the blue equates with water.

FURNISHINGS

When choosing or arranging furniture, you should aim to stimulate healthy Chi flows by choosing shapes, colors, and styles that can be seen to correspond to the elements and sectors of the eight-sided Pa Kua.

When buying furniture, for example, do select colors and designs with Feng Shui in mind. A green armchair would be suitable for the wood corners of the eastern and southeastern sectors of the room. It is also more Yin and can, therefore, be used to balance out areas where there may be too much Yang. A heavier, more rounded armchair, upholstered in red, is very Yang and would be better suited to the southern corner of the room, or areas which require Yang energy, such as the darker corners or corners that represent the southwest or northeast.

If you are having furniture made to your own specification – a dining room table, for example, or chests, cupboards, and sideboards – it pays to follow Feng Shui dimensions. The favorable dimensions are reproduced opposite for easy reference. As well as using them to assess desk, dining table, and other furniture dimensions, they can also be applied to the size of doors, windows and even business cards. These auspicious dimensions are universally followed by the carpenters of Hong Kong and Taiwan, though it is not really clear how they came about. However, the Feng Shui ruler is freely used by Feng Shui practitioners to ensure Feng Shui luck.

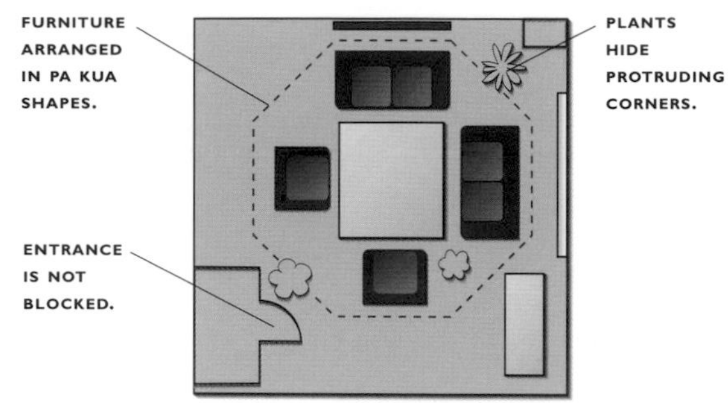

An ideal seating arrangement.

FURNITURE ARRANGEMENT

The arrangement of furniture in living areas affects the social life of the household, especially relationships with friends and relatives. The placement of sofas, chairs, and coffee tables can either enhance relationships or they can create conflicts. Good

These dining chairs are not suitable from a Feng Shui point of view. The bars on the back of the chair on the left create poison arrows.

Both of these armchairs represent the auspicious horseshoe shape, but the chair on the right is not as good because its armrests are not substantial.

AUSPICIOUS MEASUREMENTS

Auspicious dimensions exist for Yang dwellings (homes of the living) and Yin dwellings (residences of the dead). The dimensions given below are for Yang dwellings.

CHAI (MONEY LUCK)
BETWEEN 0 AND 2⅛ INCHES
BETWEEN 17 AND 19⅛ INCHES
BETWEEN 34 AND 36⅛ INCHES
BETWEEN 51 AND 53⅛ INCHES

VI (HELPFUL PEOPLE LUCK)
BETWEEN 6⅜ AND 8½ INCHES
BETWEEN 23⅜ AND 25½ INCHES
BETWEEN 40⅜ AND 42½ INCHES
BETWEEN 57⅜ AND 59½ INCHES

KWAN (CAREER AND POWER LUCK)
BETWEEN 8½ AND 10⅝ INCHES
BETWEEN 25½ AND 27⅝ INCHES
BETWEEN 42½ AND 44⅝ INCHES
BETWEEN 59½ AND 61⅝ INCHES

PUN (MONEY AND WEALTH LUCK)
BETWEEN 14¾ AND 17 INCHES
BETWEEN 31¾ AND 34 INCHES
BETWEEN 48¾ AND 51 INCHES
BETWEEN 65¾ AND 68 INCHES

This single armchair is acceptable as it has a good supporting back and armrests that support and encircle the occupant.

arrangements always ensure that none of the chairs or sofas have their backs to the door or entrance to the living room. Nor should the chairs be too close to the coffee table and other chairs; in general, arrangements should attempt to simulate the eight-sided Pa Kua. The L-shaped arrangement is actively discouraged, unless the furniture is placed against a corner of the room. This is because this shape resembles a poison arrow, which is not conducive to the smooth flow of Chi.

You should also avoid having doors opening onto furniture. This is because the flow of Chi into the room will be blocked. It is better to have the door opening onto an empty space.

Sofas with rounded backs are auspicious because they simulate the protective turtle.

This sofa is not so auspicious because its back is not very high and so would not provide a great deal of protection.

Cavalier
SHOES
BAILEY BANKS & BIDDLE
GODIVA

PART FOUR

FURTHER APPLICATIONS OF FENG SHUI

Chapter Ten

SUCCESS IN BUSINESS

There are several ways to use Feng Shui as a tool to enhance business success. These vary from methods aimed at increasing turnover at retail establishments – such as boutiques, restaurants, franchise outlets, and bank branches – to using special Compass School formulas for arranging office positions to improve the prosperity (or wealth-generating) luck of the business premises or offices.

Feng Shui features, when introduced into factories, often improve employee productivity and work flows. The business people of Hong Kong, Singapore, Malaysia, and Taiwan almost universally introduce Feng Shui features to their business establishments, and many would not make major structural or design changes without consulting a Feng Shui practitioner.

風水

IN HONG KONG, top businessmen and taxi drivers alike hold similiar reverence and respect for Feng Shui. The same holds true for the Chinese people of Taiwan, and increasingly, in recent years, of Singapore and Malaysia as well. The revival of interest in this ancient science has extended even to western-educated new generation scions who manage inherited businesses. Most acknowledge the potency of Feng Shui.

Tapping into the wisdom of this ancient science can be pleasantly rewarding. The great enticement is that very little up-front cost is required in the practice of Feng Shui. The harnessing of auspicious Feng Shui requires relatively insignificant investment in monetary terms. Nor does it require any major compromise of values or religious beliefs.

To a commercially minded person, therefore, having invested funds to start up a new business, it also makes sense to make the effort to tap into the Chi flows of the earth, if that is what it takes to harness a little bit of business advantage.

TAIWAN

In Taiwan's capital, Taipei, many high-rise buildings housing the corporate headquarters of large conglomerates incorporate Feng Shui features. Two themes that recur are the rounding off of corners and the use of large revolving doors. Rounding off corners is a friendly gesture designed to ensure that buildings do not create killing Chi for their neighbors. The sharp edges of multi-level buildings represent inauspicious poison arrows which, if pointed at the main entrance of another building, are certain to cause ill fortune, thereby inadvertently inviting retaliation.

Revolving doors are excellent purveyors of auspicious Chi flows, hence they are used at the entrance to buildings in preference to conventional hinged doors. Revolving entrances are also excellent for deflecting any killing Chi caused by poison arrows that may be hurting the main door. In London, revolving doors can be found at the north entrance to Harrods department store.

Minor but well-planned Feng Shui alterations such as increased lighting or a display of potted plants can greatly increase customer turnover in a restaurant.

THE PATH TO PROSPERITY

Feng Shui is concerned with the shapes and forms of the built-up environment, and no building can be assessed on its own as a solitary entity. Hence, in designing your own commercial structure or in assessing any building within which to place your office, shop, or showroom, it is important to examine how the building being assessed fits in with the other buildings around you.

Commercial buildings that form a disjointed and ill-planned jumble of varying heights, shapes, sizes, and forms create the kind of imbalance that is all too common in certain parts of any city. Fortunately, the ill effects of this kind of landscape can be neutralized by the generous planting of trees. The trees cause the imbalance to dissipate as the branches and leaves sway in the breeze.

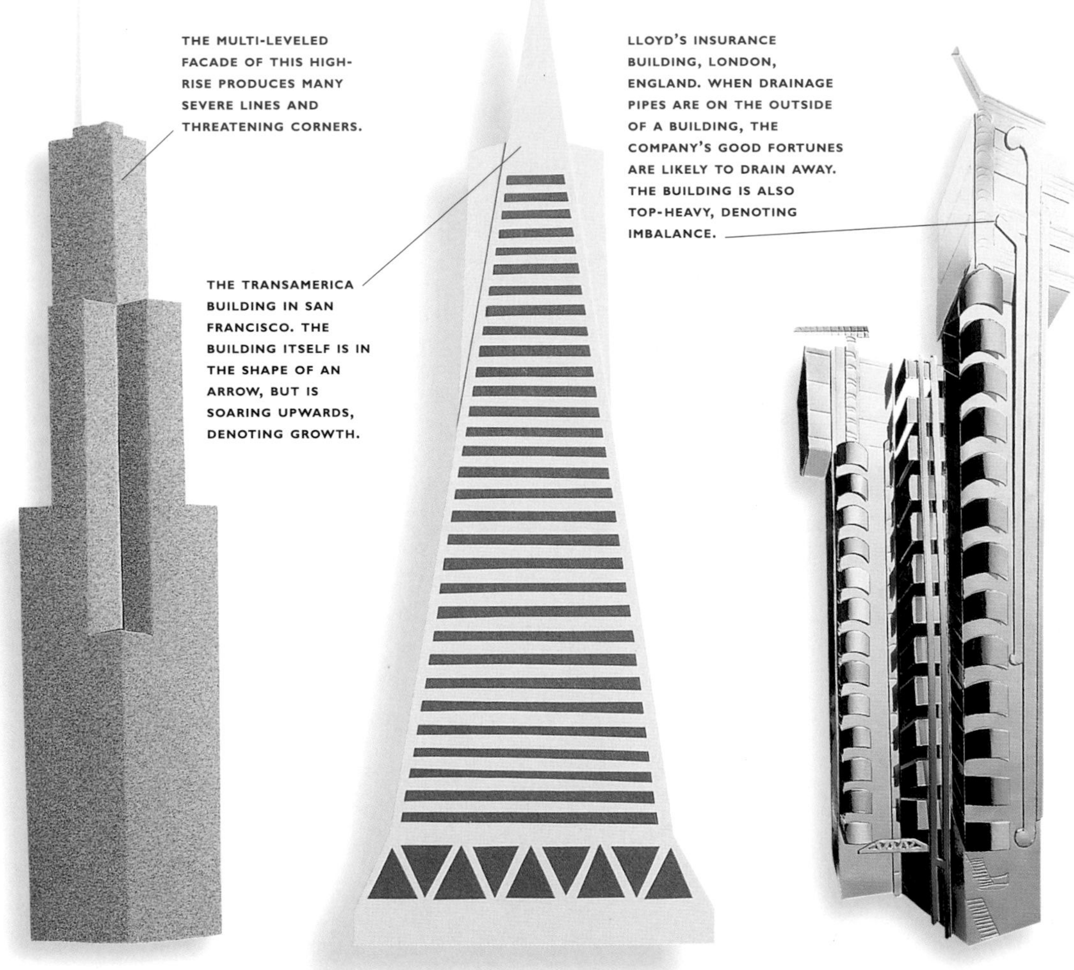

The designs of all these modern, multi-storey buildings reflect good and bad aspects of Feng Shui.

THE ROUNDED, SHELL-SHAPED ROOFS RESEMBLE THE COSMIC DRAGON.

Sydney Opera House in Australia is an example of modern architecture that is sympathetic to Feng Shui principles. It is also surrounded by the protective and auspicious water of Sydney Harbor.

Generous planting along these lines has helped to improve many parts of Kuala Lumpur, Malaysia's capital city, and is an important feature of prosperous Singapore. Malaysia is officially a Muslim country, but the fact that Feng Shui is widely practiced in the vibrant and fast growing capital is due to the multi-racial population, of which 30 percent are of Chinese origin.

The city has many wonderful examples of Feng Shui at work. One is the imposing Arab Malaysia Bank building, probably one of the most beautiful buildings in the city, but sited on a plot of land that directly faces a T-junction. Feng Shui practitioners know that main doors should never face such a junction. The owner of the building, although a Muslim, is also sensible and practical. Whether or not he believes in Feng Shui, he must have decided that there was nothing to lose in going with the flow. Thus, the building was positioned in a way that ensured the main entrance was not hit by the poison arrow of the oncoming road. The bank has gone from strength to strength.

THE CANNON AND THE CROSS

In Kuala Lumpur there is a fascinating story of a Feng Shui battle apparently being waged between two buildings. Some years ago, when a certain building – which we shall call Building A – was built, its architect designed two escalators that formed a huge cross in the foyer of the building. Unfortunately – and probably quite unintentionally – this cross adversely affected the business of the residents of Building B across the road. As their turnover declined, the sales manager at Building B called in a Feng Shui consultant, who diagnosed their problems as emanating from the cross on the other side of the road.

What could be done? How does one go about demolishing your neighbor's escalators? The Feng Shui consultant came up with an answer: "Use a cannon," he advised, which is how a cannon came to be installed just outside Building B, aimed directly at the cross (and thus the heart) of Building A. The result was that business at Building B improved, while that at Building A began to slide.

Now wise to Feng Shui considerations, the managers of Building A also called in an expert to fix matters. Unfortunately for them, the antique cannon had probably been fired at some time in its history – a bad omen, since such a cannon is regarded as being the more powerful for having tasted blood. All the Feng Shui expert could offer was the suggestion that a mirror be installed to reflect the cannon back.

Some Feng Shui tools, such as a cannon, can be used to divert killing Chi.

CHOOSING PREMISES

When looking for business premises, start by checking the overall Feng Shui of the building. Look out for poison arrows, obstacles, and inauspicious positions. Always check the characteristics of nearby roads, traffic directions, and neighboring buildings, and search for auspicious features, such as rivers, waterways, and hills.

Buildings that seem to be gently embraced by roads with slow moving traffic enjoy good Feng Shui, as do buildings that face a park or garden. Indeed, the presence of an empty space in front of the main entrance offers auspicious business luck, because good-luck Chi has a chance to settle and gather potency before entering the building.

This particular principle was deemed so important that senior managers at the Hong Kong Bank went to great pains to ensure that their Hong Kong head office would always have an empty space in front of it, thereby also enjoying an unencumbered view of the harbor. They achieved this by purchasing the land in front of the building and donating it to the government on condition that it remained undeveloped and was used only as a public space.

Trees and higher land or structures at the back of a building represent protection

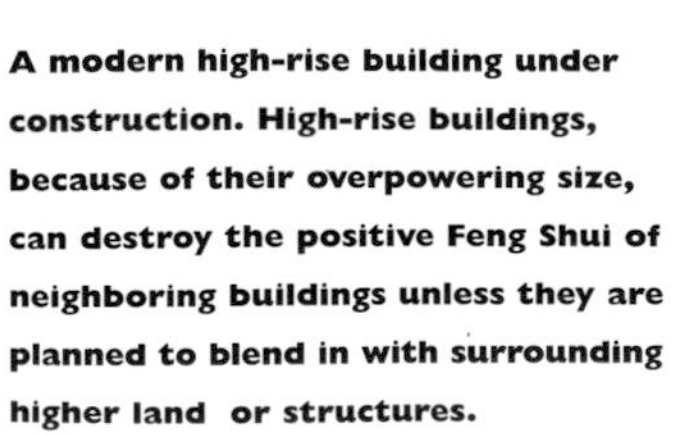

A modern high-rise building under construction. High-rise buildings, because of their overpowering size, can destroy the positive Feng Shui of neighboring buildings unless they are planned to blend in with surrounding higher land or structures.

The Hong Kong Bank (left in the picture). The Feng Shui of this massive building was improved by the open land in front of it.

while buildings on the left should be slightly higher than buildings on the right, thereby simulating the classical green dragon/white tiger configuration of the Form School of Feng Shui.

It is always useful to investigate the flow of roads and traffic moving around any building, as these offer indications of Chi flows in the vicinity of the office. Also examine the shapes and size of neighboring buildings – their heights and dimensions. If you are hemmed in by buildings larger and taller than yours, it is most inauspicious. If the land the building stands on is irregular in shape, make sure there are lights placed at the irregular corners to simulate balance.

APPROACH ROADS

Look particularly at the approach roads to an office building, and observe the direction of traffic flow. T-junctions are bad, but if there are several roads leading obliquely toward the building, and these are inclined gently downwards, it is believed to be very good Feng Shui, signifying that lucky Chi is being channeled toward the building. If the incline is too steep, the Chi becomes too strong and is then inauspicious.

Buildings that face a roundabout are also believed to enjoy good Feng Shui as the traffic brings circulating Chi flows toward the building. The effect is especially auspicious when several roads are connected to the roundabout.

Flyovers are not auspicious, as these are viewed as threatening to a building because of their resemblance to sharp knives. Sometimes the unlucky Chi is so serious it is better to move out. In the same way, buildings that face a crossroads are inauspicious. This serious Feng Shui defect can, however, be countered by planting a clump of trees to block off all views of the crossroads. Buildings facing Y-junctions and T-junctions should be scrupulously avoided.

Houses overlooking a roundabout (below) enjoy the benefits of positive Chi flows.

The outside curve of a road (above) can act as a scythe, cutting away at good fortune.

When buildings suffer from being in inauspicious positions, or when they are the subject of an offending poison arrow, all the offices within the entire building are adversely affected, although not to the same degree. Generally, the higher up the building one goes, the more the pernicious effect diminishes.

By the same token, it is possible for the effects of bad Feng Shui to be magnified on lower floors. For example, it is a very bad practice to site desks under exposed structural beams on the lower floors of a multi-storey building, since all the structural beams on every floor above will be pressing down on the unfortunate person sitting at the bottom. It is for this reason that the company's decision-makers must never have their desks situated directly beneath a structural beam.

DOORS AND MAIN ENTRANCES

Whether or not a building is auspicious or inauspicious depends to a very large extent on the Feng Shui characteristics of its main entrance. This must be in balance with the building itself, and should preferably face auspicious directions. The rules that govern the positioning of houses generally apply to buildings as well. If the building belongs to your company, position it to suit your horoscope or that of your boss. If you are renting office space within the building, use the guidelines on general positioning, which recommend facing south for good luck. Another lucky direction for businesses is southeast, which is representative of wealth. Ideally, the main door should face a direction that is auspicious for the owner or chief executive of the company, based on his or her year of birth.

From the main entrance to the building, we now move to the main entrance to your office within that building. There are certain guidelines to follow and certain dangers to avoid. For example, the main door of your office should never open directly onto a toilet. Neither should it directly face another door, as this forms a straight line, causing Chi to move too swiftly through the office. The main door should not face an open window, since this encourages vital Chi to fly out the window. This same rule applies to the back entrance to the office.

La Pyramide, Louvre, Paris. This represents excellent Feng Shui as it looks like a crystal object, symbolizing the earth, and is thus excellently placed in the center of the museum. It also brings Yang sunlight into the Yin museum.

DOOR POSITIONS: A CHECKLIST

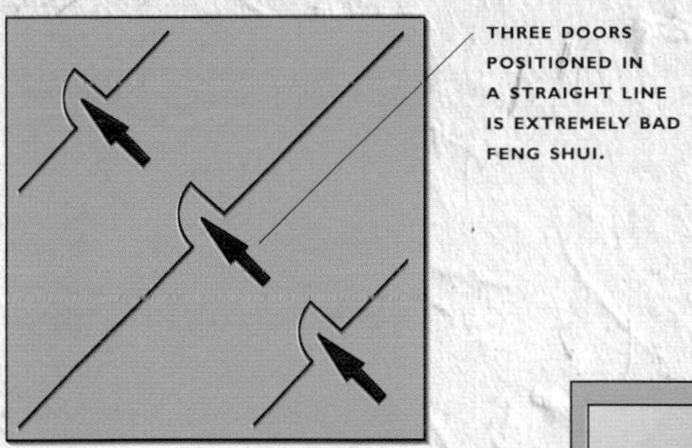

THREE DOORS POSITIONED IN A STRAIGHT LINE IS EXTREMELY BAD FENG SHUI.

Here, Chi flows too quickly through the office.

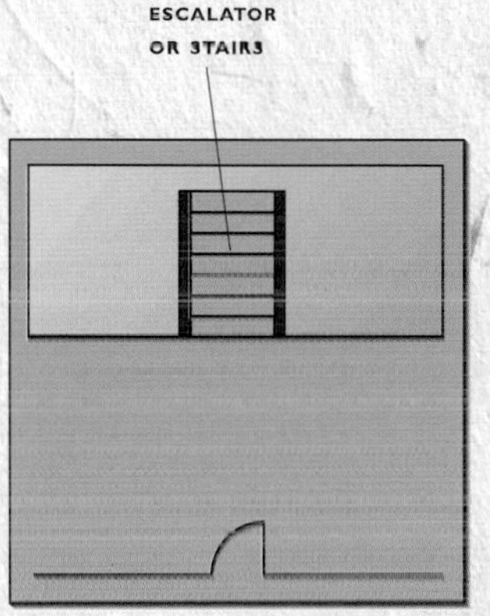

ESCALATOR OR STAIRS

Stairs or escalators channel Chi away from the foyer.

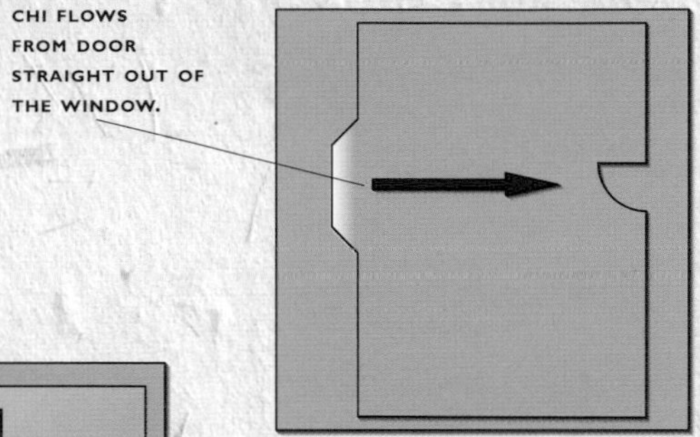

CHI FLOWS FROM DOOR STRAIGHT OUT OF THE WINDOW.

Doors facing windows allow Chi to escape.

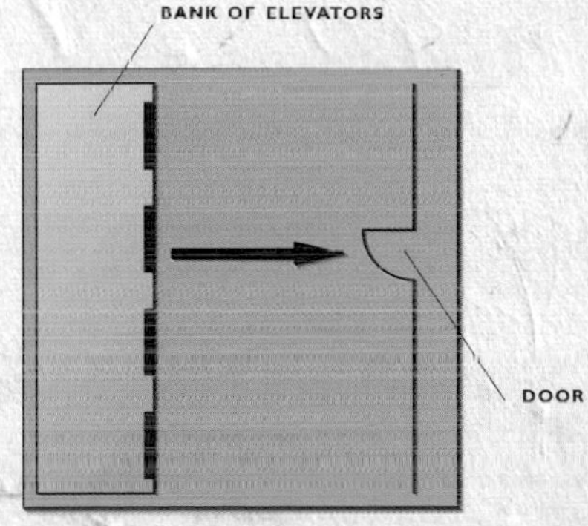

BANK OF ELEVATORS

DOOR

Elevators will carry Chi away from the entrance.

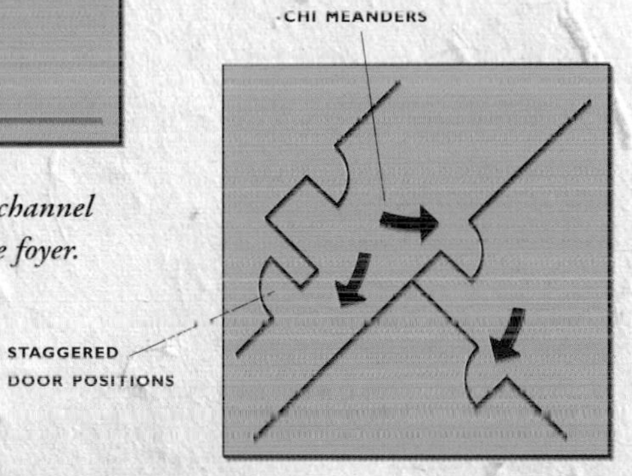

CHI MEANDERS

STAGGERED DOOR POSITIONS

A staggered arrangement allows Chi to meander.

- The main office should not face an escalator that in turn faces the building's main entrance. This is bad Feng Shui because luck seeps out. Nor should the main office door face a bank of elevators.
- Do not locate your main office door at the end of a long corridor, as this will act like a poison arrow sending harmful Shar Chi directly into your office. Your business will be badly hurt.
- If your main office door faces another main office door, make sure the doors align perfectly; otherwise, you will quarrel with your neighbor.
- Doors within an office should not be designed to form a straight line, but should be staggered so as to "meander."
- The foyer area should not be too cramped. If it is, use mirrors to enhance the feeling of space. Mirrors should not directly face the entrance, however.
- Make sure the foyer is well lit. Poor lighting causes Chi to stagnate or die.
- If there is a receptionist stationed in the foyer, he or she should not directly face the main door. It is also a good idea to have a wall divider in the foyer that conceals the inside office.

OFFICE LAYOUTS

All the basic principles that apply to the layout of a home also apply to the design of an office. As with residential dwellings, the process starts with clearing and protecting business premises from the effects of killing Chi caused by all sorts of pointed and hostile structures. Start by protecting the front doors and blocking off hidden poison arrows.

Then start investigating how the individual offices should be laid out, what design features ought to be incorporated into the plan and what features ought to be avoided. Consider the dimensions and shapes of the various rooms, the position of the managers' offices, the arrangement of desks and furniture, the flow of traffic in large open areas, and the most ideal locations for each of the different departments.

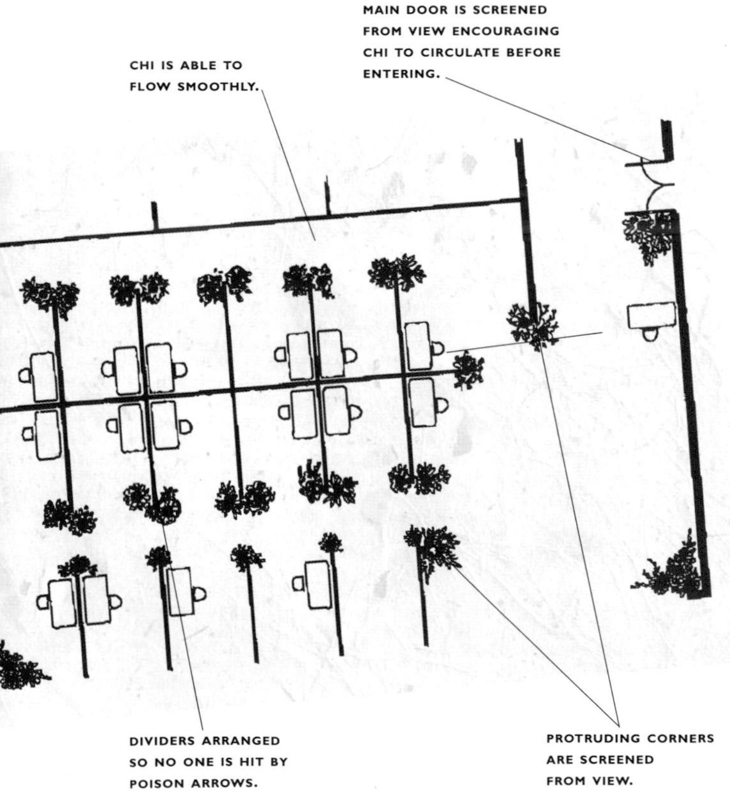

Your Feng Shui analysis should stress features and positions that promote good interpersonal relationships between employees and managers. If offices suffer from the pernicious effect of bad Shar Chi, incessant bickering and a great deal of counterproductive argument will be the result. Health problems and high levels of absenteeism could also result. Harmony and balance are important concepts that, when applied to the place of work, will promote an environment of cooperative goodwill, enhancing productivity and attracting auspicious good fortune for the businesses and companies that are housed in workplaces designed along these lines.

Office layouts should be designed to facilitate the auspicious flow of Chi. Dividers and desks should be placed in such a way as to ensure that nobody directly faces a sharp corner. Plants are vital for disguising poison arrows and for reducing their effects. They are also very useful for balancing the Yin/Yang elements, bringing nature's materials into a largely man-made environment.

Protruding corners are inauspicious, being comparable to sharp knives or hostile fingers pointing directly at the person they hit. Also, beware corners that are directed at important filing cabinets or the door of the manager's office. There are several ways to cure the bad Chi of such corners: using full-length mirrors on both sides of the corner has the effect of making it "disappear," or you can hang a faceted crystal ball from the corner. This dissolves bad Chi coming out of the corner and effectively shields the occupants of the room. If you have several corners like these in the office, it is a good idea to vary the treatment.

This layout shows good Feng Shui features. There are no stand-alone columns to block Chi flows, and the inner office door does not open directly from the main door.

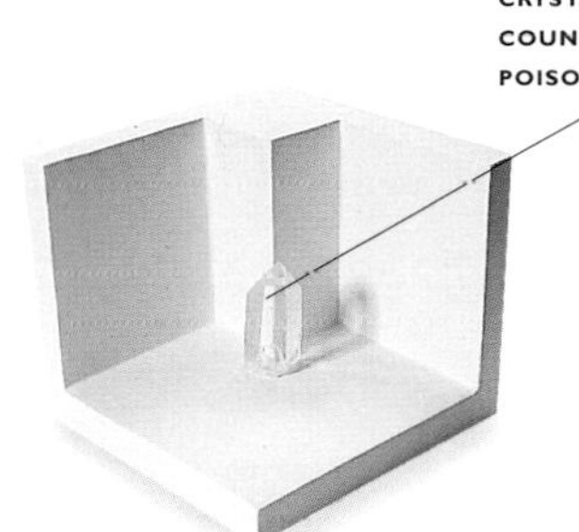

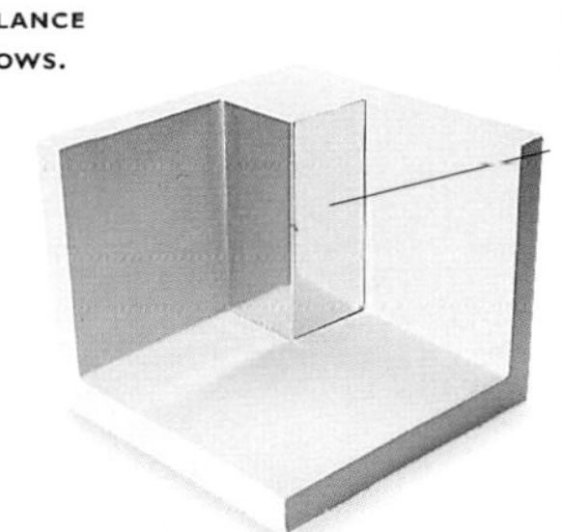

Poison arrows created by protruding corners must be disguised to dissolve the Shar Chi. Here, three well-tried remedies are illustrated – plants, crystals, and mirrors.

The best way to deal with exposed beams in the office is to camouflage them all with false ceilings, but you must take note of where they are and ensure that you do not place desks or chairs directly under them. Such beams resemble blockages that will severely affect the flow of Chi within the office. Where the beams appear in a manager's room, they should be treated immediately or his entire department might suffer. Beams can also affect creativity and cause headaches. Try to avoid them at all costs, and, if this is not possible, keep them well hidden from view.

RECEPTION AREAS

Reception areas should ideally be well lit and spacious. Poor lighting will encourage the Chi entering the office to stagnate and die, even before it has the chance to enter the rest of the business premises. If foyers are cramped, try using mirrors to give the feeling of space. Mirrors should not, however, directly face the entrance. Sofas or other seats and reception counters should not face the door directly. Dividers placed opposite the door will force the Chi coming into the office to meander, thereby slowing it down and encouraging it to settle before entering the rest of the premises.

RECEPTIONIST SHOULD SIT WITH HIS OR HER BACK TO A SOLID WALL FOR SUPPORT.

A SCREEN PLACED OPPOSITE THE DOOR ENCOURAGES CHI ENTERING THE ROOM TO CURVE AROUND IT AND SLOW DOWN.

A receptionist stationed in the foyer should be seated away from the direct view of the main door, out of the path of the Chi entering the office.

MANAGERS' OFFICES AND BOARDROOMS

The fortunes of the office are greatly influenced by the Feng Shui of the manager's office. If you are the manager, do make sure your room follows Feng Shui guidelines if you wish to enjoy good fortune.

Correct desk placement plays a large part in enhancing office Feng Shui. Examine these detailed guidelines:

- the main manager's office should ideally be located deep inside the building, but not at the end of a long corridor
- if the office is L-shaped, correct it with mirrors or lights
- deal with projecting corners, beams, or columns immediately.

FOUNTAINS AND AQUARIUMS

It is a good idea to activate the wealth sector of the office – the southeast corner – by introducing water into the area in the form of an aquarium with live fish to symbolize growth, or a small revolving fountain to represent continuous turnover, because water creates wood, which is the ruling element of the sector.

Fresh, flowing water energizes the office and brings prosperity.

BAD DESK PLACEMENT

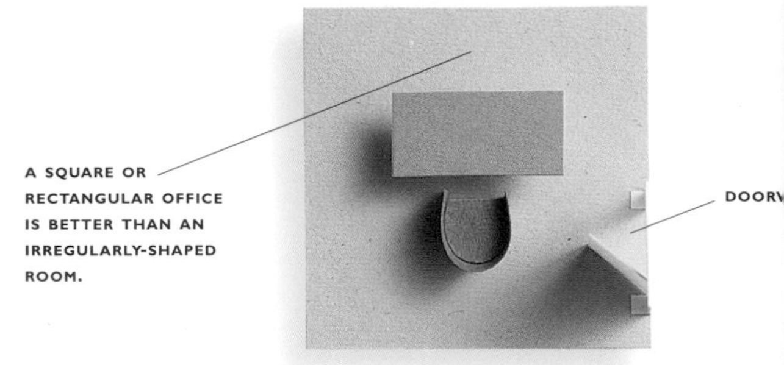

Never sit too near to the door; you will be continually distracted.

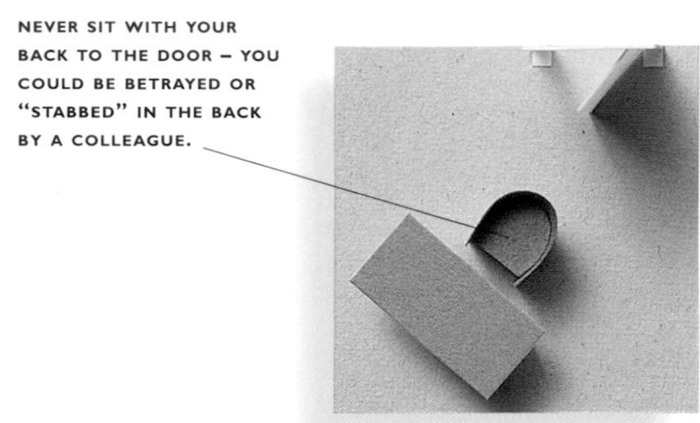

The door behind the chair creates a dangerous poison arrow and leaves you vulnerable to office politics.

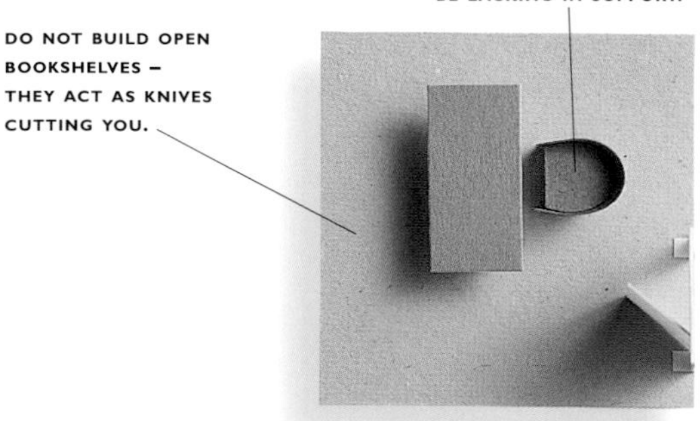

With the door behind or beside you, your concentration is affected and your authority is undermined.

GOOD DESK PLACEMENT

The best position is in the corner opposite the door, where the two walls act as a protector.

Try to sit facing the door at whatever angle you like, but make sure none of the corners are cutting at you.

Try not to face the door directly; the incoming Chi could be overpowering.

BOARDROOMS

When designing boardrooms, be sure to protect the chairman's position. This should preferably be away from the entrance, and his or her back should be properly supported by a solid wall. Do not have too many doors opening into the boardroom, as it leads to quarrels and misunderstandings and is not conducive to harmony. Since boardrooms are used for important negotiations, it is a good idea for the chief negotiator to face his or her most auspicious direction as indicated by the Pa-Kua Lo-Shu formula. The boardroom then becomes a source of luck for the business.

Another useful Feng Shui tip on boardrooms is to examine which element is best for the chairman or the person who regularly uses the room. This is obtained by checking their ruling element in the year of their birth. If water is good for them, install a fish tank for luck, designing its location in a way that merges with the decor. If fire is the element that brings them luck, use red as part of the decor. If wood is good, incorporate plenty of plants. If metal is good, use a wind chime. If earth is good, use a crystal.

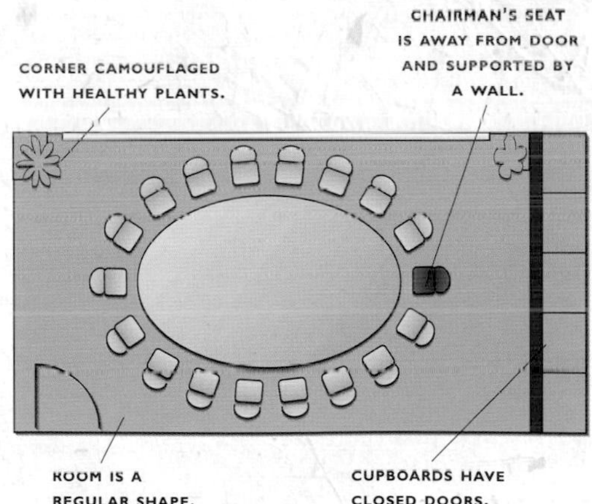

An example of a good boardroom arrangement that is spacious and well-balanced.

ACTIVATING THE WEALTH SECTOR

Every aspect of your business that involves cash and profitability should be located in the money or wealth sector (the southeastern corner of the building). This is where you should place the cash register or accounts office.

Feng Shui masters advise using old Chinese coins to activate this sector. Coins have always been a symbol of prosperity in China, and the usage of old and antique coins as amulets and for Feng Shui purposes is fairly widespread, even up until the present day. Ancient Chinese coins are round and have a square hole in the center. The method involves tying three old coins together with auspicious red thread, then attaching them to the top of your invoice and order books to attract excellent business and wealth luck.

Using water is a popular method of activating the wealth sector. Fish swimming in an aquarium will further encourage good Chi flows.

There are several variations of this practice. You can use eight coins to magnify the effect. You can also hang replica coins on the wall of the sales manager's office, or you can display them on your desk. Proprietors of retail outlets can also create a pathway of eight stepping stones, designed in the shape of coins, leading up to the shop's main entrance in a symbolic gesture in the hope of attracting wealth to the front door.

MODERN EQUIVALENTS

If you are unable to find these old coins, modern coins will do just as well. Attach them to red material and display them above your invoice books and diaries. Alternatively, you could substitute them with a photograph or image of coins.

I activate my southeastern corner with a blue-colored bowl lined with red velvet and filled with small change left over from my travels.

Good-luck coins tied together with auspicious red thread should be hung in the sales office or near a cash register to attract wealth to your business enterprise.

WATER FOR WEALTH

Water represents money and signifies the flow of wealth. To activate this symbol of prosperity, focus on the flow of water as it passes near your home. If you live in an apartment, relate the flow of water to the whole building. Differentiate between "big water," which generally describes rivers, lakes, and seas, and "small water," or artificial ponds and household drains. To activate the wealth luck of both big and small water, you should follow these two rules:

- make sure that the water – rivers, ponds, or drains – is in full view of the main front door; water flowing past the back of the property suggests missed opportunities
- make sure that the water flows past the main door in an auspicious direction.

These guidelines are based on the Water Dragon formula, which offers auspicious directions based on the direction of the main front door.

Water should flow from right to left for homes with main doors directly facing the following compass directions:

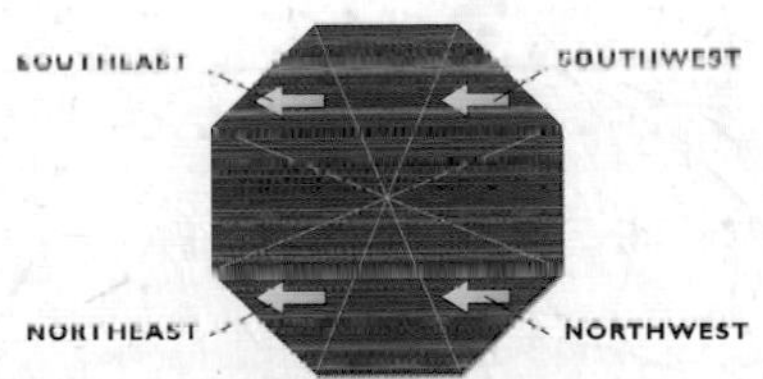

Water should flow from left to right for homes with main doors directly facing the remaining compass directions:

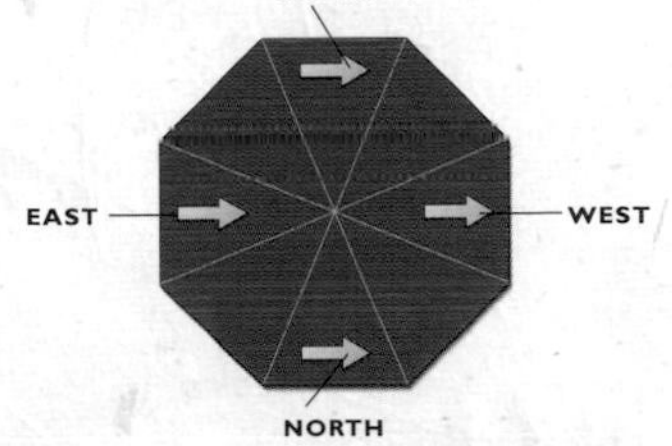

The direction in which water flows past your property affects your wealth luck.

Positioning a mirror to reflect the cash register will increase business turnover.

Another method of enhancing business turnover, especially of retail establishments, is to focus your Feng Shui techniques on the cash register. Make sure that it is not located where it faces a toilet or kitchen. Ideally, it should be near the main doorway, but not directly facing it. It should be backed by a solid wall for protection. It is a good idea to install a mirror on the side wall, so that it reflects the cash register. This represents a doubling of turnover.

An alternative method is to hang two flutes linked by a red thread above the cash register. The mouthpiece of the flutes should be at the bottom, and the flutes should slant towards each other, thereby simulating the Pa Kua shape. This channels prosperity towards the cash register. The flutes encourage Chi to flow upwards and to settle around the area of the cash register, thereby causing it to "fill with money."

FENG SHUI FOR EVERY BUSINESS

One method of enhancing the prosperity of your business is to activate the element with which it is associated.

FIERY RESTAURANT DECOR

If you are engaged in the restaurant trade, try to concentrate especially on getting the Feng Shui of the kitchen right. Restaurants that have a red decor tend to do well because this color complements the natural fire element of the business. Well-lit restaurants also have the power to pull in the customers – perhaps because lights also belong to the element of fire.

Dimly-lit restaurants seldom do as well – but do differentiate between a restaurant and a bar, which belongs to the water element. In such cases the color red, and bright lights, would be unsuitable. Instead, the complementary color to use is black or dark blue. Hence, it is preferable that such establishments are dimly lit.

Red decor in a restaurant is lucky.

Restaurants with wall mirrors, symbolizing the doubling of customers, also do well, as do restaurants that display live fish (for eating) in a glass tank, though these must be placed in either the north (water) or eastern and southeastern (wood) sectors of the restaurant's dining area.

Finally, it is auspicious for restaurants to display large figurines depicting happiness and a full tummy. It is for this reason that Chinese restaurants often display a large (sometimes life-size) statue of the laughing Buddha, complete with his fat stomach.

EARTH AND REAL ESTATE

If you are in the business of buying and selling houses and apartments, if you are engaged in the development of real estate, or if you are an architect or contractor, then the element representing your business is earth. You should therefore try to activate the earth sectors of your office. These are either the center of the office or the southwestern and northeastern corners. Locate people crucial to your business in these corners and activate the earth element in these sectors with natural quartz crystals or with carvings of marble and other forms of stone.

WATER AND MONEY TRANSACTIONS

Water is the element of those whose business involves dealing with cash and money – banking, insurance, money-changing, and so on. Water is symbolized by the colors black or blue. Such companies do well if they incorporate these colors into their decor or logo. Their business premises should be softly-lit, and the decor should include paintings with a watery theme that are placed in the northern corner of the office. Also, because metal produces water, wind chimes are an excellent enhancement. Other businesses represented by water include trading, shipping, and also the travel industry.

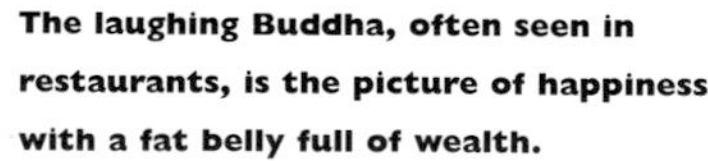

The laughing Buddha, often seen in restaurants, is the picture of happiness, with a fat belly full of wealth.

Jewellers will prosper if they activate their western corners with metallic artefacts.

CRAFTED IN METAL

If yours is a jewellery business, your element is metal and the use of wind chimes would be ideal for your business. Activate the western and north-western corners of your establishment. Do not use red in your decor because fire destoys metal, but do use the three coins method to stimulate business. Other examples of metal businesses are mining companies, engineering firms, car assemblers, and machinery and equipment enterprises.

WOODWORKING

Businesses that fall into the wood-element category are forestry, farming, paper production, horticulture, gardening, lumber merchants, furniture-makers, and sawmills. The wood directions are east and southeast. Place live or artificial plants in these corners. Water is also an acceptable enhancer because water produces wood and is, therefore, the complementary element.

LOGOS AND SIGNS

The same principles should apply to your logo and sign which are considered vital elements of the overall Feng Shui of a business. The dimensions of signs should follow the general Feng Shui precepts of balance and harmony. Attention to auspicious dimensions will also increase prosperity.

In selecting colors for logos and signs, Feng Shui experts recommend an analysis of the proprietor's element and the use of a color that is compatible. Thus, if the proprietor was born in a year whose element was wood, then red, the color of fire, would be good because wood creates fire.

When choosing the shape of a logo, there are no hard or fast rules, but some shapes are more auspicious than others. Anything that seems unbalanced or incomplete, or that represents an inauspicious symbol, should be avoided. Crosses and triangles are therefore not recommended; nor are arrows that point downwards. Circles and squares are, however, considered auspicious.

Appropriate animal symbolism can be auspicious. Dragons are often used by the Chinese in their logos, as they symbolize power, authority, vitality and courage. The phoenix, tortoise, lion, bat and deer are also considered to be good luck, as they represent continuity and strength, determination and material wealth.

Consider activating your wood element if you are in the farming business.

CASE STUDIES – A TALE OF TWO BANKS

Just about everyone in Hong Kong believes in, and practices, Feng Shui. Behind every high-rise building, there is a Feng Shui story to tell or a Feng Shui reason that accounts for its principal design features. Two prominent examples are the head office of the Hong Kong Bank and the Bank of China building, both of which are modern and striking structures – as well as being the kind of buildings that attract controversy.

When the Bank of China building was first completed, its prismatic facade, featuring large crosses and angles (formed by structural steelwork), was inevitably viewed with suspicion. Many felt that the building had bad Feng Shui, and that its many angles would cause poison arrow problems for other buildings in the vicinity. Many said that the structure that would be the most badly affected by the poison arrows would be the adjacent Governor's Residence, which (it is said) used to enjoy excellent Feng Shui.

Several others, however, using sophisticated methods and calculations based on the building's position and its "natal chart," maintain that the building enjoys very auspicious Feng Shui. The building is located in an area of busy traffic flow, and several flyovers on Cotton Tree Drive and Garden Road cross the front and back of the building. In Feng Shui terms, roads and flyovers are like rivers. If the curves of a flyover bend towards a building, they are likened to a blade or a scythe cutting into the building and bringing inauspicious Chi. In this case, however, the curves embrace the building, and resemble a river meandering slowly around it. Why? Because traffic lights on the roads

The large crosses and angles of the Bank of China were thought to create very bad Feng Shui, but this seems to have been counterbalanced by the protective Chi flows along the arms of the roads that encircle and embrace the building.

slow down the traffic, thereby ensuring that Chi approaching the building does not dissipate. The flyovers, therefore, represent a benevolent configuration, bringing good fortune to the building.

The fortunes of the nearby Hong Kong Bank – whose building stands close by – have always been closely allied to the economic fortunes of Hong Kong as a whole. Many stories surround the two stone lions that guard the entrance to the building. It is widely believed that the excellent Feng Shui of the old Hong Kong Bank building contributed to the prosperity of the whole community, so that when the decision was made to demolish the old building in 1981 and replace it with a new building, residents voiced their concern. Some attributed the collapse of the Hong Kong stock market in 1982–83 to the construction of the new building.

When the new and forward-looking building was completed and inaugurated in July, 1985, the colony's Feng Shui masters examined its natal chart and the physical surroundings in detail before pronouncing their approval. Based on both numerology calculations and the building's physical surroundings, it is now regarded as auspicious. Besides sitting in an auspicious dragon location, it also faces Statue Square, a place where auspicious Chi gathers and accumulates. The nearby Victoria Harbor also helps to accumulate Chi in the area. Meanwhile, the buildings alongside it – the Standard Chartered Bank building, the Princes Building, the Legco Building and the old Bank of China building – all act as dragons and tigers to form a most auspicious configuration. Traffic from Des Voeux Road flows slowly past, bringing good Chi.

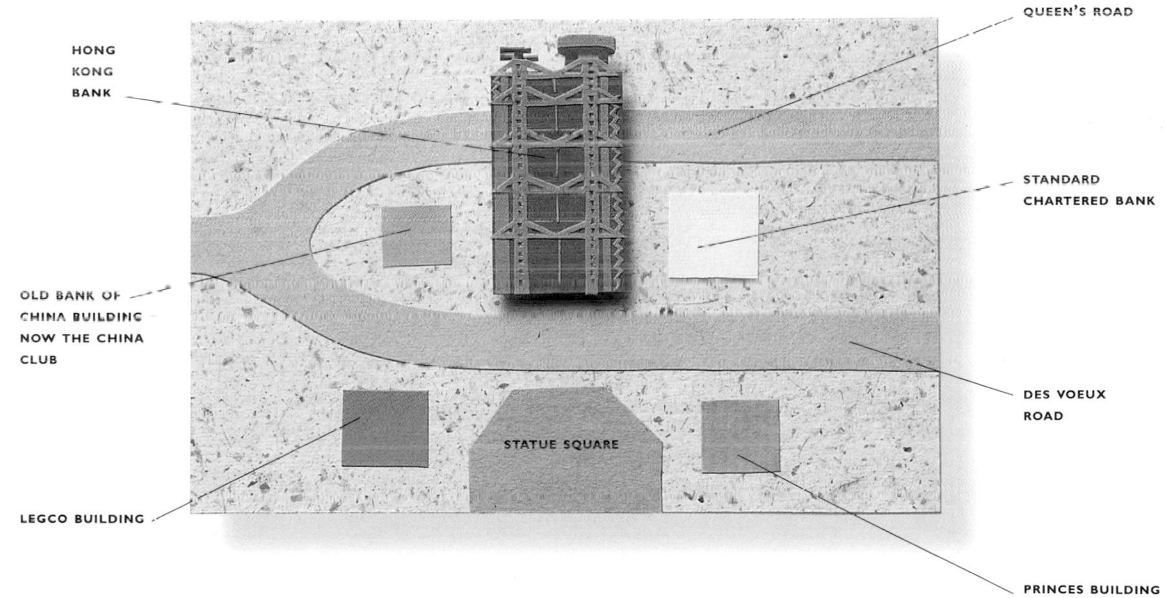

The Hong Kong Bank has met with approval from Feng Shui practitioners. The intersection of gently curved roads and the open park opposite the main entrance have enhanced its favorable Feng Shui.

Chapter Eleven

CAREER SUCCESS

As a businesswoman with a career to nurture, I have taken a strong interest in Feng Shui formulas for enhancing career prospects. Over the years, I have tried all the various formulas and methods recommended by experts, faithfully observing the outcomes to detect the flow of luck and the subtle changes I hoped for. This "testing out" of the recommended changes over time has made it possible for me to observe what works and what does not and, more importantly, which methods seem the most powerful. You are strongly advised to take a similar approach. If career success is what you want, follow the recommendations given in this chapter and success should quickly follow.

First you should focus on your bedroom. Refer to the Pa-Kua Lo-Shu formula on compass directions *(see pages 98–103)* to obtain your four most auspicious directions, and then make certain that both the location of your bedroom and the direction of your head when you are sleeping conform.

Also, check the element of your bedroom sector, and use element analysis, aided by your knowledge of the productive and destructive cycles, to enhance good luck in the bedroom. To do this, first subdivide your entire house or apartment into eight sectors, with each corner representing one of the Pa Kua directions. Find the corresponding element symbolized by the direction in which your bedroom is located.

If it is located in the northern sector of your home, then the element of your bedroom is that of water, in which case a painting of a water scene would be very auspicious. If your bedroom is located in the east wing of your house, then its element is wood – and luck in the bedroom can then be enhanced by introducing plants, or pictures of plants, and flowers.

Wood should be placed in the eastern sector of a room.

The creative use of Feng Shui in the home and office has been shown to be a contributing factor in career success.

IMPROVING YOUR SLEEPING POSITION

Focusing on the bedroom also requires analysis of your bed location. This enables the good luck Chi to flow into your head even as you sleep, thereby attracting success to flow toward you.

Make certain your bed is positioned so that you sleep facing the door. If you sleep with your back to the door, you will be symbolically encouraging people to work against you behind your back. Do not sleep with your head directly pointed at the door, either, because if you do, all your advancement luck will stagnate and die.

If you sleep facing an adjoining toilet or bathroom, you will lie directly in the path of the ill-fated Chi coming from the toilet and hence encounter severe problems at the office. This is because the Chi from the toilet is too powerfully Yin, and it weakens your Yang energy, which is so vital for career success. It goes without saying that the toilet should not be in the northern sector, or this will flush your career prospects away.

You must never sleep under a beam or near a protruding corner, or you can expect to be blamed for mistakes and for colleagues to be quarrelsome and bosses to be hostile. Worst of all, you can expect to suffer from severe migraine.

The position of the dresser in the bedroom also influences career progress, because this is where early morning Chi first affects a person. If you face your best direction when you get dressed each morning, the energy flows created will be positive, and they will have a positive impact on your work. However, you must also remember the taboos of Feng Shui – the mirror on your dresser should not face the bed or be at the foot of a bed.

Make sure your bedroom is well lit if you read or work there. Place a bright light in the career corner of your room (the northern sector). Do not put a plant in this sector since a plant here represents wood, which exhausts the water of the north. Likewise, anything representing earth (such as natural crystals, gemstones, and so on) will be detrimental to the career corner, because earth is

BUSINESS TRIPS

Carry a small compass with you wherever you go, especially if you expect to be negotiating. Also, whenever possible, sit facing your best direction in order to achieve success.

Once you have calculated your four auspicious directions using your Kua number *(see pages 100–101)* memorize them and use them in all your important business discussions.

Although natural crystals are beneficial in many aspects of daily living, they should never be used in the northern sector because they are detrimental to the career corner. They symbolize earth, which is believed to destroy the water element of this sector.

Copper or brass wind chimes can be used to enhance the career corner, but they should have hollow tubes.

believed to destroy water. But metal or gold is good for it, as metal produces water and, indeed, will enhance the career corner. Thus copper or brass wind chimes hung in the northern corner would be ideal enhancing tools.

All this may seem to be somewhat troublesome and inconvenient, but you will find your efforts to be well worthwhile. Once the bed and the dressing table are set up, observe whether your fortunes at work improve. You should expect, over a period of about three months, to find that your working life becomes more pleasant and that you are achieving more. When this happens you will know that you have successfully tapped into your good directions. If you feel that the results are discouraging, or you sense increased hostility at the office or you see opportunities passing you by, you should check your directions once more. You could have miscalculated, or even overlooked a hidden poison arrow, such as the protruding corner of a piece of furniture which could be pointing at your bed while you are sleep.

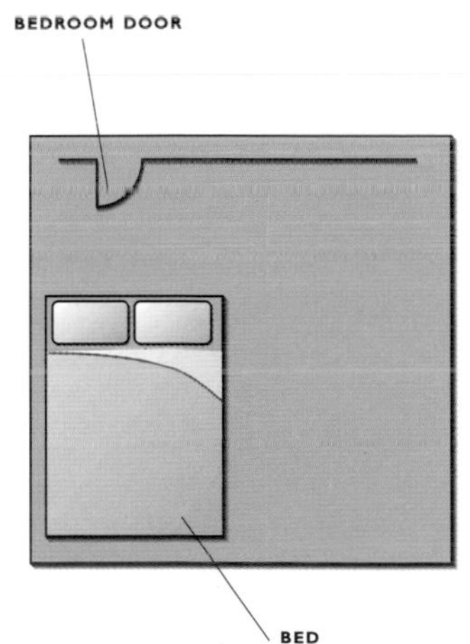

Do not sleep with your head directly pointed at the door.

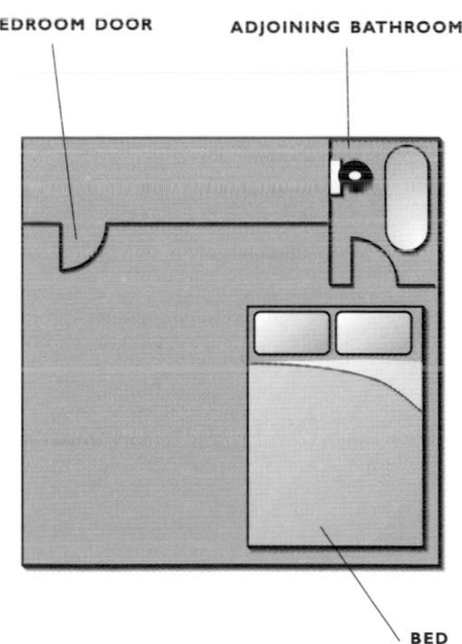

It is also inadvisable to sleep facing a toilet or a bathroom.

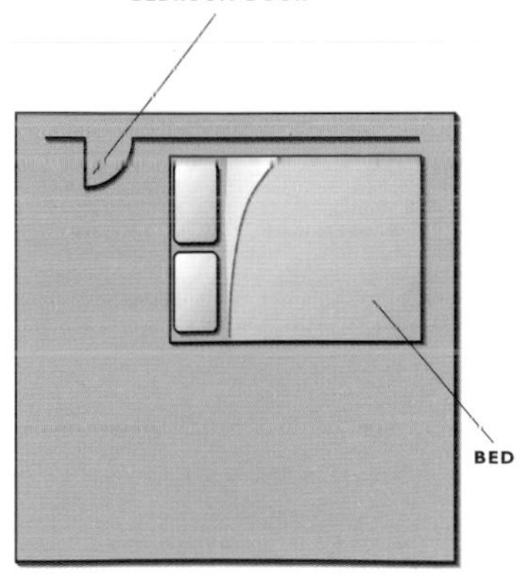

Do not sleep with your back to the door. This is bad Feng Shui.

IMPROVING YOUR OFFICE – A CASE STUDY

In early 1982 I had to relocate my office due to an internal transfer. The move required me to vacate a very nice corner office on the eleventh floor to a less auspicious, elongated room on the tenth floor, a room that had originally been occupied by someone whose fortunes with the company had left much to be desired.

My career had been pleasantly rewarding. Work had been more than satisfying and my boss was growing increasingly happy with my performance. Prospects for the future looked promising, and the dreamed of higher echelons of management seemed enticingly within reach. I was, therefore, worried about moving to a seemingly less auspicious location and environment.

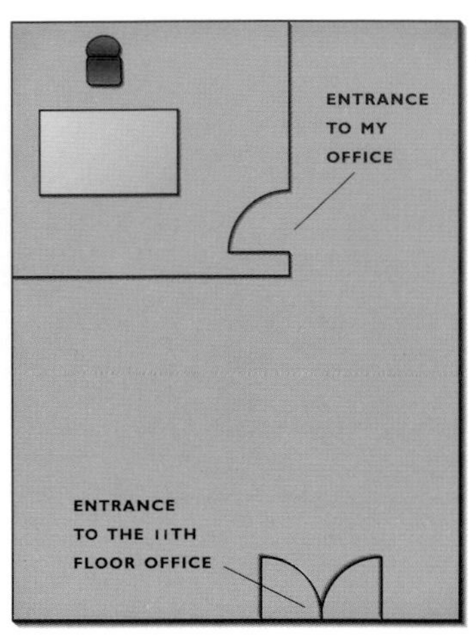

My office on the 11th floor was located across the corner from the entrance and was thus excellent Feng Shui.

The layout of my new room and its built-in furniture seemed awkward, as I would have to sit with my back to the door – and that symbolizes being stabbed in the back. I did not want any of that happening to me, so I consulted my Feng Shui advisor and together we transformed the room into something so lucky for me that my life was to change dramatically.

Indeed, the changes to my office were such auspicious Feng Shui that from day one I felt wonderful. I loved my new office and I looked forward to going to work each day. What is more, within three months of moving in, I was promoted to the position of Managing Director of Hong Leong Credit – becoming the first woman in Malaysia to become the Chief Executive Officer of a public listed company. Those were halcyon days indeed and, towards the third quarter of the same year, I was also offered the job of Managing Director of Dao Heng Bank, the group's new bank acquisition in Hong Kong – now becoming the first woman in Asia to be appointed to the position of Chief Executive Officer of a bank.

The move to another country and into another environment was definitely very far from my mind when I was so innocently designing my new room. But that is what happens when you start to activate your career luck through Feng Shui.

The models on the next page show the before and after arrangement of my office. The long office has been effectively utilized to create a work area (the desk) and a social area (the sofa), with the work area being made more important by raising my office chair on a platform *(see the tips for desk dimensions on pages 198–199).* With regard to the entrance door, the desk is in an excellent position. Various Feng Shui enhancing tools were also introduced to the office, including plants, both real and artificial, to improve the wealth corner and create good Chi flows, and a bright light to enhance the career corner. Not shown on the plan are two other auspicious features that I included in the office. These were a painting of a mountain at sunrise and a false ceiling that was installed to ensure that I did not have any exposed beams above me.

OPPOSITE *By changing the layout of my new office with the help of a Feng Shui consultant, I looked forward to going to work each day, and only three months after moving in I was promoted to Managing Director of Hong Leong Credit – becoming the first woman in the country to be made Chief Executive Officer of a public listed company.*

BEFORE

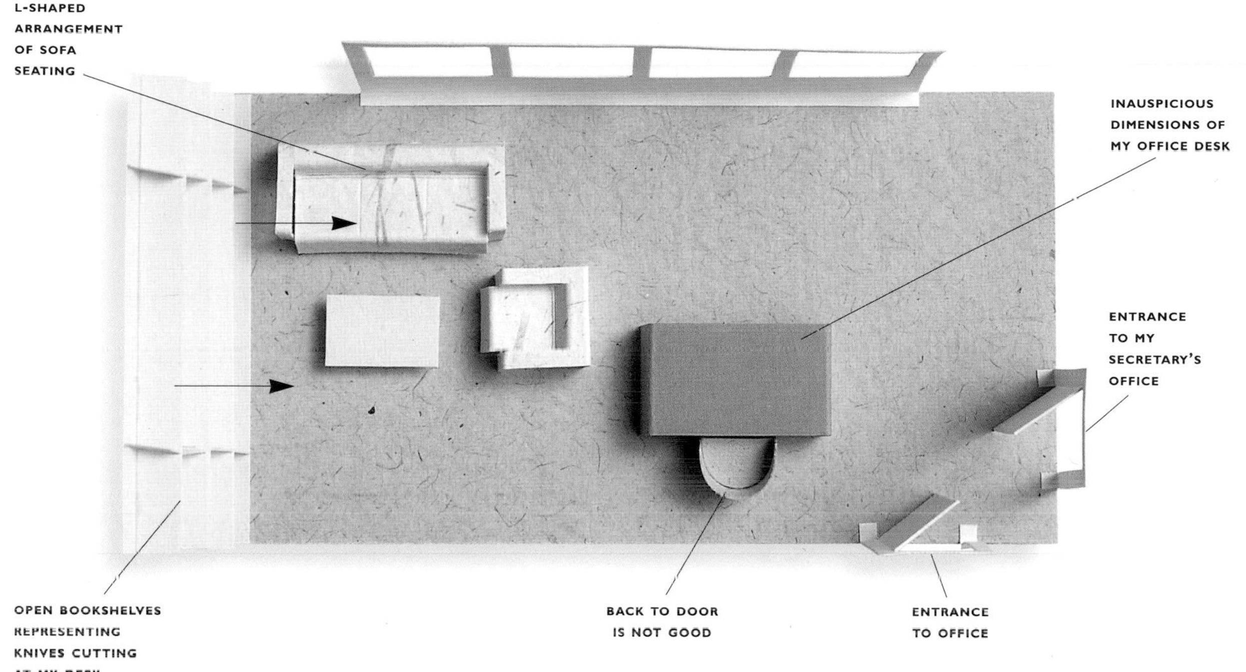

AFTER

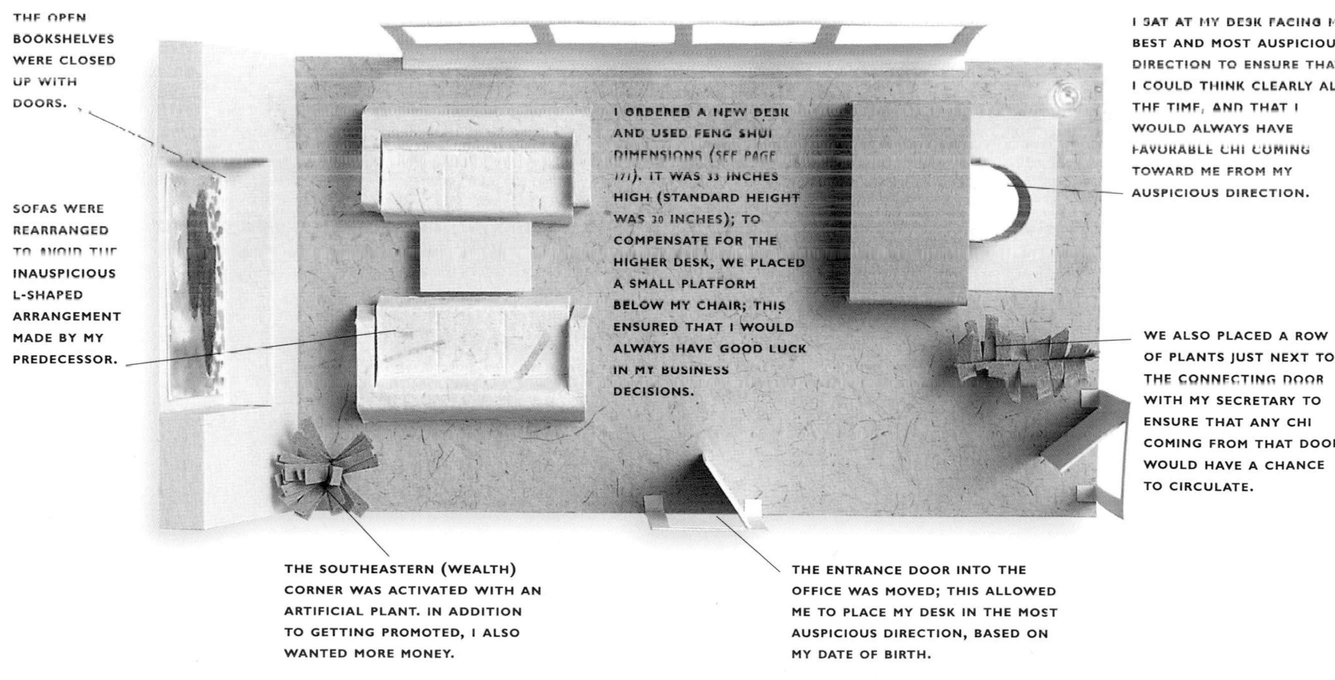

CAREER TIPS

Two key points emerge from my own personal experience of career Feng Shui as outlined on the previous pages: they are the importance of positioning your desk correctly and the value of using Feng Shui dimensions for designing your office furniture. Here we will look at these two points in more detail.

PERSONAL DEVELOPMENT

Use the Pa-Kua Lo-Shu formula to work out the most auspicious direction for personal development and advancement. Under this method, the direction you face depends on your Kua number *(see pages 102–103)*, as follows:

Kua number	Direction to face
1	North
2	Southwest
3	East
4	Southeast
5	Southwest for males; Northeast for females
6	Northwest
7	West
8	Northeast
9	South

A further refinement, is to position your main home and office doors according to your most auspicious direction for wealth creation, as follows:

Kua number	Direction to face
1	Southeast
2	Northeast
3	South
4	North
5	Northeast for males; Southwest for females
6	West
7	Northwest
8	Southwest
9	East

The direction you face when you work in the office has a very major effect on your career luck. If you sit facing an auspicious direction, you will be clear-headed, calm, and resolute when working, thinking, and making decisions.

The next thing to do is to check your desk dimensions. When your desk is of favorable

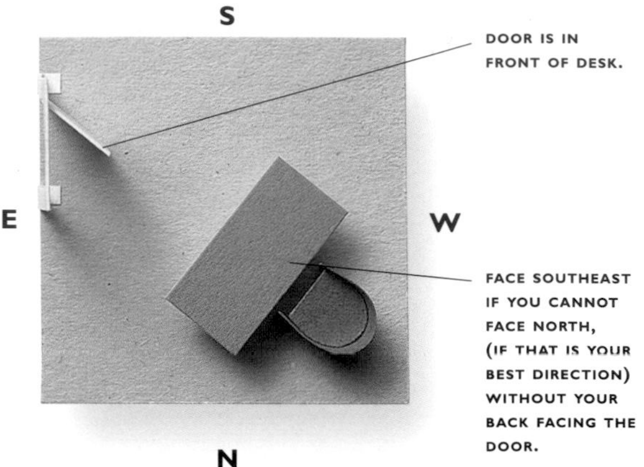

In trying to face your best direction you should not ignore other Feng Shui dictates, such as never sitting with your back to the door.

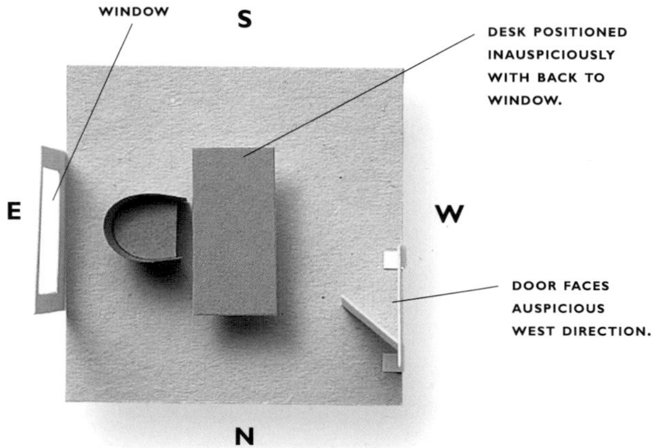

You should never sit with your back to a window. Here, if west is your best direction, try facing southwest, northwest, or northeast instead.

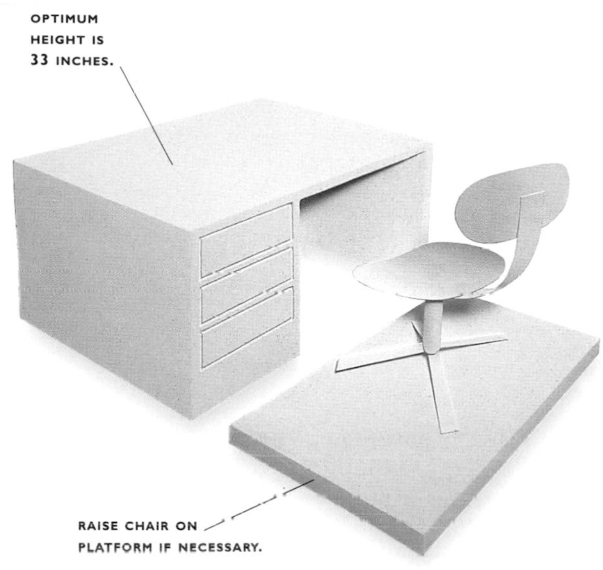

It is sometimes necessary to change the height of a working table or desk. You may also have to lift the chair higher by use of a platform.

dimensions, you will attract good fortune. The most auspicious dimensions for you have to be carefully calculated based on the Feng Shui ruler, which spells out in detail the exact type of good and bad luck for different dimensions. For desks, readers may want to consider the dimensions suggested in the following paragraphs.

A good size for a very large desk – suitable for a company director or chief executive – would be one that measures 33 inches high by 60 inches long and 34 inches wide. These dimensions are excellent for senior managers who have to work harmoniously with their staff, and are very conducive to attracting career luck.

For a smaller desk suitable for a middle manager, auspicious dimensions would be 33 inches high by 48 inches long and 32 inches wide. A secretary's desk should never be L-shaped – although this is already the common practice. Instead it should be a regular rectangular table. The perfect dimensions would be 33 inches high by 68 inches long and 26 inches wide.

In each case, the height of the desk is very auspicious, but, at 33 inches, it is higher than most conventional desks, so place a small platform underneath your chair to raise the level to a comfortable working height.

Try not to have bookcases with open shelves around you. The shelves represent unfriendly knife blades hitting at you. If you must have a bookcase, the recommended dimensions are 68 inches high, 43 inches wide, and 18 inches deep, but use doors to hide the shelves from view.

FENG SHUI AND COMPUTER STATIONS

Computers generate a huge amount of Yang energy. A room that is full of terminals will, therefore, be very auspicious. Computer screens also symbolize life and activity, both of which create and attract generous amounts of Chi – indeed, the danger is of an excess of energy.

Computer stations and dealing rooms, for example, should balance the Yang energy created with Yin color schemes such as blue and gray. Plants will also help to redress the balance, and understated lighting is preferable.

Balance Yang energy from computers with Yin colors and plants.

DOORWAYS TO A BETTER CAREER

The location and direction of doors and entrances influences individual fortunes just as much as it does the fortunes of a company or household. Your own personal career fortune can be enhanced by checking the building in which you work for an entrance that is most auspicious for you, depending on your birth sign, and using this entrance daily *(see pages 100–101 to find your most auspicious directions according to the Pa-Kua Lo-Shu theory)*. If the main entrance is not in your best direction (or your Sheng Chi direction), see if it is in any of your other good directions. If not, then look to see if there is another entrance to the building that you could use instead, one that is in one of your auspicious directions. Alternatively, use any entrance in the northern sector of the building, this being the sector that is responsible for career fortune.

Several successful businessmen in Kuala Lumpur and Hong Kong, who head large corporations with impressive head-office buildings, rather than enter or leave by the main entrance, always use a side entrance because they have been advised that the direction of the main entrance is not auspicious for them (even if it may be auspicious for their companies). It is useful to remember that companies also have birthdates, which can differ from that of the chairman or managing director.

Having ascertained which entrance you should use to enter the building, it is then advisable to use the same methods to calculate whether your office door is in one of your auspicious directions.

Margaret Thatcher was constrained to leave her job as British Prime Minister shortly after these gates were erected at the entrance to Downing Street. The positioning of the gates had created a "no way out" situation for the residents.

FISH FOR FORTUNE

Many offices and business premises in parts of the world where Chinese people have settled have an aquarium placed in a strategic position to ensure good fortune. Different kinds of fish are kept, but the very best for attracting wealth and prosperity are the arrowanas, especially if the aquarium is placed in the southeastern corner of your office or home. In Hong Kong, Malaysia, and Singapore, arrowanas are known as the "Feng Shui fish" because they are supposed to attract good fortune and great prosperity to their owners.

Angel fish, with their poison arrow-like fins (above), are not auspicious. Eight red goldfish and one black are ideal but carp (below) are also acceptable.

Arrowanas are not easy to find. They are tropical fish native to the jungles of Indonesia, Thailand, Malaysia, and Borneo. For the purposes of Feng Shui, they are best kept singly, in threes, or in fives, and always with nothing else in the aquarium. They are carnivorous and should be fed on a diet of live goldfish, which makes their scales turn gold and pink - a sure sign that money is about to arrive on your doorstep. Arrowanas are expensive fish to keep, but the cost will easily be recouped if you use this method of activating the wealth corner of any room or home.

Other fish to keep for Feng Shui purposes are the famous Japanese carp known as koi. These stunningly colorful fish are best kept in a pond. Chinese goldfish are also recommended, and should be kept in an aquarium. The most auspicious number to keep is nine, eight of which should be red and gold in color, while the ninth should be black. The black fish will absorb any bad luck coming to you. If any fish die, replace them immediately, but do not worry, because a dead fish has absorbed any bad luck.

Chapter Twelve

HEALTH, ROMANCE, AND MARRIAGE

The Chinese believe that in every woman's lifetime she has several opportunities for marriage. Some opportunities are stronger than others, and some represent a better future than others. These opportunities are part of her heaven luck. How and what she makes of these opportunities depends on her earth luck and her man luck. It is in this context that Feng Shui can be of some help. Feng Shui is the manifestation of earth luck, and if a woman can knowingly arrange her living environment in such a way as to promote auspicious luck in the area of romance, she will have improved her chances of achieving happiness in a good marriage.

風水

FOR MEN, ROMANCE and marriage luck also work in the same way, but readers must understand that the Chinese cultural tradition accepts the arrangement of multiple wives and concubines. To the Chinese mind, marital arrangements comprise the chief wife and secondary wives. It is the "number one wife" who is recognized as the mistress of the household, though a prosperous man is expected to choose and support secondary wives and even mistresses.

In modern Chinese households, especially those of overseas Chinese people who have lived in western cultures for generations, this tradition is no longer considered valid. Nevertheless, the Feng Shui classics are written from this perspective, and the benefits of tapping Feng Shui luck must be understood in this context.

Good marriage luck for women means that they will become happy first wives, and that, even if the husband strays or has a wandering eye, he will continue to respect and provide for the first wife, and that his children by her will take precedence at all family occasions.

Thus, Feng Shui strenuously advises women against having mirrors in the bedrooms, having a fish pond or aquarium on the right hand side of the main door of their homes, or having the toilet placed in the marriage or family corners of the home. These and other guidelines are part of both landscape and Compass School Feng Shui.

Good marriage Feng Shui also means a happy family life, in which quarrels and misunderstandings between husband and wife and between siblings are the exception rather than the rule, and where children grow up obedient and loving toward their parents – bringing honor to the family name.

In addition, where there is good Feng Shui, auspicious and balanced Chi also brings balance into the physical bodies of the individuals in the household, thereby promoting good health and a general absence of illnesses and disease.

This chapter thus focuses on the specific methods that can be used to harness these nonmaterial, but nonetheless attractive, benefits that can be gained from the practice of Feng Shui.

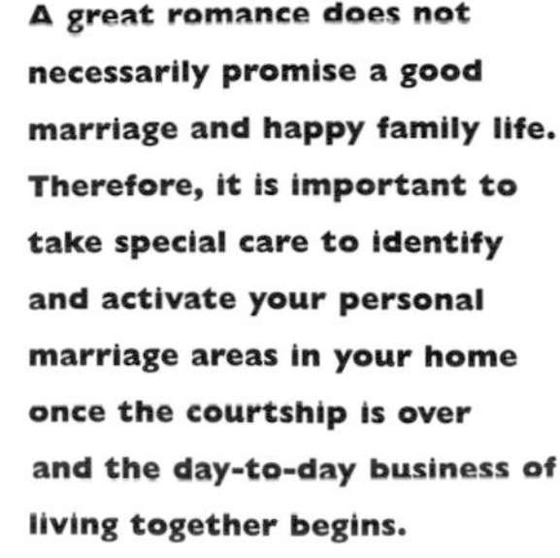

A great romance does not necessarily promise a good marriage and happy family life. Therefore, it is important to take special care to identify and activate your personal marriage areas in your home once the courtship is over and the day-to-day business of living together begins.

ACTIVATING YOUR MARRIAGE PROSPECTS

According to the "Eight Life Aspirations" method of activating Feng Shui luck, every house or apartment has a marriage corner *(see pages 78–81)*. This is represented by the trigram Kun, which symbolizes the earth mother. Kun is also symbolic of strong Yin energy and represents fertility. The marriage corner is thus represented by the southwestern corner of the house, and this is the corner that you should concentrate on activating to enhance the social life and marital prospects of any unmarried daughters or sons in the family. It is, however, equally useful to activate the personal marriage corner of the family member concerned, or the Nien Yen family corner, according to the Pa-Kua Lo-Shu theory *(see pages 98–103 and the table opposite)*. Finally, try to sit or sleep facing your personal marriage direction.

If you find that your marriage corner is missing because you have an irregular-shaped house, Feng Shui recommends that you extend this corner outward by placing a mirror on a side of the wall.

Red heart shapes can be used to activate the marriage sector, symbolizing romance and the auspicious fire element.

The Chinese character for double happiness symbolizes conjugal bliss. Placed in the marriage corner, it will encourage romantic luck.

PERSONAL MARRIAGE SECTORS

To find your personal marriage sector, first calculate your Kua number using the tables on page 101, and then find your corresponding corner based on the following table.

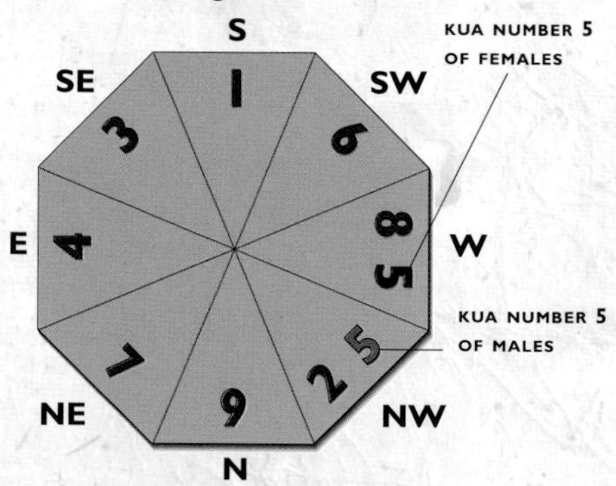

The Nien Yen or family corners according to the Pa-Kua Lo-Shu formula.

ROOM ASSOCIATIONS

Once you have identified the corner, try to make sure that the toilet, kitchen, and storeroom are not situated there. If you find that your toilet is in this sector, try to stop using that particular toilet – otherwise, your marriage prospects will be flushed away. You should not store brooms and mops in this corner either, as these symbolize sweeping away good fortune.

ENHANCING TOOLS

Instead, you should use your imagination to activate the corner by placing symbols of conjugal bliss in this sector: mandarin ducks or peacocks are possible symbols. If you cannot find mandarin ducks, try using western love birds or budgerigars. Just make sure that you hang everything in pairs to signify two people. Do not be like a friend of mine, who put a picture of a bride in her marriage corner without the groom – it did not work.

Other symbols that you can use are a painting of a peony or a wedding bouquet, a Chinese marriage knot, or the Chinese characters signifying double happiness (the symbol of conjugal bliss). These last two items can be easily purchased from any Chinese emporium at very little cost.

Since the southwestern sector is symbolized by the earth element, placing natural crystals in this corner can also be a very effective way of activating this corner. These are traditionally tied with red ribbons. Red is representative of the fire element, and since fire creates earth, red can be very effective in enhancing this corner. Useful red-coloured activators are bright lamps, perhaps with a red bulb, a vase of red roses – real or artificial – and paintings that have red as the dominant color.

Natural quartz crystals activate the earth element of the southwestern marriage sector.

Red roses are excellent symbols of romance in Feng Shui terms, and would not look out of place in Western homes.

ENHANCING THE MARRIAGE

When the honeymoon is over and two people start to live together as husband and wife, things can sometimes go horribly wrong. Sometimes when quarrels and misunderstandings start to cause rifts and unhappiness, it can be due to inauspicious Feng Shui.

Newly married couples usually start their lives together in a new home. If the Feng Shui of the house or apartment is unsuitable, even the best marriages can come under stress. It is, therefore, a good idea to look at the Feng Shui of any newly rented or newly purchased home. There are some standard guidelines that ensure that the marriage does not come under more stress than is already caused under normal circumstances.

THE GOLDEN RULES FOR MARRIAGE

Rule No. 1: never have large mirrors in the bedroom that either face you each time you get up, or are situated above you, reflecting you when you sleep. Mirrors in the bedroom are very bad Feng Shui for relationships, since, in reflecting the couple, they suggest the intrusion of third parties coming between them, either encouraging them to be unfaithful or causing trouble between husband and wife. If you need mirrors for dressing and makeup purposes, locate them in a special dressing area or in the bathroom.

Rule No. 2: never have a fish pond or an aquarium or anything to do with water located anywhere on the right-hand side of the main front door (on the right, that is, as you look out of the door). This is a taboo that Feng Shui masters stress many times over in the course of consultations. They are unable to explain the origin of this tenet, but while having a fishpond near the front door can be extremely auspicious in some circumstances – bringing great wealth to the household when other compass directions are properly formulated – the fish pond must never be on the right-hand side, but on the left-hand side of the door.

If it is on the right-hand side, it may bring success or wealth, but the husband will have a tendency to stray. This happened to a pregnant friend of mine. She installed a beautiful pond on the right-hand side of her front door, but it caused predictable heartbreak. Happily, she told me about it in time. I immediately forced her to cover up her pond, and her husband came to his senses soon after that.

A fish pond, especially with gold-colored fish associated with wealth, is very auspicious. But if placed on the right-hand side of the front door, a fish pond could cause unhappiness in your marriage.

WHAT TO DO IF THINGS GO WRONG

If you suddenly experience problems in your marriage after a major redecoration or soon after you have moved into a new house (and if things had been going well for you before that), you might suspect that something had gone wrong with the Feng Shui of your home. Having checked out the two golden rules, the next thing you should check is the location and position of the master bedroom and the conjugal bed.

Ideally, your bed should be located in the most auspicious corner of the house for you, depending on your Kua number, and you should sleep with your head in this direction, too. Obviously there is a problem with practicing this aspect of Compass School Feng Shui if you and your spouse have different Kua numbers and belong to different groups – one belonging to the west group and the other to the east.

The Prince and Princess of Wales, for example, are incompatible, as they belong to different groups. Princess Diana was born on July 1, 1961. Her Kua number is 3, and her best directions are south, north, southeast, and east. Prince Charles was born on November 14, 1948. His Kua number is 7, and his most auspicious directions are northwest, southwest, northeast, and west.

From the above, it is easy to see that what is good for one is bad for the other. It is, therefore, not surprising that these two people cannot live together harmoniously. Further analysis of their year elements indicates that she belongs to the realm of gold or metal, while he belongs to the earth element. Under the cycle of relationships, earth produces gold – thus Prince Charles "made" Princess Diana. It was he who brought fame to her.

Unfortunately, gold exhausts earth, so she caused him much exasperation and grief. Fortunately for him, he is not of the wood element, otherwise she might well destroy him and, fortunately for her, she is not of the water element, or he might destroy her.

Even fairytale marriages, which hold so much promise for the future, are doomed to failure if the man and woman belong to groups with incompatible needs. Harmonious living becomes impossible under such conditions.

JAZZING UP YOUR LOVE LIFE – A CASE STUDY

Can romance and marriage be made sweeter with Feng Shui? Can this thousand-year-old science jazz up your love life, rekindle the faded embers of a marriage gone sour, or even bring you the man of your dreams? Lest I am accused of getting carried away and becoming too extravagant in raising your expectations, let me say that I have personally seen Feng Shui work again and again in this important sector of life, sometimes in ways that surprise me. Let me tell you the story of Nancy, a beautiful interior decorator who was my special friend during my career days in Hong Kong.

Nancy, a single mother, was both vivacious and attractive. Originally from Singapore, she and her first husband had divorced in Hong Kong, where they had lived because of his work. Nancy had picked up the pieces of her life after the divorce, building her own decoration business and bringing up two beautiful children. For well over ten years, her business flourished and she achieved financial independence. The one thing she wanted most of all, however – to find someone kind and strong and wonderful to share her life with – eluded her. Despite brief engagements and near-misses, Nancy remained frustratingly single – until we discovered the reason why.

Her luxurious apartment, beautifully decorated (as you would expect from someone in her profession), was laid out in a way that sent "six killings" to her marriage chances, day after day. An elaborate bathroom was located smack in the marriage corner of her apartment – the southwest. The southwest also coincided with her own personal

Wooden carvings of mandarin ducks are good symbols for the marriage corner, but stick to displaying one pair – unless you want two marriages.

family/marriage direction. The toilet was thus flushing all her marriage chances down the drain, and, because the southwest was doubly significant in her case, the effect had been especially potent.

I advised her to relocate the toilet, and instead to put all the symbols of conjugal bliss and romance in this corner of her apartment. Nancy went to work with a vengeance. Contractors were brought in, and Nancy got herself a list of things that represented good marriage luck and went shopping. She was determined to get every suitable Feng Shui activator to place in this all-important corner.

Nancy has never been a halfhearted person, so that by the time she had finished implementing all my suggestions, the southwestern corner of her apartment, which was located next to her bedroom, looked delightfully romantic. She bought Chinese love knots, which she hung on the walls, had her favourite calligrapher write out the double happiness symbol (which also signifies marriage), and she cleverly converted this into a table top by placing it under glass. She bought wooden carvings of mandarin ducks, which she displayed under the coffee table, and she also hung a beautiful painting of the mountain flower (the peony) on the wall of her room. This is another wonderful symbol of fidelity between lovers.

If you wish to find a loving and faithful partner, try placing a peony, either real, silk, or even a painting, in your marriage sector.

Three months after making these changes, Nancy met Ray at a dinner party, and a year later they got married. The last I heard, Nancy and Ray had left Hong Kong and are now living in blissful retirement in the suburbs of Sydney, Australia. Those of you keen on adding some sparkle into your love life and enhancing your marriage prospects can try exactly what Nancy did.

DO NOT OVERDO THINGS

While it does no harm to put all the symbols of love and romance that you can possibly think of into the marriage corner, do refrain from being over-zealous. One pair of ducks, for instance is enough. If you have too many ducks, then things could well go wrong. One double happiness symbol is enough – two signifies two marriages. Try to practice moderation.

ESSENTIAL RULES FOR GOOD HEALTH

To make the most of romance, you must enjoy good health and physical well-being. Generally, it is believed that if you live in a home which has auspicious Feng Shui vibrations, where the good luck Chi flows gently in and around the rooms, you will enjoy good health.

Indeed, one of the first indications that all may not be right with your Feng Shui is when you observe members of your family constantly becoming sick, or worse, constantly being admitted to hospital. This is especially true in households with young children. If you notice that your children are constantly succumbing to one flu virus after another – especially if you have just renovated your home or moved into a new house – it might be useful to undertake a quick check of your general Feng Shui, following the simple rules outlined here.

A healthy, happy, family life across the generations can be activated by proper regard for Feng Shui practices and rigorous attention to the four golden rules for health.

PERSONAL HEALTH SECTORS

For this to work, the person who is ill will have to sleep in the room that corresponds to their most auspicious health direction, and sleep with their head pointing in the same direction.

To find a personal health sector, calculate the person's Kua number *(see page 101)* and find the corresponding sector on the diagram below.

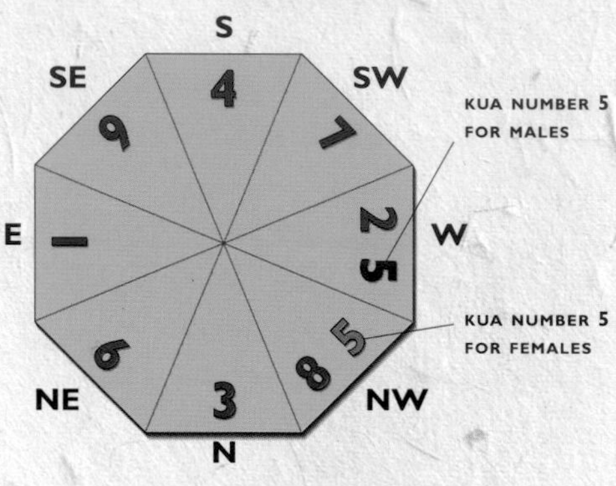

The Tien Yi, or Doctor from Heaven corners according to the Pa-Kua Lo-Shu formula.

THE GOLDEN RULES FOR HEALTH

Rule No. 1: guard against poison arrows from outside your home. Check that your main front door is not being hit by anything sharp or pointed. The rule is to beware anything straight, sharp, or pointed, anything angular, or anything that seems to be threatening. There is no need to worry about threatening structures that seem to be deflected away from you. Having said that, do remember that

The general health of your family is a sign of how auspicious the Feng Shui is in your home.

residents of homes that are hit by poison arrows do not usually just become sick. Usually the bad luck also takes on other equally, and sometimes more severe, forms.

Rule No. 2: beware of poison arrows inside the home, and ensure that children are not sleeping directly beneath exposed beams, as these will cause frequent illnesses, headaches, and an inability to sleep peacefully.

It is also advisable not to fill your home with antiques and collectibles that could cause bad luck. Examples include antique miniature cannons or even firearms. Properly displayed inside cabinets and directed away from residents, they are harmless. But openly displayed on tables, they could cause Shar Chi to build up within the home and cause harm to its occupants. Antiques are doubly inauspicious, as you are unlikely to know the luck of the people who owned the artefacts before. In the case of firearms, they also stand the chance of having once been fired in anger and of having drawn blood, which is very bad Feng Shui.

Rule No. 3: if there is someone who is really ill at home, it is possible to use Feng Shui to help them to recover. This is done using the Pa-Kua Lo-Shu formula and involves finding that person's Tien Yi, or Doctor from Heaven direction based on his or her date of birth *(see the tables for calculating your Kua number on pages 100–101 and the table opposite).* Once you have identified the sector, then you should locate the person's bedroom in that corner of the home and place their bed so that they are sleeping in the Tien Yi direction (calculate this from the inside of the house looking out).

Rule No. 4: finally, to ensure the general health of residents in your home, you should make sure that your stove is placed in a way that allows the gas or electricity to flow to it from any of your four auspicious directions, based on the Pa-Kua Lo-Shu formula. This is a difficult rule to follow where there are people of different Kua numbers living in the same house. When in doubt, use the directions of the head of the household. In extreme cases, use different ovens.

ENDWORD

The practice of Feng Shui can be as simple or as complex as your own attitudes and your own good sense dictate. Feng Shui is neither spiritual nor religious. It is an ancient Chinese science that can be easily and effectively adapted to the modern living environment. Feng Shui is not magic and it cannot bring you overnight success. But it can enhance your periods of good fortune, just as it can mitigate your times of misfortune.

By investing time and effort in studying the principles of Feng Shui, you will be well on your way to improving your lifestyle and happiness.

風水

WEALTH, SUCCESS, AND LOVE – ALL FROM FENG SHUI

Now you know that Feng Shui is about harnessing vital energy lines – which the Chinese colorfully refer to as "the dragon's cosmic breath," or Chi, to use the Chinese term. The earth's atmosphere, we are told, is crowded with these energy lines. Some of this energy is auspicious and positive, while some is pernicious and threatening.

The positive Sheng Chi (benign breath) brings tremendous good luck, much prosperity, and a great deal of happiness. Bring Sheng Chi into your living space and you will enjoy good fortune. Negative energy, on the other hand, creates "killing breath," termed Shar Chi. When hit by Shar Chi, you will suffer losses, illness (sometimes fatal), and become inundated with a battalion of problems.

These Chi lines are like the energy lines that we now know swirl around the atmosphere (analogous to radio waves and satellite transmissions). Feng Shui's Chi is everywhere. And to enjoy success, become wealthy, and have a great family and love life, all we need to do is tap the Sheng Chi and avoid all the Shar Chi that swirls around us.

How to go about doing this is what the science is about. I call it a science because, in the course of well over twenty years' exposure to this knowledge, I have discovered there is nothing mysterious or spiritual about it. Implement Feng Shui guidelines accurately, apply the formulas correctly, and anyone can get it right.

The basics of Feng Shui are easy to learn. Its concepts are neither so profound nor so complicated that you cannot grasp them with a little effort.

Astrology reveals your heaven luck which you cannot control. Feng Shui can enhance your earth luck.

At the same time, introducing Feng Shui into your life can be fun. Try applying the tips and suggestions contained in this book, and watch subtle but discernible changes occur.

A girlfriend of mine (an unbeliever) complained of massive headaches and annoying problems at the office. She was constantly unwell. I visited her one day and discovered she was sitting right in front of a massive square pillar. Its sharp edge was pointing directly at her. I suggested she place a plant at the corner of her table. She bought a trailing money plant, and within a week she not only felt better, she also came into some unexpected money!

For two months, everything improved, and for the first time she actually felt good about her job. Then things started getting bad again. In desperation she called me. I asked her how the plant was doing. "The plant is dying. What shall I do?" she wailed. "The plant cannot survive in the enclosed atmosphere of the office so change the plant" I told her, "and keep changing the plant every two months!"

So, you see, Feng Shui is also about common sense!

Feng Shui represents the luck from the earth, what the Chinese refer to as "ti choy," which complements the "tien choy" (heaven luck) and "ren choy" (man luck) that we are born with. This is the trinity of luck that is believed to determine our destiny. Control your earth luck and your man luck through Feng Shui practices and you will supplement your heaven luck.

CHINESE ASTROLOGY AND THE ELEMENTS

Feng Shui and Chinese astrology are both based, to a large extent, upon the *I Ching* and on the interactions of the five elements. Chinese astrology reveals the destiny bestowed by heaven, or heaven luck, while Feng Shui is linked to the harnessing of the earth's Chi, or earth luck. Feng Shui experts will usually cast a glance at a person's birth chart when asked to advise a client to determine the strength of that person's heaven luck for a particular year, and also their ruling element.

Chinese astrology is based on the lunar calendar, which dates back to the time of the Emperor Huang Ti (about 2600 B.C.). It divides time into 60-year cycles, made up of twelve years and five elements. Each year is, therefore, linked to an element and these are shown in the chart below.

It is important to note that whereas the Western calendar is based on the cycle of the sun, and, therefore, New Year in the West always falls on the first day of January, the Chinese calculate New Year according to the lunar cycle and, therefore, New Year falls on the second New Moon following the winter solstice. This means that the lunar New Year can occur at any time between mid-January and mid-February, and the Chinese calculate birth years accordingly.

YEAR	FROM	TO	ELEMENT
1900	*31 January 1900* –	*18 February 1901*	**Metal**
1901	*19 February 1901* –	*7 February 1902*	**Metal**
1902	*8 February 1902* –	*28 January 1903*	**Water**
1903	*29 January 1903* –	*15 February 1904*	**Water**
1904	*16 February 1904* –	*3 February 1905*	**Wood**
1905	*4 February 1905* –	*24 January 1906*	**Wood**
1906	*25 January 1906* –	*12 February 1907*	**Fire**
1907	*13 February 1907* –	*1 February 1908*	**Fire**
1908	*2 February 1908* –	*21 January 1909*	**Earth**
1909	*22 January 1909* –	*9 February 1910*	**Earth**
1910	*10 February 1910* –	*29 January 1911*	**Metal**
1911	*30 January 1911* –	*17 February 1912*	**Metal**
1912	*18 February 1912* –	*5 February 1913*	**Water**
1913	*6 February 1913* –	*25 January 1914*	**Water**
1914	*26 January 1914* –	*13 February 1915*	**Wood**
1915	*14 February 1915* –	*2 February 1916*	**Wood**
1916	*3 February 1916* –	*22 January 1917*	**Fire**
1917	*23 January 1917* –	*10 February 1918*	**Fire**
1918	*11 February 1918* –	*31 January 1919*	**Earth**
1919	*1 February 1919* –	*19 February 1920*	**Earth**

YEAR	FROM	TO	ELEMENT
1920	*20February 1920* –	*7 February 1921*	**Metal**
1921	*8 February 1921* –	*27 January 1922*	**Metal**
1922	*28 January 1922* –	*15 February 1923*	**Water**
1923	*16 February 1923* –	*4 February 1924*	**Water**
1924	*5 February 1924* –	*24 January 1925*	**Wood**
1925	*25 January 1925* –	*12 February 1926*	**Wood**
1926	*13 February 1926* –	*1 February 1927*	**Fire**
1927	*2February 1927* –	*22 January 1928*	**Fire**
1928	*23 January 1928* –	*9 February 1929*	**Earth**
1929	*10 February 1929* –	*29 January 1930*	**Earth**
1930	*30 January 1930* –	*16 February 1931*	**Metal**
1931	*17 February 1931* –	*5 February 1932*	**Metal**
1932	*6 February 1932* –	*25 January 1933*	**Water**
1933	*26 January 1933* –	*13 February 1934*	**Water**
1934	*14 February 1934* –	*3 February 1935*	**Wood**
1935	*4 February 1935* –	*23 January 1936*	**Wood**
1936	*24 January 1936* –	*10 February 1937*	**Fire**
1937	*11 February 1937* –	*30 January 1938*	**Fire**
1938	*31 January 1938* –	*18 February 1939*	**Earth**
1939	*19 February 1939* –	*7 February 1940*	**Earth**

YEAR	FROM		TO	ELEMENT
1940	*8 February 1940*	–	*26 January 1941*	Metal
1941	*27 January 1941*	–	*14 February 1942*	Metal
1942	*15 February 1942*	–	*4 February 1943*	Water
1943	*5 February 1943*	–	*24 January 1944*	Water
1944	*25 January 1944*	–	*12 February 1945*	Wood
1945	*13 February 1945*	–	*1 February 1946*	Wood
1946	*2 February 1946*		*21 January 1947*	Fire
1947	*22 January 1947*	–	*9 February 1948*	Fire
1948	*10 February 1948*	–	*28 January 1949*	Earth
1949	*29 January 1949*	–	*16 February 1950*	Earth
1950	*17 February 1950*	–	*5 February 1951*	Metal
1951	*6 February 1951*	–	*26 January 1952*	Metal
1952	*27 January 1952*	–	*13 February 1953*	Water
1953	*14 February 1953*	–	*2 February 1954*	Water
1954	*3 February 1954*	–	*23 January 1955*	Wood
1955	*24 January 1955*	–	*11 February 1956*	Wood
1956	*12 February 1956*	–	*30 January 1957*	Fire
1957	*31 January 1957*	–	*17 February 1958*	Fire
1958	*18 February 1958*	–	*7 February 1959*	Earth
1959	*8 February 1959*	–	*27 January 1960*	Earth
1960	*28 January 1960*	–	*14 February 1961*	Metal
1961	*15 February 1961*	–	*4 February 1962*	Metal
1962	*5 February 1962*	–	*24 January 1963*	Water
1963	*25 January 1963*	–	*12 February 1964*	Water
1964	*13 February 1964*	–	*1 February 1965*	Wood
1965	*2 February 1965*	–	*20 January 1966*	Wood
1966	*21 January 1966*	–	*8 February 1967*	Fire
1967	*9 February 1967*	–	*29 January 1968*	Fire
1968	*30 January 1968*	–	*16 February 1969*	Earth
1969	*17 February 1969*	–	*5 February 1970*	Earth
1970	*6 February 1970*	–	*26 January 1971*	Metal
1971	*27 January 1971*	–	*15 January 1972*	Metal
1972	*16 January 1972*	–	*2 February 1973*	Water
1973	*3 February 1973*	–	*22 January 1974*	Water

YEAR	FROM		TO	ELEMENT
1974	*23 January 1974*	–	*10 February 1975*	Wood
1975	*11 February 1975*	–	*30 January 1976*	Wood
1976	*31 January 1976*	–	*17 February 1977*	Fire
1977	*18 February 1977*	–	*6 February 1978*	Fire
1978	*7 February 1978*	–	*27 January 1979*	Earth
1979	*28 January 1979*	–	*15 February 1980*	Earth
1980	*16 February 1980*	–	*4 February 1981*	Metal
1981	*5 February 1981*	–	*24 January 1982*	Metal
1982	*25 January 1982*	–	*12 February 1983*	Water
1983	*13 February 1983*	–	*1 February 1984*	Water
1984	*2 February 1984*	–	*19 February 1985*	Wood
1985	*20 February 1985*	–	*8 February 1986*	Wood
1986	*9 February 1986*	–	*28 January 1987*	Fire
1987	*29 January 1987*	–	*16 February 1988*	Fire
1988	*17 February 1988*	–	*5 February 1989*	Earth
1989	*6 February 1989*	–	*26 January 1990*	Earth
1990	*27 January 1990*	–	*14 February 1991*	Metal
1991	*15 February 1991*	–	*3 February 1992*	Metal
1992	*4 February 1992*	–	*22 January 1993*	Water
1993	*23 January 1993*	–	*9 February 1994*	Water
1994	*10 February 1994*	–	*30 January 1995*	Wood
1995	*31 January 1995*	–	*18 February 1996*	Wood
1996	*19 February 1996*	–	*7 February 1997*	Fire
1997	*8 February 1997*	–	*27 January 1998*	Fire
1998	*28 January 1998*	–	*15 February 1999*	Earth
1999	*16 February 1999*	–	*4 February 2000*	Earth
2000	*5 February 2000*	–	*23 January 2001*	Metal
2001	*24 January 2001*	–	*11 February 2002*	Metal
2002	*12 February 2002*	–	*31 January 2003*	Water
2003	*1 February 2003*	–	*21 January 2004*	Water
2004	*22 January 2004*	–	*8 February 2005*	Wood
2005	*9 February 2005*	–	*28 January 2006*	Wood
2006	*29 January 2006*	–	*17 February 2007*	Fire
2007	*18 February 2007*	–	*6 February 2008*	Fire

GLOSSARY

C

Chen The Arousing trigram, whose direction is east and number is 3.
Chen Lung Pak Fu Green dragon/white tiger formation.
Chi The life force or vital energy of the universe. Chi can be either auspicious or inauspicious.
Chien The Creative trigram, whose direction is northwest and number is 6.
Chueh Ming Literally, "total loss of descendants," the location that represents the worst possible kind of disaster or bad luck that can befall any family.
Compass School The Feng Shui school that uses compass formulas to diagnose the quality of Feng Shui directions and locations.
Confucius The renowned Chinese philosopher (551–479 B.C.) and great moral teacher, who spent a lifetime studying the *I Ching*.

D

Dragon's cosmic breath *see* **Sheng Chi**

E

Early Heaven arrangement One of the two Pa Kua arrangements, used when considering the Feng Shui of Yin dwellings, or the abodes of the dead.
Eight Life Aspirations method A method of allocating corners in a room that identifies various life aspirations.
Elements The five elements in Chinese belief – earth, wood, fire, metal, and water – that provide vital clues to the practice of Feng Shui.

F

Feng Shui Literally, "wind/water," the Chinese system of balancing the energy patterns of the physical environment.
Flying Star Feng Shui The formula that determines good and bad time dimension Feng Shui for homes and buildings based on the Lo Shu square.
Form School The Feng Shui school that focuses predominantly on the contours of physical landscapes – their shapes, sizes, and courses.
Fu Wei Literally, "overall harmony," the location for achieving peace.
Fuk The Chinese god of wealth and happiness.

H

Hexagram A figure of six lines, of which there are 64 in the *I Ching*, symbolizing the universal archetypes of human consciousness.
Ho Hai Literally "accidents and mishaps," the location that leads to financial loss and intermittent difficulty.

I

I Ching A Chinese classic known in the West as *The Book of Changes.*

K

Kan The Abysmal trigram, whose direction is north and number is 1.
Ken The Mountain trigram, whose direction is northeast and number is 8.
Killing breath *see* **Shar Chi**
Kua One of the eight sides of the Pa Kua. Each individual's Kua number identifies his or her auspicious and inauspicious locations.
Kun The Receptive trigram, whose direction is southwest and number is 2.

L

Later Heaven arrangement One of the two Pa Kua arrangements, used when considering the Feng Shui of Yang dwellings, or abodes of the living.
Li The Clinging trigram, whose direction is south and number is 9.
Lo Shu The magic square, comprising an arrangement of nine numbers into a three-by-three grid, which first appeared about 4,000 years ago on the back of a turtle. The square exerted a powerful and mythical influence on Chinese cultural symbolism.
Lui Sha Literally, "six killings," the location that represents grievous harm to you and your family.
Luo Pan The Chinese Feng Shui compass, which contains all the clues and symbols that indicate good or bad Feng Shui.

Luk The Chinese god of high rank and affluence.

N

Nien Yen Literally, "longevity with rich descendants," the best location for enhancing the quality of home life and family relationships.

P

Pa Kua The eight-sided symbol used to help interpret good or bad Feng Shui. It corresponds to the four cardinal points of the compass and the four sub-directions and derives its significance from the eight trigrams of the *I Ching.*
Pa-Kua Lo-Shu theory The theory, based on the Pa-Kua and Lo-Shu, that every abode can be divided into eight sectors, each representing an auspicious or inauspicious situation.
Poison arrow Any sharp or straight structure from which foul energy or Shar Chi emanates, carrying with it ill fortune and other odious effects.

S

Sau The Chinese god of health and longevity.
Shar Chi Literally, "disruptive Chi from the west" or inauspicious energy lines, caused by the presence of sharp, pointed objects or structures that channel bad Feng Shui; also known as "killing breath."
Sheng Chi Literally, "growing chi from the east" or auspicious energy lines, which travel in a meandering fashion. Also known as "dragon's cosmic breath" or benign breath.
Sheng Chi When referring to a location, literally "generating breath," the best location for attracting prosperity.
Sun The Gentle trigram, whose direction is southwest and number is 4.

T

Tao "The Way," a philosophy and way of life – the eternal principle of heaven and earth in harmony.
Tao Te Ching An important Chinese philosophical text, traditionally ascribed to Lao Tzu, and one of the keys to philosophical Taoism.
Taoism The philosophical system set forth in the *Tao Te Ching.*
Tian ling di li ren he The six-character phrase meaning "auspicious heavenly influence, beneficial topography, harmonious human actions: that is often used to describe Feng Shui in classical texts.
Tien Ti Ren Heaven luck, earth luck and, man luck.
Tien Yi Literally, "doctor from heaven," the best location for members of the household who are ill.
Trigram A figure made up of three lines, either broken or complete, symbolizing the trinity of heaven, earth, and man.
Tui The Joyous trigram, whose direction is west and number is 7.

W

Water Dragon Classic A formula that offers twelve water flow and exit directions across a plot of land; also the title of one of the source texts for Feng Shui practice, about the relative merits of waterways.
Wu Kwei Literally, "five ghosts," the location that generates the kind of bad luck that results in fires, burglary, and loss of income or employment.

Y

Yang Creative energy, one aspect of the complementary opposites in Chinese philosophy. It reflects the more active, moving, warmer aspects; *see also* **Yin.**
Yang Dwelling Classic One of the classic Feng Shui manuscripts, which lays down guidelines on house and room positioning.
Yang Yun-Sang, Master Principal advisor to the court of the Tang emperor Hi Tsang (A.D. 888) and widely acknowledged as the founder of Feng Shui.
Yin Receptive energy, one aspect of the complementary opposites in Chinese philosophy. It reflects the more passive, still, reflective aspects; *see also* **Yang.**

FURTHER READING

CHINESE ASTROLOGY

Kwok, Man-Ho with Palmer, Martin and O'Brien, Joanne, *Authentic Chinese Horoscopes,* ARROW, LONDON, 1987

FENG SHUI

Eitel, Ernest, *Feng Shui, The Science of the Sacred Landscape of Old China,* SYNERGETIC PRESS, TUCSON, ARIZONA, 1993

Kwok, Man-Ho and O'Brien, Joanne, *The Elements of Feng Shui,* ELEMENT BOOKS, SHAFTESBURY, 1991

Lo, Raymond, *Feng Shui and Destiny,* TYNRON, 1992

Lo, Raymond, *Feng Shui: The Pillars of Destiny (Understanding Your Fate and Fortune),* TIMES EDITIONS, SINGAPORE, 1995

Lo, Raymond, *Feng Shui and Destiny for Managers,* TIMES EDITIONS, SINGAPORE, 1995

Rosbach, Sarah, *Feng Shui,* RIDER, LONDON, 1984

Rosbach, Sarah, *Interior Design with Feng Shui,* RIDER, LONDON, 1987

Skinner, Stephen, *Living Earth Manual of Feng Shui: Chinese Geomancy,* PENGUIN, 1989

Too, Lillian, *Applied Pa-Kua and Lo Shu Feng Shui,* KONSEP BOOKS, KUALA LUMPUR, 1993

Too, Lillian, *Chinese Numerology in Feng Shui,* KONSEP BOOKS, KUALA LUMPUR, 1994

Too, Lillian, *Feng Shui,* KONSEP BOOKS, KUALA LUMPUR, 1993

Too, Lillian, *Practical Applications of Feng Shui,* KONSEP BOOKS, KUALA LUMPUR, 1994

Too, Lillian, *Water Feng Shui for Wealth,* KONSEP BOOKS, KUALA LUMPUR, 1995

Walters, Derek, *Feng Shui Handbook: A Practical Guide to Chinese Geomancy and Environmental Harmony,* AQUARIAN PRESS, 1991

GENERAL

Eberhard, Wolfram, *A Dictionary of Chinese Symbols,* ROUTLEDGE & KEGAN PAUL, NEW YORK, 1986

Kwok, Man-Ho (trans.) and O'Brien, Joanne (ed.), *Chinese Myths and Legends,* ARROW, LONDON, 1990

I CHING

Karcher, Stephen L. and Ritsema, Rudolph, *I Ching,* ELEMENT BOOKS, SHAFTESBURY, 1994

Wilhelm, Richard (trans), *The I Ching or Book of Changes,* 3RD EDN, ROUTLEDGE & KEGAN PAUL, 1968

TAO TE CHING

Freke, Timothy and Palmer, Martin, *Tao Te Ching,* PIATKUS, LONDON, 1995

Kwok, Man-Ho, Palmer, Martin and Ramsay, Jay, *Tao Te Ching: The New Translation,* ELEMENT BOOKS, SHAFTESBURY, 1993

Kwok, Man-Ho, Palmer, Martin and Ramsay, Jay, *The Illustrated Tao Te Ching: The New Translation,* ELEMENT BOOKS, SHAFTESBURY, 1993

Mabry, John R, *The Little Book of the Tao Te Ching,* ELEMENT BOOKS, SHAFTESBURY, 1995

Mitchell, Stephen (trans), *Tao Te Ching,* HARPER PERENNIAL, NEW YORK, 1991

USEFUL ADDRESSES

AUSTRALASIA

Feng Shui Design Studio
PO Box 705
Glebe
Sydney NSW 2037
Australia
Tel: 61 2 315 8258

Feng Shui Society of Australia
PO Box 1565
Rozelle
Sydney NSW 2039
Australia

GREAT BRITAIN

The Geomancer
P.O. Box 250
Woking, GU21 1YJ
Tel: 44 1483 839898
Fax: 44 1483 488998

Feng Shui Association
31 Woburn Place
Brighton BN1 9GA
Tel/Fax: 44 1273 693844

Feng Shui Network International
PO Box 2133
London W1A 1RL
Tel: 44 171 935 8935
Fax: 44 171 935 9295

Feng Shui Society
18 Alacross Road
London W5 4HT
Tel/Fax: 44 181 567 2043

Midlands Feng Shui
34 Banbury Road
Ettington
Stratford-upon-Avon
Warwickshire
CV37 7SU
Tel/Fax: 44 1789 740116

NORTH AMERICA

Earth Design
PO Box 530725
Miami Shores
FL 33153
Tel: 1 305 756 6426
Fax: 1 305 751 9995

Feng Shui Designs
PO Box 399
Nevada City
CA 95959
Tel: 1 800 551 2482

The Feng Shui Institute of America
PO Box 488
Wabasso
FL 32970
Tel: 1 407 589 9900
Fax: 1 407 589 1611

Feng Shui Warehouse
PO Box 3005
San Diego
CA 92163
Tel: 1 800 399 1599
Fax: 1 800 997 9831

Macrobiotic Association of Connecticut
24 Village Green Drive
Litchfield
CT 06759
Tel: 1 860 567 8801

Transformational Institute
20 Butlertown Road
Waterford
CT 06385
Tel: 1 203 44 37330

Vital Environments Inc
PO Box 277
Stanhope
NJ 07874

INDEX

AUTHOR'S ACKNOWLEDGMENTS

Writing about Feng Shui always gives me enormous pleasure but seeing my manuscript transformed into this stunningly beautiful book just takes my breath away, for which I truly must thank Element Books.

To Sonia Land, my agent, must go the credit for seeing the great promise of a tie-up with Element Books. To Julia McCutchen a huge hug for her vision; to Caro Ness a warm embrace for her patience and sensitivity and to the team at the Bridgewater Book Company grateful acknowledgement of their creativity and meticulous attention to detail.

I must also acknowledge all the Feng Shui experts whose input progressively enhanced my knowledge of this great science as they successively passed through my life – but most of all, I owe a huge debt of gratitude to Master Yap Cheng Hai, my friend and Si Fu for his wonderful generosity in sharing Feng Shui kung fu (wisdom), *and secret computations with me, formulas that successfully provided the key to unlocking Feng Shui's many complexities . . . I am so enormously grateful to him. And finally, to all my readers and friends in Malaysia and in Singapore. It was their support and encouragement that provided the impetus for me to carry on writing.*

LILLIAN TOO

Grateful acknowledgment must go to Thomas Wang for the material on Feng Shui and western science on pages 30–33 which is an abridged version of his essay.

*Lillian Too may be contacted on: The World Wide Web URL http://*www.asiaconnect.com.my/lillian-too *or* http://www.wwwmktg.com/fengshui/ *or E-mail* ltoo@asiaconnect.com.my *or* ltoo@jaring.com.my

PUBLISHER'S ACKNOWLEDGMENTS

The publishers wish to thank the following for the use of pictures:

Ancient Art & Architecture Collection: pp.13R, 31B, 75TL
Berita Publishing Sdn. Bhd. (Her World Home Scene magazine, vol 1, 1994): pp.60L, 61, 67L, 67R
Bridgeman Art Library: pp.62, 86 (Victoria & Albert Museum)
Christie's Images: pp.8/9
e.t.archive: pp.65T, 162B, 209; 19B, 25 (National Palace Museum, Taiwan); 23 (Science Museum, London); 50 (William Rockhill Nelson Gallery, Kansas); 167L (Brera Milan); 212 (Victoria & Albert Museum); 213 (British Museum)
The Garden Picture Library: pp.46 (Brian Carter); 60TR (Juliette Wade); 60BR (Henk Dickman)
Habitat: pp.170BL, 170BCL, 170BCR, 170BR, 171L, 171TR, 171BR
Hulton Deutsch Collection Ltd: pp.27T, 207B; 37 (Ross Kinnaird)
The Image Bank: pp.136BL; 2/3 (Tadao Kimura); 10 (estudio Francisco Rajo); 12T, 17BR (Jeff Spielman); 12B, 17BCL, 146R, 146L,178T (Romilly Lockyer); 16BL (Alan Becker); 16BR (M Pasdzior); 17BL (Michael Salas); 17BCR (D Berwin); 28, 33, 59R (P & G Bowater); 31T (Steve Satushek); 34 (Antonio M Rosario); 36B (Real Life); 38 (Marc Grimberg); 41T (Marvin E Newman); 43B (Steve Allen); 48/49 (Zhen Ge Peng); 53R, 180 (Grant V Faint); 54L (Rob Atkins); 58 (Peter Frey); 59L (B Martin); 64L, 166BL (Harald Sund); 69T (Zao Grimberg); 87, 136TL (Kaz Mori); 96B (Gary Ross); 98T, 99L (Yellow Dog Prods); 106/107 (Pete Turner); 109B, 136BC (Hans Wolf); 109T (Derek Redfearn); 110 (Antony Edwards); 112 (Terje Rakke); 113T (Nick Pavloff); 114L (Gary Cralle); 114R (F Roiter); 116B (Cesar Lucas); 118L (Jun Ling); 136TR (Ancrea Pistolesi); 136BR, 148BL (Steve Dunwell); 138 (Dag Sundberg); 139R (F Rojo Alvarez); 144L (A Choisnet); 144R (Tom Knibbs); 145BR (H Willig); 146CL (Ivor Wood); 146CR (Herb Hartmann); 147L (Stephen Marks); 147CL (Robert Morris); 147CR, 184BL, 207T (Infocus International); 147R (Eddie Hironaka); 153TL (Patti McConville); 157R (Chuck Lawliss); 172/173 (David Brownell); 174 (Patrick Doherty); 178B (Hank de Lespinasse); 179 (Jeff Hunter); 179R (John Banagan); 193B (Miguel Martin); 206 (James Meyer)
Images Colour Library: p.202
The Kobal Collection: pp.203B, 203T
The Stock House Ltd: pp.18; 26 (James Montgomery); 29T (Steve Vidler); 117T (Dallas & John Heaton); 175 (Timothy Liu)
Syndication International: pp.36R
Lillian Too: pp.7, 47
Zefa Picture Library: pp.11R, 19T, 43T, 65R, 69B, 89TR, 105B, 108, 111T, 115R, 117B, 118/119, 120, 126, 127T, 139L, 145T, 168L, 211; 24, 142 (J Becker); 30 (Davies); 115L (Naegele); 127B (Barone); 152L (Grinsven); 153BL (F Thomas); 160 (Schi Aback); 210L (A Edgeworth)

Special thanks go to:
Bonsai-Ko, Brighton, East Sussex
Bright Ideas, Lewes, East Sussex
Dixons Ltd, Lewes, East Sussex
Habitat Designs Ltd
Vokins, Brighton, East Sussex
for help with properties.